The Good Beach Guide 1992

A guide to over 450 of Britain's best beaches

Marine Conservation Society

Edited and extensively revised by
Guy Linley-Adams

Based on work originally done by
Dr Anne Scott and Richard Caines

VERMILION
LONDON

Published by Vermilion, an imprint of Ebury Press
Random Century House, 20 Vauxhall Bridge Road, London SW1V 2SA

First impression 1988
Reprinted twice 1988
Revised and updated 1989, 1990, 1991 and 1992

Illustrations by Kate Simunek
Edited by Gillian Haslam
Designed by Gwyn Lewis
Front cover photograph by Val Corbett/Landscape Only

A catalogue record for this book is available from the British Library.
ISBN 0 09 175266 3

Typeset in Souvenir by Textype Typesetters, Cambridge
Printed and bound in Great Britain at The Bath Press, Avon

Contents

The Marine Conservation Society and Heinz **4**

Foreword by David Bellamy **6**

An Introduction To The Guide **7**

So What Is Wrong With Our Beaches? **8**

You Still Want To Go To The Seaside? **14**

Key To The Heinz Good Beach Guide Star System **19**

South-West England **20**

South-East England **74**

The East Coast **94**

North-West England **114**

Scotland **122**

Wales **156**

Northern Ireland **186**

What Can You Do To Help Clean Up The Beaches? **196**

Index **202**

Marine Conservation Society Membership Form **207**

The Marine Conservation Society

The Marine Conservation Society is the only environmental organisation that works exclusively to safeguard the marine environment across the whole range of conservation issues. The Society is a registered charity with an expanding membership (over 5,000 in 1991) which encourages members to take part in projects to help provide a sound research base for campaigns.

This year sees the launch of the 'Seas Fit For Life' appeal – write to us to see how you can help raise funds for help save our seas!

Membership is £12 per year and among other items, members receive our quarterly magazine 'Marine Conservation'. The more readers of the Heinz Good Beach Guide, the more pressure we can bring to bear on your behalf to change attitudes within government and industry alike. There is a membership form at the back of the Guide – use it today!

The Heinz Good Beach Guide forms one part of the Society's work, but has had a massive impact on the debate over the state of Britain's beaches and the continuing pollution of the seas by raw sewage. By producing the Guide each year with the help of Heinz and Ebury Press, the Marine Conservation Society has forced the Government to take note of the problem.

Evidence given by the Society to the House of Commons Environment Committee in 1990 was welcomed and adopted in the Committee's final recommendations to the Government. The National Rivers Authority described the 1991 Good Beach Guide as 'excellent' – this one is even better!

AT LAST WE ARE HAVING AN IMPACT!
HELP US TO DO EVEN MORE – JOIN US TODAY!

Heinz

Heinz is a major sponsor of British conservation programmes and has been closely involved with the Marine Conservation Society since 1988 as sponsors of The Heinz Good Beach Guide.

The Company has a long and on-going commitment to the environment and actively recognises its responsibilities both operationally and at a wider educational level.

Heinz cares about the quality of life and the world we live in; the development of best practice on environmental issues is an integral part of the company's business philosophy.

In 1986, Heinz launched a major conservation programme, entitled 'Guardians of the Countryside'. Aimed at protecting wildlife species and habitats, the programme has supported many projects, both land and marine based.

Projects have included the funding of coastal wardening at several sites in the UK, sponsorship of a marine conservation officer and the Marine Conservation Society's 'Coastal Directory'. Through the programme a large number of important sites have been protected including Helford River and sites in Devon, Dorset and Northumberland.

The purchase of Cape Cornwall (including Priest's Cove) and Dunwich Heath in Suffolk for the National Trust have been important steps for Heinz, underlining its commitment to Britain's environment. The company is proud to be sponsors, for a fifth year, of The Heinz Good Beach Guide and will continue to support environmentally beneficial initiatives.

All information received from local authorities, the National Rivers Authority and water companies up to 1 January 1992 has been included in this revised edition. Marine Conservation Society and Ebury Press take no responsibility for data that has been altered and amended after *The Heinz Good Beach Guide 1992* has been compiled.

**MARINE CONSERVATION
SOCIETY**

Foreword
by David Bellamy

A trip to the beach means different things to different people, from the rush to the coast on a Bank Holiday, a much-needed escape from the madness of commuter-life, to the traditional British family seaside holiday.

But we have all heard the horror stories about the presence of sewage in the water, people contracting strange illnesses and finding sewage-related debris on the beach. This is not a new problem. It is certainly not an insurmountable one.

We all know who produces the stuff in the first place and that the technological know-how to recycle and re-use it and stop beach pollution exists. The water service companies are investing money under pressure from organisations such as the Marine Conservation Society, but we must keep up the pressure.

Quite simply, everyone who visits the seaside can make a difference.

Until all the beaches of the UK are clean and the seas are free of raw sewage, we must:

* vote with our feet and not go to dirty beaches!

* write to all in power to protest until the Post Office beg us to stop!

* make it quite clear that sewage must be used in one of the many constructive ways already available – we expect no less!

* shame those responsible into action!

And remember, if none of us acts, then we will all be responsible for the ruin of the seas, guilty by indifference of neglecting our marine heritage.

An Introduction To The Guide

Around the United Kingdom we have over 7,000 miles (11,000km) of coastline, with thousands of beaches. The range of beaches offers something for everyone, from the quiet isolation of 'wilderness' beaches, to the sunburnt splendour of the resort promenade on an August Bank Holiday.

We are blessed with some of the most spectacular coastline in the world, from the chalk cliffs of the Seven Sisters to the saltmarshes of the Lincolnshire coast and the sandy beaches of the West Country. Many are remote beaches, of great nature conservation value, off the beaten track and largely undeveloped.

Others are bustling with activity. Sun, sea and surf attract watersports enthusiasts and sunbathers alike. The beaches and bathing waters support immensely popular resorts such as Brighton, Bournemouth and Blackpool. Without the beaches, these resorts would never have evolved. Atlantic rollers have made beaches in Cornwall world centres for surfing.

Still more beaches support smaller towns, such as Whitby, an east coast fishing port. Such towns may still be centred around a commercial activity – towns with a trade – but inevitably are becoming more reliant on the tourists they attract. Luckily many are doing this without losing the charm and character that are their best assets.

In the 1992 Heinz Good Beach Guide, we at the Marine Conservation Society have attempted to give the reader a definitive guide to all the 'resort style' or 'managed' beaches of Great Britain and Northern Ireland.

The choice about which beach to visit, where to bathe, surf, dive and go sailboarding or yachting is entirely up to the reader. The Guide is just that – your guide to the popular and the best beaches in the United Kingdom. At a time when holidays at home are becoming popular again, it is an essential ally in the hunt for clean, safe beaches and bathing waters.

So What Is Wrong With Our Beaches?

The state of the beaches and bathing waters of the UK has been the subject of vociferous debates for the last four decades since the establishment of the Coastal Anti-Pollution League by Mr. Tony Wakefield and his late wife Daphne. They lost their daughter to an illness contracted while swimming off a British beach. The water was heavily contaminated with sewage.

Thirty four years after that tragedy, there are still bathing waters in the UK that present a real risk to human health. While it is thankfully very rare for potentially fatal illnesses to be caught, the Government's own studies show us that we have a good chance of catching ear, nose and throat infections in the water, or ending up with diarrhoea and vomiting after a day at the sea.

Sewage in the water

We pump 300 million gallons of sewage into the sea every day – about two-and-a-half bucketfuls per person per day.

The majority of it is untreated – it enters the sea just as it disappears round the U-bend in your toilet. That includes the bleach that you throw down the pan and the various plastic items that get flushed away 'out of sight and out of mind'.

Sewage is an amazing mixture of domestic wastewater, cleaning agents, industrial and trade effluent, solid litter and stormwater (run-off from road surfaces). Typical sewage will contain viruses and bacteria that cause human diseases, engine oils from trade and domestic uses, fat balls from domestic and trade kitchens, old pesticides disposed of down the drains and a range of heavy metal contaminants (mercury, lead, cadmium, arsenic, copper) from trade effluent, detergents and road surface run-off.

When you consider just what sewage is and just how much of it is produced in the UK, then comprehensive treatment would seem essential in order to protect ourselves and the marine environment. But what is sewage treatment? And how much of our sewage do we treat?

There are many different ways of treating sewage. So that this Guide can be more easily understood, there is a summary of sewage treatment methods below and figures as to how much receives treatment before discharge together with the law concerning sewage pollution.

Sewage treatment and the law

A comprehensive sewage treatment system is described below. It is important to note just how little treatment most of the sewage discharged to sea around the UK receives.

The first stage is to remove all the larger solids, such as plastics, nappies and all manner of debris that finds its way into the sewers. This is done by screening the sewage, a type of very coarse filtering. This is called **preliminary treatment**. The material screened out is largely unrecyclable and may be landfilled or incinerated. Preliminary treatment may include a process called **maceration** – a process similar to putting the sewage through a blender.

The sewage will still have between 220–500mg/litre suspended solids and so the next step in a comprehensive treatment system is to allow the solids to settle out. This is known as **primary treatment**. A standard sewage treatment works will allow for several hours of sedimentation, before the effluent is passed on to the next stage. Primary treatment will remove 50–60% suspended solids, 30–40% of oxygen demand (the amount of oxygen that the effluent will need to be broken down completely in the sea) and between 0–50% of bacteria and viruses. A large volume of sludge is produced by primary treatment.

The effluent from primary treatment is then subject to **secondary treatment**. This is biological treatment designed to reduce the oxygen demand of the sewage. Secondary treatment may be achieved by drip-trickle through gravel beds, or the use of activated sludge processes. Both methods generate more sludge. Secondary treatment can remove 90–95% of suspended solids, 80–90% of oxygen demand, 75–99% of bacteria and viruses and about 50% of heavy metal contamination.

In some cases, although this is very rare in the UK, **tertiary treatment** may be used to reduce the nitrogen and phosphorus levels in the effluent in order to reduce its 'fertiliser effect'. This is also known as 'nutrient stripping'. This is important since nutrients in sewage can severely disrupt the marine ecosystem causing algal blooms and the death of marine life.

There are now novel methods of treating sewage to a very high standard, without the conventional stage just described. Write to the Pollution Officer, Marine Conservation Society for factsheets about *membrane technology* and also *reed bed technology*. Please enclose an SAE and a small donation to cover costs.

Outfall pipes can be of varying length. Many discharge a matter of a few metres below the low water mark and hence bathing waters may be badly contaminated with sewage. Some even discharge above the line of low tide. In the past, the long sea outfall was seen as the solution to contaminated bathing waters, but it is now regarded on all sides of the debate as no substitute for treatment, as there are significant ecological problems with raw sewage wherever it is discharged. Sewage slicks from long sea outfalls may also be washed back towards beaches by wind, waves and currents.

The **sludge** generated by sewage treatment can be used in a variety of ways. It should be not be regarded as a waste to be disposed of as quickly and cheaply as possible, but as a resource to be exploited for the production of agricultural fertilisers, soil conditioners, peat substitutes, methane production for electricity generation, and even oil production. The House of Commons Environment Committee Enquiry into Pollution of Beaches in 1989/90 adopted this recommendation proposed by the Marine Conservation Society and we now see the Department of the Environment showing enthusiasm in this area – evidence that we can make a difference!

At whatever stage the effluent is discharged to sea, be it raw or having received secondary treatment, **chemical disinfection** may be applied. The chemicals used may be sodium hypochlorite, peracetic acid or ozone. None of these systems has been adequately tested to ensure their safety to marine life and human health. As there is also doubt about the efficiency of these methods in killing disease-causing agents in the effluent, the water service companies may be lulling us into a false sense of security by using chemical disinfection. Chemical disinfection is no substitute for comprehensive sewage treatment.

The following table gives a good idea about the extent of UK sewage discharges to sea.

COASTAL SEWAGE DISCHARGES AROUND THE UK
(serving over 10,000 people).

OUTFALLS	%	No	Pop'n Served
Raw sewage	42	49	1,645,000
Preliminary treatment	46	54	3,359,000
Primary treatment	10	11	395,000
Secondary treatment	2	3	443,000

(Source: Study of Coastal Discharges Vol 3. CES Ltd/DoE Oct'90)

Note that about 88% of outfall pipes carry raw or simply screened sewage. 42% of outfall pipes do not even have screens to remove large objects like sanitary towels, nappies and panty liners. Note, also, that there are very many outfall pipes serving populations of less than 10,000 people that are not included in the table. The estimated number of such outfalls is over 1,000, the vast majority of which carry untreated raw sewage.

Added to all these routinely discharging outfalls are the overflow outfalls. During storm incidents, raw sewage is released from works that normally treat sewage. Works are usually designed to cope with three times the average daily flow of sewage. This is often exceeded in the UK. On average storm water and overflow outfalls are used 10 times a year as treatment works become overloaded and sewers fill up.

The water service companies have control over all discharges and are directly responsible for cleaning up this deliberate mass pollution of our seas. Action is needed now, preferably unilateral, but by legal pressure if necessary. There are three main laws and legal systems that refer directly to sewage discharge to the sea:

The Water Act 1989 and the National Rivers Authority

Under this Act, the National Rivers Authority must give consents to discharge to the water companies for each sewage discharge to sea. These should be designed to protect the waters into which the sewage is being discharged. The NRA should put a limit on the amount of sewage that can be discharged to sea. In practice, the system does not always work effectively to reduce the polluting impact of sewage, but simply maintains the status quo.

A major review of sewage discharge consents is long overdue. Some coastal discharges regularly breach the consents. Many simply do not have numerical consents, meaning no limit is put on what volume of raw sewage goes down the outfall pipe.

The EC Urban Waste Water Directive

A new European Community law called the Urban Waste Water Directive was adopted by the UK government in 1991. It seeks to make secondary treatment the norm of all coastal sewage discharges serving populations of more than 10,000 people (or the equivalent) and estuarine discharges serving more than 2,000.

However, the numerous 'smaller' outfalls are not covered. There is also an exception whereby primary treatment will be considered adequate for the 'large' outfalls if the coastal waters are declared 'less sensitive', a description that has yet to be clearly defined. If the initial half-hearted approach to the EC Bathing Waters Directive is anything to go by, then we should expect the worst.

Marpol Annex IV

The UK government is now considering the ratification of Annex IV of the International Agreement on the Prevention of Pollution from Ships (MARPOL). Annex IV makes it an offence in many cases to discharge sewage from ships and large boats and yachts without treatment. Holding tanks on ships are to be encouraged so that sewage can be discharged to land-based sewage treatment works at ports and harbours. Reception facilities at ports must be adequate to cope. However, there is no point in bringing raw sewage back to land, if the land-based treatment is simply to discharge it back to sea via an outfall pipe!

While this is a step in the right direction, many countries with large shipping fleets operating around the UK coastline do not recognise the MARPOL Agreement and still discharge raw sewage.

Despite all these treatment methods available and the legal framework designed to protect the seas, the simple fact is that the vast majority of sewage from coastal populations is discharged raw or simply screened. And while that is the case, those using beaches and bathing waters will still suffer from illnesses caught in the water and be disgusted by the debris on the beach.

Litter on the beaches

Many beaches are still liberally littered with sewage debris. How do you explain to your kids what a sanitary towel or a condom is and what it is doing washed up on the beach? This may sound a little alarmist, but bear in mind that in 1991, thirteen beaches lost their European Blue Flags for having sewage-related debris on the beach (see 'European Blue Flags', page 17). If that is happening on what have been billed as our best beaches, then it is not hard to see that the problem is indeed real and serious.

The Environmental Protection Act 1990 made it illegal to drop litter in public places on land including beaches, though it is impossible to find a beach around the coastline that has not been tainted by litter dropped not by the careless, but by the couldn't-care-less.

It is also illegal under the International Agreement on the Prevention of Pollution from Ships (MARPOL) Annex V to throw garbage overboard from ships and boats. Much illegal fly-tipping goes on around our coast. Ships undoubtedly still dump rubbish over the side while at sea. A jar of Soviet coffee was given to us in 1991 – it was stamped with the date 1990 and found at the foot of Beachy Head in Sussex among plastic drums of 'ships' detergent' and tubes of industrial lubricating grease, all obviously thrown overboard and washed ashore.

Despite very poor compliance with these two laws and the difficulties of enforcing them, some effort has been made by the Government to tackle the problem. It is therefore strange and inconsistent of the authorities to continue to allow water companies to pump plastic and other debris out to sea with the sewage. The installation of screening at all sewage discharges cannot be argued against on financial grounds – the only conclusion is that the water companies do not care enough about the seas.

However, we can all help with the sewage debris problem. Simply refraining from flushing sanitary items and condoms, but binning them instead will help clean up the beaches and bathing waters, as well as making the water companies' treatment of sewage before discharge to sea (such as it is) easier; the machinery would be subject to fewer breakdowns with less debris in the sewers. The variety of items that get carried out to sea in domestic sewage defies belief.

If you go to the seaside, just as you should in the countryside or in the city centre, put all rubbish in the bin or take it home with you. It is now a criminal offence to drop litter anywhere in public. Drink cans and glass bottles are particularly dangerous – there is no excuse at all for leaving these lying around, especially since they can be taken for recycling in most towns in the UK.

Oil pollution at sea and on the beach

After the horrific oil spills in the Gulf in 1991 and from the Exxon Valdez in Alaska in 1989, you could be forgiven for thinking that major disasters were the main source of oil pollution of the seas. The truth is very different. The bulk of oil that finds it way into the sea comes from routine and hence controllable discharges. Deliberate and illegal flushing of tanks at sea by the bulk oil carriers and other ships is probably the major source. Spills at on-shore and off-shore oil installations during the on- and off-loading of tankers and pipeline fractures also contribute to the tonnes of oil that escape into the seas each year.

The most visible sign of oil pollution is the sticky tar found on most UK beaches. Murphy's Law says that it will always manage to get on your clothes and your shoes, however careful you think you've been to tip-toe around it.

That tar is a minor problem compared to the clogging and smothering effects of oil on seabirds. About 60% of dead seabirds found around the UK are oiled. In the English Channel this figure rises to 75%. Marine life under the water is also at risk. Not all oil floats! The heavier fractions of an oil slick will sink to the sea bed where bottom-dwelling animals and plants are unable to escape.

You Still Want To Go To The Seaside?

After all that, you may be thinking that it would be best to stay at home and watch TV and avoid the seaside with all its polluted waters and mucky beaches. That is the last thing you should do!

We want more people enjoying a break at the seaside! The more people that use our beaches and bathing waters, the more will learn to cherish the sea and take action with the Marine Conservation Society to protect it from all sorts of abuse. Why not join us?

The picture is not one of complete doom and gloom. There are beaches that have good water quality and are not badly contaminated with sewage. The water companies and local authorities are slowly beginning to clean up their act. Beaches and bathing waters are getting better.

But there is still a long way to go, and while that is so, the difficulty comes in finding out which ones are good and which are not safe. What about your particular favourite beaches – is the water safe? Is there sewage discharged nearby? Is it treated?

Ever since Tony Wakefield published his first *Golden List of Britain's Beaches* in 1960, there has been help at hand for the public to find out which beaches are safe. Many years on, the Heinz Good Beach Guide 1992 is an essential read for swimmers, surfers, sailboarders and most importantly families visiting the seaside.

How To Use The Guide

The Guide can be used in many ways, but by far the best way to use it is to sit down and plan your trip around a good beach and safe waters. A good beach is the central feature of a seaside holiday or weekend break. The waters are the most important feature for surfers, sailboarders, divers and swimmers. Select one of the best 150 or so beaches that the Guide describes in detail – make sure the description matches what you require.

If, however, you are limited by the difficulties of travel or have already chosen which beach you are going to visit, or if you wish to find out more about your own favourite beach, the Guide has a list, descended and considerably expanded from the original *Golden*

List. This gives details for over 600 beaches of:

* water quality in terms of compliance with European law
* the number of outfalls found on or near the beach
* the type of treatment that the sewage has received
* whether the discharge is above or below low tide
* the track record of the bathing water over the last 6 years.

There are also remarks about the type of beach (sandy, rocky or shingle) and whether there are any known dangers at the beach.

The water quality information is given using our own Marine Conservation Society star system. This is based on the European Community Bathing Water Directive (1976). Under this law, about 450 designated bathing waters have been identified in the UK. These are regularly monitored for sewage pollution by the National Rivers Authority (NRA), River Purification Boards and DoE – Northern Ireland, throughout the bathing season from May to September inclusive. They measure for the number of coliform bacteria in the water.

Coliform bacteria are found in the gut of every person. They do not cause diseases in man, but are used as an indicator of the amount of sewage contamination in the water. Sewage itself may carry enteric viruses, salmonella, hepatitis A virus and many other disease-causing agents. The Directive does allow for the monitoring of enteric viruses and salmonella but since the UK government bases its results only on the faecal and total coliform counts, we have to use their raw data. However we process into five much finer water quality classes – not simply a crude pass-fail standard used by the Department of the Environment.

Adding to the potential confusion, there are not one but two sets of standards laid down by the Directive. These are the Imperative (also called the Mandatory or minimum standards) and the much stricter Guideline standards:

	Imperative	*Guideline*
Faecal coliforms (number/ 100ml)	2,000	100
Total coliforms	10,000	500

NB It is only the Imperative standards that are involved when a beach is given a pass or a fail. *It must always be remembered that if a beach achieves a pass, it is not declaring itself sewage-free. It simply means that the sewage has reached a certain dilution.*

The track record is a new feature to the Heinz Good Beach Guide. It is based simply on a pass or fail of the minimum standards of the Directive, but will help to highlight all those beaches whose water have been consistently failing (such as Blackpool or Great Yarmouth's South Beach) and equally those that have been consistently passing (such as Poole's Sandbanks Beach).

A key to the star system is on page 19.

Other Information

The Seashore Code

This is one of many educational packages produced by the Marine Conservation Society. It covers the seashore and how everyone should act when at the seaside (copies are available from MCS Sales 0989-62834).

* Show respect for sea creatures
* Take photos not living animals
* Take your rubbish home with you
* Drive on roads not beaches
* Be careful near cliffs
* Avoid disturbing wildlife

'Take nothing but photos, leave nothing but footprints, waste nothing but time.'

European Blue Flag Awards

In 1991, a total of 35 beaches were awarded Blue Flags. The award is sponsored by the Commission of the European Community and administered by the Tidy Britain Group. The award aims to indicate good beach cleanliness and suitable visitor facilities (such as a dog ban from May to September).

However, to qualify at all, the bathing waters off the beach must have achieved the minimum standards of the EC Bathing Waters Directive. The water quality criteria for 1991 Blue Flags are now considered by many experts (including the Marine Conservation Society) not to be strict enough. For this reason it is imperative that the reader should consider the Blue Flag only in terms of amenity (car parks, toilets, dog bans) and not as an indicator of the best water quality.

Furthermore, 63 beaches applied for the Award in 1991, but nearly half failed, many due to the presence of sewage-related litter on the beaches. The 35 winners represent a pathetically small sample of all beaches potentially eligible for an award.

In 1992, the criteria that must be met to achieve Blue Flag status will be tightened. The water will have to have met the Guideline standards of the EC Bathing Waters Directive in 1991 to get a Blue Flag in 1992. If that had been applied in 1991 there would have been many irate tourist department bosses around the coast of the UK without their annual Blue Flag! This tightening of the standards indicates just how borderline the water is at many beaches awarded Blue Flags in 1991.

Our advice is don't take much notice of Blue Flags awarded in 1991. They can be very misleading. Consult the MCS star system for an indication of water quality.

Nevertheless, the winners in 1991 were:

Cullercoats, Filey, Bridlington North, Bridlington South, Hunstanton, Lowestoft, Southwold, Clacton, Sheerness, Camber, Bexhill, Eastbourne, Christchurch (Friars Cliff), Bournemouth, Poole Sandbanks, Swanage, Weymouth, Seaton, Jacobs Ladder (Sidmouth), Budleigh Salterton, Teignmouth, Oddicombe, Ansteys Cove (Redgate), Meadfoot, Paignton (Paignton Sands), Crinnis, Sennen Cove, Porthmeor, Porthminster, Woolacombe, Weston-super-Mare, Caswell, Pembrey, Tenby, Magilligan (Benone)

Golden Starfish Awards

These are the baby brothers of the Blue Flag Awards, given to those beaches that do not have extensive visitor facilities. Among the criteria for qualification, there must be a 'guardian' of the beach to keep it spotlessly clean, such as a local youth group. There were 13 awards given in 1991, although 21 applied. The winners were:

Sandend, Inverboyndie, Bamburgh, Beadnell Bay, Kessingland, Bournemouth (Hengistbury), Harlyn Bay, Polzeath, Sandymouth, Trebarwith Strand, Treyarnon Bay, Crackington Haven, Constantine Bay

Naturist Beaches

These are a growing number of specialist naturist beaches in the UK. There may be others indicated in the listing section. Any information about naturist beaches will be gratefully received.

The list below and overleaf gives several beaches used by naturists.

South-West:
Wild Pear Beach, near Combe Martin, Devon
Polgaver Bay, Carlyon Bay, Cornwall
Pilchard Cove, Slapton Sands, Devon
Labrador Bay, Shaldon, Devon
Studland Beach (mid-section), Dorset

South-East:
Brighton East Beach, Brighton, East Sussex
Fairlight Cove, Hastings, East Sussex
Long Rock Beach, Swalecliffe, Whitstable, Kent
Shellness, near Leysdown, Isle of Sheppey, Kent
St Osyth, Essex
Corton Sands, near Lowestoft, Suffolk
Holkham, Norfolk

East Coast:
Fraisthorpe Sands, Bridlington, North Humberside

Scotland:
Ardeer Beach, Stevenston, Ayrshire
Cleat's Shore, Lagg, Isle of Arran

RYA Windsurfing

RYA Windsurfing is the National Governing Body of the sport and operates as a department of the Royal Yachting Association. It is responsible for producing training schemes for children and adults which are taught in over 250 recognised Centres in the UK and Mediterranean. Competition training activities cover all aspects of the sport from the Under 12s right up to Olympic representatives. Its main function, however, is to promote the sport of windsurfing to newcomers and look after the rights and needs of participating sailors. Over the past few years the rights of windsurfers to access clean water around our coasts has become a major concern. Because of windsurfer's intimate contact with the water, the RYA Windsurfing sees it as being essential to support the MCS and other similar groups with, amongst other things, information on the water quality at popular sailing beaches. It is their aim to help the MCS to expand the Heinz Good Beach Guide to include wind-surfing access and suitability information, making the book the bible of windsurfing access information. If you feel able to provide information relating to the water quality and windsurfing suitability of any beach please contact them for a report form at the address below:

RYA Windsurfing, RYA House, Romsey Road, Eastleigh, Hampshire SO5 4YA.

Key To The Heinz Good Beach Guide Star System

Here is the key to the star system in the following list.

**** – all the samples taken have met the Guideline standards. There is very little sewage, if any. *COME ON IN, THE WATER'S LOVELY.*

*** – all the samples met the Imperative standards, but not all the samples met the Guideline standards. The water is probably affected by sewage but may still be safe.

** – not all the samples met the Imperative standards, but over the season the waters achieved a pass. The water is almost certainly affected by sewage – the choice is yours.!

f** – not all the samples met the Imperative standards and over the season the waters failed. Swimming and other immersion sports may make you ill. *VOTE WITH YOUR FEET – GO TO ANOTHER BEACH.*

f* – over one third of the sample failed the Imperative standards. The waters failed badly. Swimming or other immersion sports are not at all advisable. *AGAIN, VOTE WITH YOUR FEET – GO TO ANOTHER BEACH.*

If two gradings are given separated by a '/', there was insufficient data to distinguish the waters further.

Track record p = passed the minimum coliform standards of the EC Bathing Waters Directive. f = failed those standards

The track record shows how consistent the water quality has been at beaches around the UK. This is particularly useful for pinpointing those that have either failed or passed consistently for the last six years!

Abbreviations The following abbreviations are used in the lists (see page 9 for details of sewage treatment).

HWM = high water mark *(all figures are in metres unless otherwise stated)* LWM = low water mark SSO = short sea outfall LSO = long sea outfall

South-West England

f = failed to meet EC minimum coliform standards for bathing water in 1991.
Numbered beaches are included in the following chapter.
p = passed
p/f = some sites passed, some failed

Long distance coastal paths
South West Coast Path
562 miles (904km), but made up of four main sections:
(1) Minehead to Padstow 131 miles (211km).
(2) Padstow to Falmouth 158 miles (254km).
(3) Falmouth to Exmouth 174 miles (280km).
(4) Exmouth to Poole 99 miles (159km).

Isle of Wight Coastal Path
A circuit of the island 60 miles (97km).

Solent Way
Milford on Sea to Portsmouth 60 miles (97km).

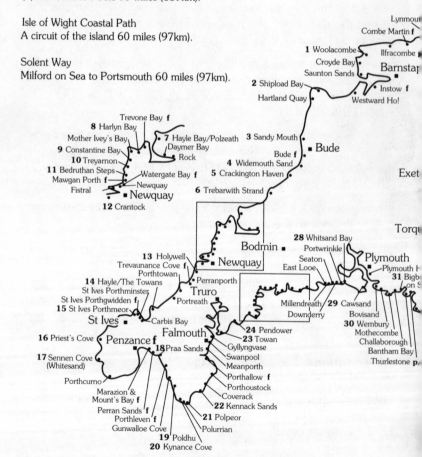

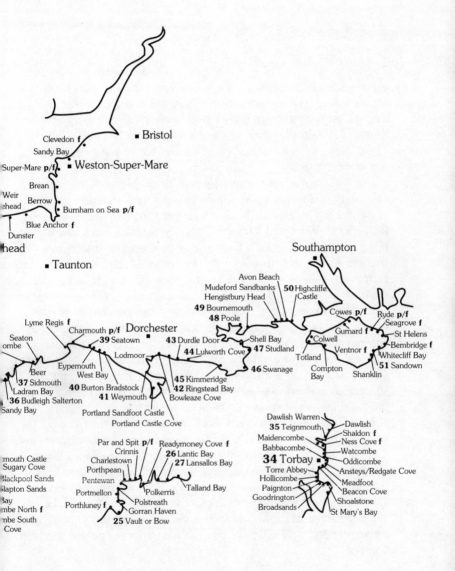

Clevedon **f**

Sandy Bay

■ **Bristol**

Super-Mare **p/f** ■ **Weston-Super-Mare**

Brean

Weir
ehead

Berrow

Burnham on Sea **p/f**

Blue Anchor **f**

Dunster

head

■ **Taunton**

Southampton

Avon Beach

Mudeford Sandbanks

Hengistbury Head **50** Highcliffe
Castle

49 Bournemouth Cowes **p/f** Ryde **p/f**

Lyme Regis **f** **48** Poole Seagrove **f**

Charmouth **p/f** ■ **Dorchester** Gurnard **f** St Helens

Seaton **39** Seatown **43** Durdle Door Shell Bay Colwell Bembridge **f**

ombe **47** Studland Ventnor **f** Whitecliff Bay

Lodmoor **44** Lulworth Cove Totland **51** Sandown

Beer Eypemouth **46** Swanage Compton Shanklin

37 Sidmouth West Bay Bay

Ladram Bay **45** Kimmeridge

36 Budleigh Salterton **40** Burton Bradstock **42** Ringstead Bay

Sandy Bay **41** Weymouth Bowleaze Cove

Portland Sandfoot Castle

Portland Castle Cove

Dawlish Warren

35 Teignmouth Dawlish

Par and Spit **p/f** Readymoney Cove **f** Maidencombe Shaldon **f**

Crinnis Babbacombe Ness Cove **f**

mouth Castle **26** Lantic Bay Watcombe

Sugary Cove Charlestown **27** Lansallos Bay **34** Torbay ■ Oddicombe

lackpool Sands Porthpean Torre Abbey Ansteys/Redgate Cove

lapton Sands Pentewan Hollicombe Meadfoot

Bay Polkerris Paignton Beacon Cove

mbe North **f** Portmellon Talland Bay Goodrington Shoalstone

mbe South Porthluney **f** Polstreath Broadsands

Cove Gorran Haven St Mary's Bay

25 Vault or Bow

South-West England

There are hundreds of miles of glorious coastline along the south-west peninsula. Long sweeping bays and small secluded coves are separated by rugged headlands. There are spectacular rocky cliffs to contrast with smooth turfed slopes where wild flowers abound. Some of Britain's loveliest unspoilt scenery is to be found along this coast. Many of our cleanest beaches and bathing waters are found in the west country.

But the area is not completely free of problems. Various forms of pollution affect several beaches; untreated sewage discharged close inshore is washed back on to the sands at popular resorts. Both South-West and Wessex Water companies have investment programmes to deal with the sewage problems of the region, but there is a long way to go. In the immediate future it appears the surfers of Newquay will still be plagued by sewage and related debris.

In other areas, the china clay industry has covered some sands with a film of white dust and the Cornish tin mining industry discharges waste either directly into the sea or into rivers flowing to the sea; for instance one of the beautiful beaches on the eastern side of St Ives Bay is affected by a 'red' river. The river, containing suspended mining waste, flows across the sand, turns the waves pink and the waste is washed back on to the shore.

Large numbers of tourists flocking to the beaches during the summer can cause problems. Long queues of traffic develop on the narrow lanes and the picturesque Cornish fishing villages become congested. The beaches become crowded and this can lead to damage; for example, the erosion of dunes is a particular problem. Careless visitors leaving rubbish can ruin an otherwise lovely beach. To avoid some of these problems a visit in the spring or autumn is recommended, and in winter you can have miles of golden sands to yourself.

The South-West   See page 19 for further details

Beach No on Map	Rating. The more stars the better. f=failed	Resort	Pass/Fail track record	Sewage outlets	Population discharging from outlet	Type of treatment	Discharge point relative to low water mark, unless otherwise stated. Distance given in metres	Remarks
AVON								
		Clevedon:		1	60,000	Fine	At HWM	Rocks and mud. Crude
	f ★★	**Bay**	FFFFPF			screening,		discharges now removed.
	f ★★	Marine Lake				filtration,		All flow to STW at
	★★	Layde Bay				settlement		Kingston Seymour.
		Weston-Super-Mare:		1	75,000	Fine screening, disinfection	400m below LWM	Improvement scheme completed 1990.
	★★	Uphill Slipway						
	f ★★	Sanatorium						
	f ★★	Tropicana						
	f ★★	Grand Pier						
	★★★	Marine Lake						
	★★★	Weston Anchor Head (Birnbeck Pier)						
	★★★	Weston Sand Bay	PFPPPP					
SOMERSET								
		Berrow:						
	★★★	**North**						
	★★★	**South**	PPFPPP					Sandy.
	★★★	**Brean**	PPPPPP					Sandy.
		Burnham-on-Sea:		1	36,000	Fine	At HWM	All flow to West
	f ★★	Yacht Club				screening,		Huntspill STW.
	★★	Jetty				filtration,		
	f ★★	Paddling Pool				settlement		
		East Quantoxhead		1	800	Maceration	At LWM	Rocks and sand. Water quality not monitored by NRA.
	f ★	Doniford		1	5,000	Fine screened	100 above LWM	Sand and mud.
	f ★★	Watchet		1	4,500	Raw	100 above LWM	Sand and mud.
	f ★★	**Blue Anchor**	PFPPPF					Sand and shingle. Flows to Minehead headworks.
		Dunster:						
	★★	**North West**						
	★★★	**South East**	FFFFPP					Sand and shingle. Flows to Minehead headworks.

Beach No on Map	Rating. The more stars the better. f=failed	Resort	Pass/Fail track record	Sewage outlets	Population discharging from outlet	Type of treatment	Discharge point relative to low water mark, unless otherwise stated. Distance given in metres	Remarks
	★★★ ★★ ★★★ ★★	**Minehead:** West of harbour (Only five samples) Terminus The Strand Warren Point		1	35,000	Screening. Long sea outfall and tidal discharge	750 below LWM	Sandy. Headworks and outfall completed 1989.
	★★★	**Porlock Bay: Porlock Weir**	PFPPPP	3	850 1,200 450	Raw Raw Raw	At LWM At LWM At LWM	Pebbles.
NORTH DEVON								
	f ★★	**Lynmouth**	FFPFFF	1	4,349	Raw	110 below	Pebbles. New primary treatment works and outfall planned for 1995.
	f ★★	**Combe Martin**	FFFFPF	1	3,522	Raw	65 below	Pebbles and sand. New full treatment works and 500 m outfall planned by 1995.
	f ★★ ★★ ★★★	**Ilfracombe:** **Hele Beach** **Capstone Beach** Tunnels	FFPPPP	2	22,022 744	Raw Raw	235 below 30 below	Sandy. Bathing safe. Improvements planned to include enclosed primary treatment works and medium sea outfall by 1995.
	★★★★	Rockham Bay						Rocky.
	★★	Barricane Bay						Sandy cove surrounded by rocks.
1	★★★★ ★★★	**Woolacombe:** **Putsborough** **Village**	PPPPPP	1	11,000	Secondary	100 below	Sandy. Surfing popular.
	★★★	**Croyde Bay**	PPPPPP	1	6,431	Maceration	At LWM	Sandy. Surf bathing. Strong undertow at all times. Lifeguards. Problems with sewage-related debris.
	★★★	**Saunton Sands**	PPPPPP					Sandy. Safe bathing except near river mouth. Lifeguards.
	f ★★	**Instow**	FFFPFF					Polluted by River Taw and Torridge. £62.4m scheme to provide secondary treatment, long sea outfall and sludge digestion by 1997.

Beach No on Map	Rating. The more stars the better. f=failed	Resort	Pass/Fail track record	Sewage outlets	Population discharging from outlet	Type of treatment	Discharge point relative to low water mark, unless otherwise stated. Distance given in metres	Remarks
	★★★	**Westward Ho!**	PPPPPP	1	8,521	Fine screens	10 below	Sand and pebbles. Surf bathing. Improvements as above.
	★★★	Clovelly		1	259	Raw	At LWM	Sand at low tide only.
2	★★★★	Shipload Bay						Pebbles, sand at low tide.
	★★★	**Hartland Quay**	PPPPPP					Rocks and pebbles.
	★★★★	Welcombe Mouth						Pebbles and rocks;some sand at low tide.
CORNWALL								
3	★★★	**Sandy Mouth**						Sandy. Swimming dangerous at low tide. Surf bathing. Lifeguards.
f ★★		**Bude Crooklets**	FFFPPF					Sandy. Surf bathing.
f ★★		**Bude Summerleaze**		1	13,143	Tidal tank	75 below	Scheme to resite outfall and provide primary treatment and sludge digestion by 1993.
4	★★★	**Widemouth Sand**	PPPPPP					Sandy. Bathing dangerous at low tide. Lifeguards.
5	★★	**Crackington Haven**						Sandy. Safe bathing in centre of bay. Lifeguards.
		Boscastle		1	1,285	Raw	At LWM	Harbour outfall inaccessible. Water quality not monitored by NRA.
		Tintagel		1	1,724	Raw	At LWM	Shingle. Water quality not monitored by NRA.
6	★★★	**Trebarwith Strand**						Sand and rocks. Swimming can be dangerous. Lifeguards.
		Port Isaac		1	1,910	Secondary	At LWM	Fishing port. Water quality not monitored by NRA.
7	★★	**Polzeath**	PPPPPP	1	656	Primary	At LWM	Sandy. Bathing can be dangerous at low water. Lifeguards.

Beach No on Map	Rating. The more stars the better. f=failed	Resort	Pass/Fail track record	Sewage outlets	Population discharging from outlet	Type of treatment	Discharge point relative to low water mark, unless otherwise stated. Distance given in metres	Remarks
	★★★	**Daymer Bay**	PPPPPP					Sandy. Safe swimming.
	★★	**Rock**	FFPPPP					Sandy. Good sailing. Swimmers beware currents.
		Padstow		1	3,874	Fine screens		Small harbour. No swimming. Water quality not monitored by NRA.
	f ★★	**Trevone Bay**	FFFPPF	1	1,104	Raw	At LWM	Sandy. Bathing can be dangerous. Lifeguards. Improvements planned to give higher degree of treatment and sludge digestion in 1995.
8	★★★	**Harlyn Bay**	PPPPPP	1	3,202	Secondary (summer)	At LWM	Sandy. Safe bathing. Lifeguards.
	★★★	**Mother Ivey's Bay**	~PPPPP					Sandy. Safe bathing. Pedestrian access.
9	★★★	**Constantine Bay**	~PPPPP					Sandy. Bathing dangerous.
10	★★	**Treyarnon Beach**	PPPPPP					Sandy. Surfing dangerous at low tide.
	f ★★	**Mawgan Porth**	FFPFFF					Sandy. Surfing dangerous at low tide. Improvements planned to construct reed bed at St Columb Major STW by 1994.
11		Bedruthan Steps						Sand and rocks. Bathing dangerous.
	f ★★	**Watergate Bay**	PPPPPF					Sandy.
	f ★★	**Porth Beach**		1		Maceration/ screens	75 below	Sandy. Surfing. Lifeguards.
	★★★	**Newquay Bay: Towan Beach**	PPPPPP	1	50,078	Maceration/ screens		
	★★★	**Fistral Bay**	PPPPPP					Sandy. Strong currents when rough. Litter and sewage pollution reported in 1991.

Beach No on Map	Rating. The more stars the better. **f**=failed	Resort	Pass/Fail track record	Sewage outlets	Population discharging from outlet	Type of treatment	Discharge point relative to low water mark, unless otherwise stated. Distance given in metres	Remarks
12 ★★★		**Crantock**	PPPPPP					Sandy. Surfing. Swimming dangerous at low water and near Gannel estuary.
13 ★★★		**Holywell Bay**						Sandy. Surfing dangerous at low tide. Lifeguards.
	★★★ f ★★	**Perranporth:** Penhale Village Village End Beach		1	11,872	Maceration	At LWM	Sandy. Good surfing. Dangerous at low tide. Lifeguards.
	f ★★	**Trevaunance Cove**	FFPPPF	1	4,140	Fine screening	At LWM	Sandy. Powerful surf. New £2.3 m improvement scheme.
	★★	**Porthtowan**	PPPPPP					Sandy. Surfing dangerous at low water. Lifeguards.
	★★★	**Portreath**	PPPPPP	1	24,143	Screening	At LWM	Sandy. Surfing. Swimming dangerous near pier. Lifeguards.
		Deadman's Cove		1	25,000	Raw	At LWM	Sand and rocks. Water quality not monitored by NRA.
14 ★★ ★★★		**The Towans – Hayle** **The Towans – Godrevy**	PPPPPP					Sandy. Surfing. Swimming dangerous at low water. Lifeguards.
	f ★★ ★★★	**Carbis Bay:** Porth Kidney Sands Station Beach						Sandy and sheltered.
	★★★	**St Ives Porthminster**	PPPFPP					Sandy. Sheltered. Safe swimming. Well managed beach.
	f ★★	**St Ives Porthgwidden**	FPFFFF					Sandy beach. All discharges ceased.
15 ★★★		**St Ives Porthmeor**	PPPPPP	1	50	Fine screened	150 from harbour wall	Sandy. Surfing.
16		St Just Priest's Cove						Shingle.
17 ★★★		**Sennen Cove**	PPPPPP	1	1,489	Maceration	130 from sea wall	Sandy. Surfing north of beach is dangerous. Lifeguards.

Beach No on Map	Rating. The more stars the better. f=failed	Resort	Pass/Fail track record	Sewage outlets	Population discharging from outlet	Type of treatment	Discharge point relative to low water mark, unless otherwise stated. Distance given in metres	Remarks
		Porthgwarra						Sandy at low tide. All discharges ceased.
	★★★	**Porthcurno**	PPPPPP	1	211	Maceration	At LWM	Sandy.
		Lamorna Cove		1		Tidal tank	At LWM	Sand and rocks. Water quality not monitored by NRA.
		Mousehole		1	2,100	Raw	At LWM	Fishing port. Water quality not monitored by NRA.
	 f ★ f ★ f ★★ ★★★	**Marazion and Mount's Bay:** Wherrytown Heliport **Penzance** Little Hogus	 FFFFFF	12	37,585	Raw	11 at LWM, 1 at 50 below	Sand and shingle. New £ 48.7 m scheme proposed for Newlyn and Penzance for completion in 1995 to provide secondary treatment, sludge treatment, two storm water outfalls and a long sea outfall.
	f ★★	**Perran Sands**	PPPPPF	1	1,615	Raw	At LWM	Sandy.
18	 ★★★ ★★★	**Praa Sands:** West East	 PPPPPP PPPPPP					Sandy. Surfing. Lifeguards.
	 f ★★	**Porthleven** **West**	 FFFPFF	1	3,852	Raw	At HWM	Flint and pebbles. Bathing dangerous. £3.2 m improvement scheme planned to provide full treatment at inland STW and discharge via medium sea outfall.
	★★★	**Gunwalloe Cove**	PPPPPP					Swimming dangerous in rough weather. Lifeguards.
19 ★★★		**Poldhu Cove**	PPPPPP					Sandy. Bathing dangerous at low tide. Lifeguards.
	★★	Polurrian Cove	PPPPPP	1	2,000	Macerated	At LWM	Sandy. Weekend lifeguards.
20		Kynance Cove						Sandy. Safe bathing.
21		Polpeor Cove						Rock and shingle. Safe bathing.

Beach No on Map	Rating. The more stars the better. f=failed	Resort	Pass/Fail track record	Sewage outlets	Population discharging from outlet	Type of treatment	Discharge point relative to low water mark, unless otherwise stated. Distance given in metres	Remarks
		Church Cove		1	4,375	Maceration	500 below	Rocky fishing cove. Water quality not monitored by NRA.
22	★★★	**Kennack Sands**	PPPPPP					Silver sands. Safe swimming in calm weather.
	★★★	**Coverack**	PPPPPP					Sand and shingle.
	★★★★	**Porthoustock**	PPPPPP					Shingle with sand at low tide.
	f ★★	**Porthallow**	FFFFPF					Grey stones. Improvements planned by 1995 to intercept numerous minor raw sewage discharges and provide treatment and short outfall.
	★★	**Maen Porth**	PFPPPP					Sand and shingle. Safe swimming except when rough. Lifeguards.
	★★★	**Swanpool Beach**	PFPPPP	1	31,156	Maceration	At LWM	Sand and shingle. £14.5m improvement scheme planned.
	★★★	**Gyllyngvase (Falmouth)**	PFPPPP					Sandy. Safe swimming. Lifeguards.
	★★★	Loe Beach Feock						Sand and shingle. Boating beach.
	★★★	St Mawes		1	1,551	Other		Sandy. Safe swimming.
	★★★★	St Anthony's Head						Sheltered bay; fine shingle at low tide.
23		Towan Beach, Portscatho		2	1,988 52	Raw Raw	At LWM At LWM	Sand and rock.
	★★★	Porthcurnick Beach						Sand, some rocks.
24	★★	**Pendower Beach**						Sand and rock. Safe bathing.
		Portloe		1	431	Maceration	At LWM	Sand and rock. Fishing village.
	★★★★	Portholland Beach						Shingle, sand at low tide. Old lime kilns on the shore.

Beach No on Map	Rating. The more stars the better. f=failed	Resort	Pass/Fail track record	Sewage outlets	Population discharging from outlet	Type of treatment	Discharge point relative to low water mark, unless otherwise stated. Distance given in metres	Remarks
	f ★★	Porthluney Cove						Sandy. Safe swimming.
	★★★	Hemmick Beach						Small sandy bay.
25		**Gorran Haven:**						
	★★★★	**Bow (or Vault)**	PFPPPP					
	★★	**Little Perhaver**		1	2,487	Raw	At LWM	Sandy, safe swimming. Improvements by 1994 to provide treatment and an extension to the existing sea outfall.
	★★★	**Portmellon**	PPPPPP					Sand and shingle.
		Mevagissey		1	5,865	Raw	At LWM	Fishing harbour. No beach. Water quality not monitored by NRA.
	★★	**Polstreath**	PPPPPP					Contaminated by the Mevagissey sewage outfall – improvements planned.
	★★★	**Pentewan**	FFFFPP					Sandy. STW and 500 m outfall to discharge effluent to St Austell Bay by 1994.
	★★★	**Porthpean**	PPPPPP	1	34	Raw	At LWM	Sandy.
	★★★	**Charlestown**	~~~~PP	1	3,248	Raw	At LWM	Sandy. Leisure complex. Improvements planned by 1993 to give secondary treatment and a long sea outfall.
	★★★	**Duporth**	~~~~FP					
		Crinnis Beach:						Sandy. Swimming dangerous near stream. Improvements as above. Well managed beach, although reports of marine debris.
	★★	Golf Links	PPPPPP					
	★★★	Leisure Centre						
	★★★	**Par Sands**	FPPPPP	1	23,263	Primary	60 below	Sandy. Dominated by china clay factory. Improvements as above.
	f ★★	Spit Beach						
	★★★	**Polkerris**	PFPPPP	1	57	Raw	5 below	Sandy.
	★★	Polridmouth Beach						Sandy beach with shelter from south-westerly winds.
	f ★★	**Readymoney Cove (Fowey)**	FFPPPF	1	3,448	Raw	At LWM	Sandy.

Beach No on Map	Rating. The more stars the better. f=failed	Resort	Pass/Fail track record	Sewage outlets	Population discharging from outlet	Type of treatment	Discharge point relative to low water mark, unless otherwise stated. Distance given in metres	Remarks
26 ★★★		Lantic Bay						Sand and shingle. Strong undertow.
27		Lansallos Bay						Sandy. Safe bathing.
		Polperro		1	3,466	Maceration	At LWM	Pebbles. Water quality not monitored by NRA.
	★★★	**East Looe**	PPPFPP					Sandy. Safe bathing.
	★★★	**Millendreath**	~PPFPP					Sandy.
	★★	Seaton Beach	FFFPPP	1	1,337	Raw	At LWM	Grey sand and pebbles. Improvement scheme for completion in 1995 to provide sewage treatment and discharge via medium sea outfall.
	★★★	**Downderry**	~FPPPP	1	938	Raw	At LWM	Silvery sand. Scheme as above.
28 ★★★		**Portwrinkle**	~FPPPP	4		3 Raw 1 Treated	At LWM	Grey sand. Improvements due in 1994.
29		Cawsand Bay		5		All raw	At LWM	Pebbles and rocks. Improvement scheme to eliminate raw sewage outfalls by 1995.
SOUTH DEVON								
		Kingsands Bay		2	157 665	Raw	5 and 12 below	Sand and shingle. Water quality not monitored by NRA.
	f ★★	**Plymouth Hoe**	FFFPFF	3	49,000 368 2,300	Primary Raw Raw		£37.6 m improvement scheme due in 1998. Providing primary treatment at Millbay.
	★★★	**Bovisand Bay**	PPPPPP					Sand and rocks. Polluted by untreated sewage from Plymouth outfalls.
30 ★★★		**Wembury**	PFPPPP	1	4,383	Primary	100 below	Silvery sand and rocks.
	★★	**Mothecombe**	PPPPPP					Sandy. Bathing safe only on incoming tide.
	★★	**Challaborough**	PFPPPP					Sandy and rocky. Bathing dangerous at low tide.

Beach No on Map	Rating. The more stars the better. f=failed	Resort	Pass/Fail track record	Sewage outlets	Population discharging from outlet	Type of treatment	Discharge point relative to low water mark, unless otherwise stated. Distance given in metres	Remarks
31		Bigbury-on-Sea:		1	1,286	Primary/other	At LWM	Sandy. Swimming dangerous near river mouth. Improvement scheme to give secondary treatment.
	★★★	North						
	★★	South	PPPPPP					
	★★★	Bantham	PPPPPP					Sand and mud. Bathing dangerous.
		Thurlestone:		1	1,161	Primary	At LWM	Red sand. Sheltered swimming. Improvement scheme planned for 1992 including tertiary treatment by reed-beds.
	f ★★	North	~~~FFF					
	★★★	South	~~~PPP					
	★★★	Hope Cove	PPPPPP	1	1,152	Primary	At LWM	Sandy.
	★★★	Soar Mill Cove						Stream crosses sands, rock pools and cliffs.
	f ★★	Salcombe North	FPPFPF	1	2,226	Raw	50 below	Sandy. Full treatment by 1994.
	★★★	Salcombe South	FPFPPP	1	21	Raw	7 below	Sandy.
	★★	Mill Bay	PFPPPP					Sandy.
	★★★	Hallsands						Shingle. Interesting ruined village nearby.
	★★★	Beesands						Shingle, steeply shelving.
	★★★	Torcross	~~~~PP	1	693	Raw	At LWM	Fishing port.
32	★★★★	Slapton Sands	PPPPPP	1	889	Primary	30 below	Tiny red pebbles. Improvement scheme.
33	★★★★	Blackpool Sands	PPPPPP					White sand. Shelves steeply.
		Leonard's Cove		2	1,051 / 1,044	Raw / Raw	At LWM / At LWM	Shingle. Water quality not monitored by NRA.
	★★★	Dartmouth Castle and Sugary Cove	PPPPPP					Shingle.
	★★★	St Mary's Bay	PPPPPP	1	90,000	Raw/maceration	220 below	Sand and pebbles. Improvement scheme.
	★★★	Shoalstone Beach	PPPPPP					Pebbles.
	★★★	Churston Cove						Shingle.

Beach No on Map	Rating. The more stars the better. f=failed	Resort	Pass/Fail track record	Sewage outlets	Population discharging from outlet	Type of treatment	Discharge point relative to low water mark, unless otherwise stated. Distance given in metres	Remarks
	★★★	**Broadsands Beach**	PPPPPP					Muddy sand and pebbles.
34		**Torbay (Goodrington to Watcombe):**						
	★★★	**Goodrington Sands**	PFPPPP	1		Screened	At LWM	Sand and pebbles. Storm water overflow.
	★★★	**Paignton Sands**	PPFPPP	1		Screened	200 below	Red sands.
	★★★	**Preston Sands**	~~~PPP	1		Screened	At LWM	Red sands. Stormwater overflows.
	★★★	**Hollicombe**	PPPPPP					
	★★★	**Torre Abbey Sands**	PPPPPP					Safe bathing.
	★★	**Beacon Cove**	~PPPPP					
	★★★	**Meadfoot Beach**	PPPPPP					Sandy at low tide.
	★★	**Anstey's Cove/ Redgate Beach**	PPPPPP	1	89,000	Fine screened	At LWM	Sand and shingle. Outfall off Hope's Nose. Improvements planned.
	★★★	**Babbacombe**	PPPPPP	1	1,000	Transfered to above.		Shingle.
	★★★	**Oddicombe**	PPPPPP					Shingle.
	★★★	**Watcombe Beach**	PPPPPP					Sandy.
	★★★	**Maidencombe**	PPPPPP					Red sand.
	f ★★	**Ness Cove**	PPPPPF					Sandy. Improvements planned – see below.
	f ★★	**Shaldon**	FFFPPF	1	1,869	Raw	At LWM	Sandy. Improvement scheme due for completion in 1994 to provide new long sea outfall and treatment at existing works inland.
35 ★★★		**Teignmouth**	PFPPPP	2	17,400	Screens/ tidal tank	At LWM	Sandy. Improvements as above.
	★★★	**Holcombe**	~~~FPP	1	1,639	Maceration	At LWM	Rocky. Improvements as above.

Beach No on Map	Rating. The more stars the better. f=failed	Resort	Pass/Fail track record	Sewage outlets	Population discharging from outlet	Type of treatment	Discharge point relative to low water mark, unless otherwise stated. Distance given in metres	Remarks
	★★★ ★★★	**Dawlish** Town Coryton Cove	PPPPPP	2	22,301	Raw	At LWM/ 330 below	Red sand/shingle. Town beach affected by sewage-related debris.
	★★★	**Dawlish Warren**	PPPPPP					Sand and dunes. Bathing dangerous near river. Sewage–related debris a problem.
	★★★	**Exmouth**	FPPPPP	1	43,009	Primary	166 below	Sandy. Improvement scheme. Sewage-related debris a problem.
	★★	**Sandy Bay**	PPPPPP					Red sand.
36	★★	**Budleigh Salterton**	PFPPPP	1	5,066	Raw	50 below HWM	Pebbles sloping steeply.
	★★	**Ladram Bay**	~PPPPP	1	3,055	Primary	At LWM	Pebbles.
37	★★	**Sidmouth**	~~~~PP	1	15,880	Maceration/ screens	400 below	Pebbles with sand.
	★★★	**Sidmouth: Jacob's Ladder**	PPPPPP					
38	★★★	Branscombe						Pebbles.
	★★	**Beer**	PPPPPP	1	3,016	Raw	At LWM	Pebbles. Steep beach.
	★★	**Seaton**	PFPPPP					Pebbles. Steep beach. Improvement scheme.
DORSET								
	f ★★ f ★ ★★★	**Lyme Regis:** **Monmouth Beach** **Church Beach** **Cobb Beach**	FFFFFF	2	32 9,519	Raw Raw	10 below 15 below	Sandy. £8.7 m improvement scheme planned for 1995 to provide primary treatment and a long sea outfall. Also sludge digesters planned.
	★★★ f ★★	**Charmouth** West East	FPPPPP					Sand and shingle. £2.7 m improvement scheme.
39	★★	**Seatown**	PPPPPP					Pebbles.
	★★★	**Eypemouth**	FPPPP					Pebbles.
	★★★	**West Bay**	PPPPPP	1	30,000	Maceration/ screens	1500 below	Shingle; steep beach.
40	★★★	Burton Bradstock						Shingle.

Beach No on Map	Rating. The more stars the better. ⚠=failed	Resort	Pass/Fail track record	Sewage outlets	Population discharging from outlet	Type of treatment	Discharge point relative to low water mark, unless otherwise stated. Distance given in metres	Remarks
	★★★★	Chesil Beach		1	86,000	Maceration/ screens	1300 below	Pebbles. Swimming very dangerous.
	★★★	**Church Ope Cove**	PPPPPP					Shingle.
	★★★★ ★★★	**Portland Harbour: Sandsfoot** **Castle Cove**	PPPPPP					Sandy. Sandy.
41	★★★ ★★★	**Weymouth:** South Central	PPPPPP					Sandy.
	★★★ ★★★	Lodmoor West Lodmoor						
	★★★	**Bowleaze**	PPPPPP					Fine shingle and sand.
42 ★★★		**Ringstead Bay**	PPPPPP					Shingle and pebbles.
43	★★★★ ★★★	**Durdle Door:** **West** East	PPPPPP					Sand and pebbles.
	★★	Stair Hole						
44 ★★★		**Lulworth Cove**	PPPPPP	1	2,000	Raw	Below LWM	Shingle. Discharge is outside the cove. Screens planned for 1994.
		Worbarrow Bay						Closed at times due to military range. Water quality not monitored by NRA. Sand and pebbles.
45 ★★★		**Kimmeridge Bay**	PPPPPP					Rocky.
46	★★ ★★★ ★★★	**Swanage:** South Central North	PPPPPP	1	20,000	Maceration	100 below	Sandy. Outfall off headland.
47 ★★★		**Studland Bay**	PFPPPP					White sand. Naturist beach.
	★★★	**Shell Bay**						Sandy. Strong currents.

Beach No on Map	Rating. The more stars the better. f=failed	Resort	Pass/Fail track record	Sewage outlets	Population discharging from outlet	Type of treatment	Discharge point relative to low water mark, unless otherwise stated. Distance given in metres	Remarks
		Poole:						
	★★★	**Rockley Sands**	FPPPPP					
	★★★	**Lake**	PPPPPP					
	★★★	**Harbour**	PPPFPP					
48	★★★	**Poole Sandbanks/ Shore Road**	PPPPPP					
	★★★	Branksome Chine						Sand and shingle. Muddy at low tide (Lake and Harbour)
	★★★	Alum Chine						Windsurfing popular.
49		**Bournemouth:**						Sandy.
	★★★	Bournemouth Pier	PPPPPP					
	★★★	Boscombe Pier						
	★★★	Southbourne						
	★★★	Hengistbury Head	PPPPPP					
		Christchurch:						
	★★	Stanpit						
	★★★	Mudeford Sandbank	PPPPPP					
	★★	Mudeford Sand Harbour						
	★★★	Mudeford Quay						
	★★★	Avon Beach	PFFPPP					
	★★★	Friars Cliff						
	★★★	Highcliffe Castle						
50	★★★	**Highcliffe**	PPPPPP					Sailing harbour. Shingle and mud. Rivers Avon and Stour contain treated sewage giving a high coliform bacterial count in the harbour.
ISLE OF WIGHT								
	★★★	**Totland**	FPPPPP	1	2,000	Maceration	300 below	Shingle. To be transferred to Norton by 1993.
	★★★	**Colwell Bay**	FPFPPP					Shingle.
		Yarmouth		1	1,000	Raw	170 below	Sailing harbour. Shingle beach. Water quality not monitored by NRA.
	★★★	Norton		1	15,000	Maceration	230 below	Sandy.

Rating. The more stars the better. **f**=failed	Resort	Pass/Fail track record	Sewage outlets	Population discharging from outlet	Type of treatment	Discharge point relative to low water mark, unless otherwise stated. Distance given in metres	Remarks
f ★★	**Gurnard Bay**	FFFPFF	1	5,800	Maceration	400 below	Shingle. Safe bathing.
	Cowes:		1	15,000	Screens	700 below LWM	Sailing centre.
f ★	West	FFFFFF					
★★★	East		3	3,000	Raw		To be abandoned in 1992.
	Ryde:		1	21,000	Maceration	3km below LWM	Sandy. Safe swimming.
f ★★	West	FFFFPF					
★★	East						
	Seaview						Sandy and rocks. Bathing safe. Sewage transfer to Ryde. Water quality not monitored by NRA.
f ★★	**Bembridge**	FFFFPF	1	7,000	Maceration/ tidal tank	800 below	Sailing centre. New scheme planned for 1995 to give preliminary treatment and a long sea outfall.
★★★	**Whitecliff Bay**	PPFFPP					Sandy. Safe bathing.
★★★	Yaverland		1	50,000	Primary	250 below	Sandy. Safe bathing.
★★★	**Sandown Esplanade**	PPPPPP					Sandy. Safe bathing in calm weather.
★★★ **★★**	**Shanklin** Shanklin Chine	PFPPPP					Sandy. Safe bathing.
f ★★	**Ventnor**	FFFFPF	2	5,300	Maceration	At LWM	Sandy. Safe bathing. Improvement scheme to give preliminary treatment and a long sea outfall by 1995.
★★★	**Compton Bay**	PPPPPP					Pebbles.
★★	**St Helens**	PFFFPP	1	1,500	Raw		Sandy. Improvements to inland tretament works in 1991.
f ★★	**Seagrove Bay**	PPFFFF					Connected to Ryde.

1 Woolacombe Sand, Woolacombe, Devon   OS Ref: SS4500

Two rugged headlands, Morte Point and Baggy Point, bound this magnificent long, straight, west-facing beach. 2 miles (3.3km) of flat sands extend south from the rocky shore at Woolacombe to the sandstone cliffs of Baggy Point at Putsborough. This end of the beach has again achieved a four-star Heinz Good Beach Guide grading for its water quality. The 380 yard (350m) wide sands are backed by extensive dunes behind which the shrub-covered slopes of Woolacombe Down rise. The beach is popular with surfers because of the crashing waves that wash the shore and with families wanting to relax on the beach. After building sand castles and exploring the rock pools you can escape from the crowds by taking a stroll on the headlands at either end of the bay. On the northern side of Woolacombe there is a pocket-sized beach, in complete contrast to the long sweeping sands to the south. The small sandy Barricane beach nestles among the rocky shore stretching to Morte Point and is overlooked by the hotels and guest houses of Woolacombe.

Water quality Beach monitored by the NRA and found to meet the EC Guideline coliform standards for bathing water in 1991; **** in this year's listing section – the second year running. One outfall serving 11,000 people discharges fully treated sewage 100m (120 yards) below low water, north of the beach.

Bathing safety It is dangerous to swim near the rocks or at low tide due to undertow currents. Lifeguards patrol the beach from Whitsun to the second week in September.

Access A turning off the approach road to Woolacombe from the B3231 leads to car parks behind the beach. There are paths through the dunes to the sands.

Parking There are several car parks behind the dunes which provide over 1,000 spaces. National Trust car park close to Baggy Point.

Toilets There are toilets in the car park behind the dunes and at the Putsborough end of the beach.

Food Cafés and shops at the Woolacombe end of the beach; shop at Putsborough car park.

Seaside activities Swimming, surfing, windsurfing, diving, sailing and fishing. Surfboards are available for hire. Hang gliding from Woolacombe Down.

Wildlife and walks The North Devon Coast Path leads in both directions from Morte Bay. To the south, the gorse-clad Baggy Point affords excellent views across the bay, as does the jagged slate headland of Morte Point. On a clear day you can see Lundy Island lying 15 miles (24km) away in the Bristol Channel. This island is a Marine Nature Reserve, renowned for the rich marine wildlife around its rocky shores. The steep cliffs that soar 130 yards (120m) above the sea are the haunt of numerous seabirds. Trips to the island to explore its superb shore in greater detail are available from Ilfracombe harbour.

2 Shipload Bay, Hartland, Devon   OS Ref: SS2428

Far removed from the seaside resort or the quaint tourist attraction, this is a small unspoilt cove on the northern side of Hartland Point. 110 yard

(100m) cliffs rise sharply above the half moon of shingle and low tide sand. There are rocky reefs at either side of the beach below the grass-covered cliffs. The steps which lead down to this sheltered beach are steep and quite difficult.

Water quality No sewage is discharged in the vicinity of this beach. Beach monitored by the NRA and found to meet the EC Guideline coliform standards for bathing water in 1991; ★★★★ in this year's listing section.

Bathing safety Safe bathing from the centre of the beach but beware of currents that may cause problems.

Access From Hartland take the road signposted to Hartland Point lighthouse. The bay lies just off the road a mile before the Point; there are steps down the steep cliffs.

Parking There is a National Trust car park on the cliff top.

Toilets None.

Food None.

Seaside activities Swimming.

Wildlife and walks The North Devon Coast Path leads along the cliff path to Hartland Point; the strenuous walk is rewarded with excellent views along the rocky shore to the south and to Lundy Island on the far horizon. From the point, you look down on to a lighthouse standing on a lower promontory (the lighthouse is not open to the public).

3 Sandy Mouth, near Bude, Cornwall   OS Ref SS200100

The National Trust watch over this superb Cornish beach. Rocks and sand, with many rock pools – this beach is in pristine condition and absolutely unspoilt. The cliffs surrounding the beach are somewhat unstable but covered in beautiful wildflowers.

Water Quality The beach is monitored by the NRA and found to meet EC minimum coliform standards for bathing water in 1991; ★★★ in this year's listing section.

Bathing safety Swimming is dangerous at low tide due to currents.

Access From A39 going north, turn left to Stibb and continue through the village to the beach car park (National Trust).

Parking NT car park, 300m behind beach.

Toilets Near car park, including disabled facilities.

Food Beach shop/café.

Seaside activities National Trust leaflet offers interpretation for the beach. Walking recommended, but keep one eye on the tide; some areas may be cut off by the incoming tide and the cliffs offer little escape.

Wildlife and Walks The area boasts an Area of Outstanding Natural Beauty, Heritage Coast, Cornish Trust for Nature Conservation and National Trust land. This is a valuable site indeed – please treat it with great care.

4 Widemouth Sand, Widemouth Bay, Cornwall   OS Ref: SS2002

In contrast to a lot of the beaches in North Cornwall, the mile of flat sands at Widemouth Bay is backed by low cliffs and undulating grassy fields which stretch down to the beach from the whitewashed houses of Widemouth village. Flat rocks, which can be too hot to lie on, stretch away in either direction from this popular surfing beach. The relatively easy access, which can be so important if you do not wish to negotiate steep cliff paths, unfortunately often means that in summer the beach also becomes very congested. The cliffs that rise on either side of the beach provide walks away from the busy sands.

Water quality Beach monitored by the NRA and found to meet the EC minimum coliform standards for bathing water in 1991; ★★★ in this year's listing section. No sewage is discharged in the vicinity of the beach.

Litter There are reports of bottles and containers being washed up on the beach. The beach is cleaned by the local authority.

Bathing safety Surf bathing is dangerous at low tide, and beware of currents near the rocks at each side of the beach. Lifeguards patrol the beach during the summer.

Access Widemouth Bay is signposted from the A39 south of Bude. Sandy slopes and steps lead from the car parks on to the beach.

Parking There are two car parks behind the beach, at either end of the bay, with spaces for approximately 200 cars in each.

Toilets At the car parks.

Food A café at the southern car park and a beach shop at the northern car park.

Seaside activities Swimming, surfing, windsurfing and fishing. Surfboards are available for hire.

Wildlife and walks The coast path leads off the road south of the beach, climbing Penhalt cliff towards Dizzards Point. There are superb views looking back along the straight coast stretching north of Bude.

5 Crackington Haven, Cornwall   OS Ref: SX1496

A steep-sided valley opens to the coast at Crackington Haven. At its mouth is a small 'V' shaped sandy beach, flanked on either side by sheer, dark cliffs. Those of Pencarrow Point on the north-eastern side of the beach rise 400 feet (120m) above the sands, which are edged with rocky outcrops. Surfers ride the waves that wash this beach, although anyone swimming or surfing should steer well clear of the rocks on either side of the bay. A perfect little beach for the family who want to spend a day on a beach with a lovely setting; there are superb walks along the coast path for those that tire of the sand and surf. Unfortunately the village can be rather congested in summer. Dogs are banned from the beach between Easter Sunday and 1st October.

Water quality Beach monitored by the NRA and found to meet the EC minimum coliform standards for bathing water in 1991; ★★ in this year's listing section. No sewage is discharged in the vicinity of this beach.

Bathing safety Bathing is safe in the centre of the bay, but the rocks on the southern shore are very dangerous. Lifeguards patrol the beach in summer.

Access Signposted from the A39, steep lanes lead down to the village where there is a small car park; it is a short walk to the sands. Grass slopes and rocky outcrops edge the beach and a road runs parallel.

Parking There is a car park in the village which fills very quickly in summer. A council car park, with picnic facilities, is close to the beach.

Toilets There are public toilets in the village.

Food There is a shop, café and two pubs in the village.

Seaside activities Swimming, surfing and fishing.

Wildlife and walks The stretch of coast that lies both north and south of this bay must be one of the wildest and most magnificent in the country. The coast path follows the grass slope which rises south of the bay: the path leads over National Trust land to High Cliff – a stretch of extremely rugged shale cliffs that rise 731 feet (222m) above the waves. As its name suggests, this is one of the highest cliffs in England. Below is a sandy beach known as The Strangles because of the numerous boats that have found their final resting place on this shore. The rock-studded sands can be reached down an extremely steep and rough path, which is not to be recommended. Bathing from the beach is very dangerous. There are superb views all along the coast path from Crackington to Boscastle; the path can be reached from the National Trust car park south of Trevigue. There is also an information point at this site.

6 Trebarwith Strand, Treknow, Cornwall   OS Ref: SX0587

The lane through a deep wooded valley ends at what can appear to be a tiny rocky cove with cliffs framing an attractive view to Gull Rock. But as the tide recedes an expanse of sand stretching north below steep cliffs is revealed. From the lane end smooth rocks must be crossed to reach the rock-studded sands. A most impressive beach but one on which great care must be taken as the rising tide can cut off the unwary visitor; signs at the entrance to the beach warn of the dangers.

Water quality No sewage is discharged in the vicinity of this beach. There are, however, concerns about the quality of the stream which flows across the sands. The beach is monitored by the NRA and was found to meet the EC minimum coliform standards for bathing water in 1991; ★★★ in this year's listing section.

Bathing safety Swimming can be dangerous at low water and close to rocks. Great care must be taken when surfing. The beach is patrolled by lifeguards during the summer months.

Access Trebarwith Strand is signposted from the B3236, Camelford to Tintagel road. The road ends at the shore, with smooth rocks leading down on to the sand.

Parking There are two car parks off the road with about 140 spaces; it is a 2 minute walk down to the beach.

Toilets At the entrance to the beach.

Food There is a café, hotel, restaurant and pub at the beach entrance.

Seaside activities Swimming, surfing. Surf school on the strand.

Wildlife and walks From the coast path which follows the cliffs there are good views of the rocky cliffs, beach and the Gull Rock (in appearance a small version of the Ailsa Craig rock on the Clyde coast). North, the path leads to Tintagel with its cliff-top castle, the legendary seat of King Arthur. In the village the Old Post Office and King Arthur's Hall can also be visited. Tintagel is a honeypot for visitors and becomes very congested in summer. The Heritage Coast Mobile Visitor Centre comes to the area regularly in the summer.

7 Polzeath, Cornwall   OS Ref SW930790

Situated in Hayle Bay in the Camel Estuary, Polzeath is a very popular small resort. The beach is flat and sandy and is cleaned regularly by volunteers from the local Residents Association, resulting in its being awarded a Golden Starfish in 1991. There is an information board on the beach which gives information about the beach and surrounding area and details of water quality.

Water quality Beach monitored by the NRA and found to meet the EC minimum coliform standards for bathing water in 1991; ★★ in this year's listing section. One outfall serving 656 people discharges primary treated sewage at low water mark.

Litter The beach is cleaned regularly.

Bathing safety Bathing can be dangerous at low water; there are lifeguards in summer.

Access A turning off the B3314 leads down a steep hill to Polzeath. The village is on a local bus route.

Parking Two private car parks adjacent to the beach; one local authority car park on the beach and another at New Polzeath close by. The Marine Conservation Society is not in favour of car parking on the beach.

Toilets Near the beach, with facilities for the disabled.

Food Hotels, pubs, cafés and takeaways in the village.

Seaside activities Swimming, surfing.

Wildlife and walks There are good walks on the National Trust property north of Polzeath with superb views from Pentire Point and the Rumps headland where there is an Iron Age fort. Tamarisk grows well in this area and is spectacular in July and August.

8 Harlyn Bay, Harlyn, Cornwall   OS Ref: SW8776

A wide bite into the cliffs on the sheltered eastern side of Trevose Head contains the sandy arc of Harlyn Bay, ⅔ mile (1km) in length. A bank of soft sand overlaid with a scattering of pebbles gives way to gently shelving surf-washed sand, backed by the dunes of Harlyn Warren which are themselves bounded by the dark grey and brown flecked cliffs towards Cataclews Point. There is a small indent in the cliffs, forming Big Guns Cove. Access to the beach is from the south-eastern corner at Harlyn Village, where a stream flows on to the beach and curves to St Cadoc's Point. The remains of an Iron Age cemetery were found below the sands behind the beach.

Water quality Beach monitored by the NRA and found to meet the EC minimum coliform standards for bathing water in 1991; ★★★ in this year's listing section. One outfall serving 3,202 people discharges secondary treated sewage at low water mark east of Cataclews Point. In winter sewage only undergoes maceration.

Litter Some sea-borne litter is washed on to the shore. The beach is cleaned by the local authority.

Bathing safety Safe bathing. Patrolled by lifeguards in summer.

Access The road from the B3276 to Harlyn runs along the south-eastern corner of the beach. There is a footpath from the car park to the sand.

Parking There is a car park off the road directly behind the beach.

Toilets At the car park.

Food Refreshments available close to the beach.

Seaside activities Swimming, surfing and fishing.

Wildlife and walks The walk along the cliffs north-east of the bay skirts Mother Ivey's Bay; a lifeboat house stands on the northern shore of this rocky cove. The footpath continues along the cliffs to the point of Trevose Head where a lighthouse stands sentinel. There are superb sea views towards Pentire Head in the north-east and south towards Newquay, with several small, rocky islands lying just east of the head.

9 Constantine Bay, Treyarnon, Cornwall   OS Ref: SW8575

This wide sweeping arc of gently shelving soft pale sands, backed by large marram-covered dunes and bounded on either side by low headlands with rocky outcrops stretching seawards, is a picture to behold. There is very limited parking and there are few facilities available at the beach.

Water quality Beach monitored by the NRA and found to meet the EC minimum coliform standards for bathing water in 1991; ★★★ in this year's listing section. No sewage is discharged in the vicinity of this beach.

Bathing safety Bathing is dangerous near the rocks.

Access A road off the B3276 at St Merryn is signposted Constantine Bay.

Parking A private car park with space for 200 cars is located 2 minutes from the beach.

Toilets At the entrance to the beach.

Food None.

Seaside activities Swimming, surfing.

Wildlife and walks The dunes behind the beach are under restoration, with marram grass being planted to stabilise the sands. There are interesting rock pools to explore. The coast path skirts the bay but the low cliffs do not provide the spectacular views that can be found elsewhere on this coastline.

10 Treyarnon Bay, Padstow, Cornwall   OS Ref SW859740

Treyarnon is a still unspoilt wide, sandy bay in an Area of Outstanding Natural Beauty, next to the larger Constantine Bay. The beach is popular with surfers and was awarded a Golden Starfish in 1991 for its cleanliness. It is very dangerous, however, to swim near the cliffs and there are warning notices.

Water quality Beach monitored by the NRA and found to meet the EC minimum coliform standards for bathing water in 1991; ★★ in this year's listing section. No sewage is discharged in the vicinity of the beach.

Litter The beach is cleaned regularly and dogs are banned.

Bathing safety Swimmers should keep to the centre of the beach. There is a lifeguard service, lifeline and reel with an emergency telephone. A natural pool in the rocks provides safe swimming at low tide.

Access There is a turning off the B3276 to Treyarnon.

Parking Car park adjacent to the beach with approximately 150 spaces.

Toilets Near the beach, with facilities for the disabled.

Food Beach shop and hotel.
Seaside activities Swimming, surfing. Surfboards available for hire.
Wildlife and walks Treyarnon is on the North Cornwall Coast Path which affords spectacular views.

11 Bedruthan Steps, Trenance, Cornwall   OS Ref: SW8469

The beach that lies below the towering grey cliffs is a visual marvel, best appreciated from the cliff top. The steep slopes of the granite cliffs are reflected in the many islands and rock stacks that have been left isolated by the retreating cliff line. At low tide the rock stacks which punctuate the beach are separated by golden sands. At high tide the beach completely disappears and the rocks are pounded by the waves that have created this wonderful scenery. From Carnewas Island the sands stretch 1¼ miles (2km) north to Park Head. Steep steps lead down the cliff to the beach. Visitors should note that swimming from the beach is dangerous and that there are areas of the beach that are quickly cut off by the rising tide. Legend says that the rocks were used by a giant, Bedruthan, as stepping stones and this gives the beach its name. The National Trust owns this section of coastline and it has provided good facilities for the numerous visitors that come to view the lovely scenery.
Water quality No sewage is discharged in the vicinity of this beach. The NRA do not monitor the water quality at this beach.
Bathing safety Bathing is dangerous, particularly at low tide.
Access Signposted from B3276 north of Trenance, the road ends at the car park. A path leads from the car park to steep steps down the cliff to the beach.
Parking There is a National Trust car park on the cliff top with space for approximately 100 cars.
Toilets Public toilets at car park.
Food There is a National Trust shop and café near the car park.
Wet weather alternatives There is a National Trust Information Centre close to the beach.
Wildlife and walks The Cornwall North Coast Path provides good walking north and south of the beach, with fine views along this beautiful rocky coastline.

12 Crantock, Cornwall   OS Ref: SW7761

An excellent sandy beach nestles between the twin headlands of Pentire Point East and Pentire Point West. The beach is backed by high dunes and Rushy Green, an area of undulating grassland behind the dunes. The tidal channel of the River Gannel bounds the northern side of the beach, below Pentire Point East. There is a deep inlet in the low cliffs on the south side of the bay, Vugga Cove, which can only be reached at low tide. There are also a number of caves; the one closest inshore – Piper's Hole – can be explored at low tide. There are many signs of man's activities around the bay; two slipways are cut into the rocks of Vugga Cove, a poem is carved on a rock in Piper's Hole and there is evidence along the Gannel of its past use as a natural harbour.

Water quality Beach monitored by the NRA and found to meet the EC minimum coliform standards for bathing water in 1991; ★★★ in this year's listing section. There is no sewage discharged in the vicinity of this beach.

Bathing safety Bathing is dangerous at low tide and near the Gannel. Red flags indicate where and when it is safe to swim. The beach is patrolled by lifeguards between mid-May and mid-September.

Access Crantock is signposted from the A3075 south of Newquay. A lane from the village leads to a car park behind the dunes. There is a path through the dunes to the beach. The beach can also be reached from West Pentire; a path leads from the village to steps down the cliffs. The Gannel can be crossed from Newquay by either ferry or tidal bridge at Fern Pit or Trethellan.

Parking There is a National Trust car park behind the dunes and another in West Pentire.

Toilets There are toilets at both car parks.

Food There are cafés, shops and pubs in Crantock and West Pentire.

Seaside activities Swimming, surfing and fishing.

Wildlife and walks There is a network of paths south of the beach providing pleasant circular walks. The footpath which follows the cliffs on the southern side of the beach passes Piper's Hole, a deep crevice in the cliffs where fulmars may be seen nesting. The path continues to the end of the headland where there is a collapsed cave and beautiful views to be enjoyed. Tucked below the headland is a tiny unspoilt cove, Porth Joke. The walker can either continue around the next headland, Kelsey Head, toward Holywell beach or make the return journey across Cubert Common.

13 Holywell Bay, Holywell, Cornwall   OS Ref: SW7559

Holywell Bay gets its name from two wells in the area said to contain waters with healing powers. ⅔ mile (1km) of lovely sands sweep south from the low cliffs of Kelsey Head to Penhale Point. The beach is backed by dunes that rise to 200 feet (60m). At the southern end a stream flows through the dunes and across the sands. A narrow cave entrance in the cliffs, at the northern end of the bay, can be explored at low tide. It contains one of the holy wells.

Water quality Beach monitored by the NRA and found to meet the EC minimum coliform standards for bathing water in 1991; ★★★ in this year's listing section. No sewage is discharged in the vicinity of this beach.

Bathing safety Bathing is only safe between the orange and red flags. Surfing is dangerous at low tide. Lifeguards patrol the beach during the summer months.

Access Holywell is signposted from the A3075 south of Newquay. A path leads from the village along the side of the stream to the beach.

Parking There is a car park in Holywell village.

Toilets There are toilets in Holywell.

Food There are shops and pubs in Holywell.

Seaside activities Swimming and surfing.

Wet weather alternatives Holywell Bay Leisure Park on the approach road to the village.

Wildlife and walks A path north along the beach follows the cliffs on to Kelsey Head, where the scant remains of a castle can be seen. From the headland there are excellent views back across the beach, north to the adjacent Pentire Point West and also over 'The Chick', a small rocky island offshore. Seals may often be seen around the island. To the south of the bay the path leads to Penhale Sands, an extensive area of sand hills stretching to Perranporth 3½ miles (5.5km) away. Unfortunately the path is sometimes closed because parts of the dunes are used by the Ministry of Defence as a firing range. A red flag indicates when access is restricted.

14 The Towans, Hayle, St Ives, Cornwall   OS Ref: SW5639

St Ives Bay has a magnificent necklace of golden beaches, backed on its southern edge by high dunes and some rocky outcrops. The approach to the beach at Hayle is uninspiring; there has been a lot of development on the landward side of the dunes which is rather unattractive and an army of telegraph poles marches across the scene. However, once down on these lovely sands all is forgotten; the 3 miles (5km) of rippled pale golden sands remain untouched by the development behind. From the mouth of the River Hayle the sands, fringed by magnificent dunes and rocky outcrops, stretch north towards Godrevy Point where Godrevy lighthouse stands on an island just offshore. Dogs are banned from the beach from Easter to 1st October.

Water quality Beach monitored by the NRA and found to meet the EC minimum coliform standards for bathing water in 1991, ** in this year's listing section. No sewage is discharged in the vicinity of this beach; an outfall is to be constructed at Gwithian to discharge St Ives and Penzance sewage.

Litter The beach is cleaned regularly.

Bathing safety There are strong currents around the river mouth which make bathing dangerous. Lifeguards patrol during the summer.

Access The beach is signposted from the A30 through Hayle. The road leads up to the car parks behind the dunes and the sands are less than 5 minutes' walk away.

Parking Car parks behind the dunes provide plenty of spaces.

Toilets At the car parks.

Food Beach shop and café at the car parks. A hotel provides snacks and meals.

Seaside activities Swimming and surfing. Surfboards are available for hire.

Wet weather alternatives Hayle Paradise Park and West Cornwall Leisure and Bowling Club.

Wildlife and walks Following the beach north brings you to the rocky shore towards Godrevy Point where the coast path leads along the cliffs to Navax Point. There are lovely views back across St Ives Bay and numerous seabirds can be seen nesting on the cliffs.

15 Porthmeor, St Ives, Cornwall   OS Ref: SW5241

The delightful old buildings which are crowded together on the narrow streets around the harbour spill directly on to the beach at Porthmeor. A row of stone houses faces on to the sands but they in no way spoil this most attractive of beaches. Below St Ives Head, also known as the Island, ⅔ mile (1km) of soft sand backed by low cliffs stretches west. Unlike the more sheltered beaches on the other side of the headland, Porthmeor is a surfer's beach with the waves from the Atlantic rolling on to the shore. A promenade at the foot of the cliffs provides all the facilities needed for a day on this lovely beach. St Ives is famous for its quality of light which has made it popular with artists, a fact reflected in the numerous art galleries and craft workshops to be found in the town. Dogs are banned from the beach from Easter until 1st October.

Water quality Beach monitored by the NRA and found to meet the EC minimum coliform standards for bathing water in 1991; ★★★ in this year's listing section. One outfall serving 50 people discharges fine screened sewage into the sea 155 yards (150m) from the harbour wall.

Litter The beach is cleaned daily in the summer.

Bathing safety Care must be taken. The beach is patrolled by lifeguards in the summer. An area for use of surfboards is marked with buoys.

Access The beach is signposted within the town but it is best to use the large car park above the town and walk down to the beach. There are steps and a lane down on to the sands.

Parking The main car park for the town is signposted on the approach roads. There are car parks at either end of the beach; each has space for about 40 cars.

Toilets At the car parks.

Food Beach shop and café on the promenade.

Seaside activities Swimming and surfing. Deck chairs, surfboards and beach huts are available for hire. Boat trips around St Ives Bay are available from the harbour.

Wet weather alternatives Art galleries, craft workshops, Barbara Hepworth Museum, St Ives museum, St Ives Leisure and Squash Club.

Wildlife and walks From the beach a coastal path leads west along the low rocky cliffs to a series of sandy and rocky coves.

16 Priest's Cove, St Just, Cornwall   OS Ref: SW3532

Cape Cornwall was presented to the National Trust by Heinz as part of their Guardians of the Countryside programme with the World Wide Fund for Nature. The headland and surroundings remain unspoilt, having escaped the commercialisation of Land's End. A tall chimney stands sentinel on the domed headland, a disused ventilation shaft for the mines far below. The rocky Priest's Cove shelters on the southern side of the Cape, its 200 feet (60m) of shingle ringed by low rugged cliffs. There are numerous quiet and unspoilt coves around the toe of Cornwall – rocky shores with a small fishing boat or two drawn up on to the pebbles. A good starting point to enjoy this rugged, windswept coastline and explore the exposed rocky shore where marine life is plentiful.

Water quality No sewage is discharged in the vicinity of this beach. The beach is not monitored by the NRA.

Bathing safety Bathing can be unsafe due to the rocky nature of the shore and the large swell that develops.

Access A narrow lane from St Just leads to a car park behind the beach. There is a path and concrete ramp to the shore.
Parking Car park with about 70 spaces behind the beach.
Toilets At the car park.
Food Occasionally an ice-cream van at the car park.
Seaside activities Swimming and fishing.
Wet weather alternatives North of St Just at Trewellard is Geevor Mine and Mining Museum and at Pendeen there is a mineral and mining museum.
Wildlife and walks There is a pleasant walk on to the Cape where you can enjoy good views along the coast towards Land's End and out to the Brison Rocks where seals can be seen. The coast path provides good walking both north and south along the rugged granite cliffs which are dotted with the remains of mines.

17 Whitesand Bay, Sennen Cove, Cornwall   OS Ref: SW3626

On the rugged Land's End Peninsula the splendid sweep of Whitesand Bay is in sharp contrast to the many rocky coves that indent the cliffs. From the picturesque little harbour of Sennen Cove the beach stretches north 1 mile (1.6km) to Aire Point, with steep cliffs ringing the northern section. The southern end of this moderately shelving beach is good for swimming and surfing, being sheltered by offshore reefs. The northern end is open to the full force of the Atlantic and conditions can be wild and dangerous. Dogs are banned from the beach between Easter and 1st October.
Water quality Beach monitored by the NRA and found to meet the EC minimum coliform standards for bathing water in 1991; ★★★ in this year's listing section. One outfall serving 1,489 people discharges macerated sewage at low water mark by the harbour. There have been some complaints of sewage slicks in the bay in the past. Litter clean-up well managed by the local authority.
Bathing safety Bathing and surfing are safe at the southern end of the bay. Lifeguards patrol the beach during the summer months.
Access A road from the A30 to Land's End leads steeply down to Sennen Cove. There is easy access to the beach.
Parking There is a car park in Sennen Cove and another on the approach road.
Toilets There are toilets in the village.
Food There are shops, cafés and a pub in the village.
Seaside activities Swimming, surfing and angling. Fishing trips are available from the harbour. Surfboards can be hired.
Wildlife and walks The granite cliffs south from Sennen Cove to Land's End are owned by the National Trust. The coast path follows the cliff top which can be wild and windswept. It is probably the best way to approach Land's End avoiding the severe summer congestion of the most westerly tip of Britain, which has been rather spoilt by uncontrolled development.

18 Praa Sands, Ashton, Helston, Cornwall   OS Ref: GR5827

This most attractive sweep of sand between rocky headlands is a popular beach for the family. Sheltered by Hoe Point cliffs to the west, the 1 mile

(1.6km) sandy strip edged by high dunes stretches east to Lesceave cliff and the granite Rinsey Headland. At low water 110 yards (100m) of gently sloping sand is exposed, with rockpools at either end containing an interesting variety of marine life. There is a car park on the headland and a path leads down to the quiet sandy cove of Porthcew. Caravan parks close by make the beach busy.

Water quality Beach monitored by the NRA and found to meet the EC minimum coliform standards for bathing water in 1991; both East and West Beaches have ★★★ in this year's listing section. No sewage is discharged in the vicinity of this beach.

Litter Although the beach is cleaned regularly by the National Trust, seaborne litter is frequently washed ashore.

Bathing safety A rip current makes bathing at low tide very unsafe; the beach is patrolled by lifeguards during the summer season.

Access Praa Sands are signposted from the A394 between Helston and Penzance. From the car park there is a short walk down a sloping path to the beach. From the car park further up the hill there are steps and a steeper path to the beach.

Parking On the road down to the beach there is a car park with 100 spaces. At the bottom of the hill, adjacent to the beach entrance, there is another small car park.

Toilets At the entrance to the beach.

Food Cafés/takeaways and a pub/restaurant at the beach entrance.

Seaside activities Swimming, diving, surfing, windsurfing, sailing, raft racing and fishing.

Wildlife and walks The coast path from the eastern end of the beach leads away from the often crowded sands up Lesceave cliff and on to Rinsey Head. Wheal Prosper, the engine house of an old copper mine, stands on the headland; the property and surrounding land is owned by the National Trust. The mine shaft has been capped and the building restored. A mile (1.6km) further east the ruin of another mine stands on Trewavas Head. To the west of Praa Sands the coast path rises over the cliffs at Hoe Point, passing Kenneggy Sands and Prussia Cove before reaching Cudden Point.

19 Poldhu Cove, Mullion, Cornwall   OS Ref: GR6620

A stream crosses this sheltered, sandy cove backed by dunes and bordered by steep, turf-covered slopes. At high tide there is a fair-sized beach, and the falling tide reveals wide, gently sloping sands washed by clear green seas. This cove is easily accessible, making it popular and often busy. It can be a good starting point for reaching coves north and south which are quieter. The Cornwall South Coast Path leads south to the Marconi Memorial ¾ mile (1.2km) away, and north to Church and Dollar coves. Both are fine, sandy coves framed by low, rocky cliffs, but they are unsafe for swimming at low tide. On the rocks of Church Cove stands the 15th-century church of St Winwaloe.

Water quality Beach monitored by the NRA and found to meet the EC minimum coliform standards for bathing water in 1991; ★★★ in this year's listing section. There is no sewage discharged into Poldhu Cove.

Bathing safety Signs warn that it is unsafe to swim for one hour either side of low tide. The beach is patrolled by lifeguards during the summer season.

Access A lane north-west of Mullion, signposted to Poldhu, leads down to the car park behind the beach. There is a path to the sands.

Parking There is a car park with 100 spaces close to the beach. There is another car park behind Church Cove.

Toilets There are toilets on the beach.

Food There is a beach shop/café.

Seaside activities Swimming, surfing, windsurfing and fishing from the beach, but no hiring facilities for boards etc.

Wildlife and walks There are pools among the rocks that fringe the beach, with plenty of marine life to be examined.

20 Kynance Cove, The Lizard, Cornwall   OS Ref: GR6912

A classic Cornish cove which is extremely well known for its magnificent cliff scenery and is therefore popular with visitors. 200 foot (60m) cliffs shadow the golden sands which are revealed at low tide. Softer layers of rock between the richly-coloured serpentine have been eroded to form some spectacular cliff formations, impressive isolated stacks, arches and caves. This includes 'The Devil's Bellows' stacks which tower as high as the cliffs; they are surrounded by the sands of the cove at low tide. The beach completely disappears at high tide, so great care is required not to get cut off by the rising tide.

Water quality No sewage is discharged in the vicinity of this beach. The NRA does not monitor this beach.

Bathing safety Safe bathing away from the rocks.

Access A toll road from the A3083 north of The Lizard leads to a car park on the cliff top. It is a 5-minute walk to the cove down a valley path to the north of the car park.

Parking There is a National Trust car park on the cliff top.

Toilets In the car park.

Food Beach café. Seasonal refreshments in the car park.

Seaside activities Swimming.

Wildlife and walks There is good walking on the coast path along the cliffs from which the seabirds nesting on the cliffs and stacks can be best appreciated. There are caves that can be explored at low tide.

21 Polpeor, The Lizard, Cornwall   OS Ref: SW7012

The Lizard Peninsula is beautiful and remote, with much of interest for the naturalist. Unfortunately, in the summer it is overwhelmed by visitors and the narrow roads become congested with traffic. If you want to appreciate the lovely coves around the headland, make your visit early or late in the season to avoid some of the crowds. Polpeor is a small rock and shingle cove at the southernmost tip of the Lizard, framed by the cliffs of the Lizard Head and the Lizard Point, a rocky promontory that shelters the beach. The 110 yard (100m) beach disappears at high water. A former lifeboat house and slipway adjoins the beach on to which a few boats are still drawn. The turning of the local marble-like serpentine rock has become a small local industry with many of the items sold locally.

Water quality No sewage is discharged from this beach. The NRA does not monitor this beach.

Bathing safety Safe bathing.

Access There is a path from the car park 500 yards (450m) from the beach.

Parking There are two car parks with 100 spaces.

Toilets On the beach.

Food Cafés close to the beach.

Seaside activities Swimming and fishing.

Wet weather alternatives Museum of Cornish History in the village, lighthouse and lifeboat house open to the public.

Wildlife and walks Several rare plant species flourish in the mild climate of the Lizard Peninsula, particularly those of the maritime heathland which is a feature of the headland.

22 Kennack Sands, Kuggar, Cornwall   OS Ref: SW7316

Probably the best swimming beach on the Lizard, Kennack Sands gained a four-star water quality rating in 1991. Two separate 550 yard (500m) beaches merge at low tide to form one wide, gently sloping sandy beach. The pale sands, on the sheltered eastern side of the Lizard Peninsula, are fringed by dunes. At either end of the bay the sand gives way to shingle, which is bounded landwards by cliffs. This is a popular family beach.

Water quality Beach monitored by the NRA and found to meet the EC minimum coliform standards for bathing water in 1991; ★★★ in this year's listing section. No sewage is discharged in the vicinity of this beach.

Bathing safety Safe bathing.

Access A road from Kuggar village signposted for Kennack ends behind the beach; there is a short walk through dunes to the sands.

Parking There is a car park at the beach entrance with 250 spaces.

Toilets There is a toilet in the car park.

Food Cafés at the entrance to the beach.

Seaside activities Swimming, surfing, diving, windsurfing and fishing. Surfboards are available for hire adjacent to the beach.

Wildlife and walks The Cornwall South Coast Path proceeds east from the beach along the cliff tops towards Black Head with good sea views.

23 Towan Beach, Portscatho, Cornwall   OS Ref: SW8733

A safe and sandy beach south of the fishing village of Portscatho. 550 yards (500m) of sand and pebbles are encircled by low shale cliffs on which wild flowers abound. St Anthony's Head, south-east of the beach, guards the entrance to Carrick Roads.

Water quality No sewage is discharged in the vicinity of this beach. The NRA does not monitor this beach.

Litter Fishing materials and a lot of plastics are frequently washed up on the beach; however, it is cleaned by the owners, the National Trust.

Bathing safety Safe bathing.

Access From Portscatho take the road to St Anthony's Head. The car park is off this road. There is a 330 yard (300m) level walk from the car park behind the beach to the sands.

Parking There is a National Trust car park behind the beach at Porth Farm with 200 spaces.

Toilets Toilets, including disabled facilities, 275 yards (250m) from beach.

Food None.

Seaside activities Swimming, windsurfing, diving and fishing.

Wildlife and walks The beach lies on the Cornwall South Coast Path, which can be followed in either direction. There is a 6 mile (9.6km) circular route starting at the beach; follow the path inland along Froe Creek, turning east along the Percuil to Carricknath Point and beach. From there continue to the lighthouse on St Anthony's Head, where there is a superb panorama of Falmouth Bay and the Black Rock. The path returns to Towan beach along the cliff top.

24 Pendower Beach, Veryan, Cornwall   OS Ref: SW9038

A lovely, unspoilt beach with an attractive setting facing Gerrans Bay; there are good views from the beach towards the gorse-covered cliffs of Nare Head. There is a ⅔ mile (1km) strip of coarse sand fringed by dunes which have suffered from erosion. In order to repair the damage, access is restricted with areas fenced off. Further west the sand gives way to the rocky outcrops and sand of Carne Beach. There are rocky platforms below the steeply sloping cliffs towards Nare Head. A good family beach with easy access.

Water quality Beach monitored by the NRA and found to meet the EC minimum coliform standards for bathing water in 1991; ★★ in this year's listing section. No sewage is discharged in the vicinity of the beach.

Bathing safety Safe bathing.

Access A turning off the A3078 leads to the car park behind the beach. Do not take cars right to the end of road as there is only parking for hotel patrons. There are board walks across the dunes suitable for wheelchairs.

Parking National Trust car park behind the dunes has 200 spaces.

Toilets There are toilets in the car park.

Food The Pendower House Hotel and café overlook the beach.

Seaside activities Swimming, windsurfing, diving, sailing, canoeing, waterskiing and fishing.

Wet weather alternatives Veryan Sports Club.

Wildlife and walks There is abundant marine life to be found in the rockpools along the shore. The coast path follows the cliffs that rise to the southeast of the beach. There are excellent views from Nare Head and from Carne Beacon. The panorama along the coast stretches from Zone Point in the west to Dodman Point in the east.

25 Bow or Vault Beach, Gorran Haven, Cornwall OS Ref: SX0141

Sheltered on the eastern side of Dodman Point is the superb Vault Beach, a sweep of sand and shingle below steep, bracken- and heather-clad cliffs. From Maenease Point the beach curves for ⅔ mile (1km) to the rock outcrop of Penover Point. The cliffs rise beyond to the impressive 370 foot (110m) bulk of Dodman Point.

Water quality Beach monitored by the NRA and found to meet the EC Guideline coliform standards for bathing water in 1991; ★★★★ in this year's listing section. One sewage outfall serving 2,487 people discharges untreated sewage at low water mark on the north side of Maenease Point.

Litter There is only a very small amount of litter on this beach.

Bathing safety Bathing is safe with care.

Access The coast path must be followed south from Gorran Haven to reach a steep path down the cliffs. Alternatively, there is a path down from Lamledra Farm.

Parking There is a National Trust car park at Lamledra Farm, above the beach.

Toilets None.

Food None.

Seaside activities Swimming.

Wildlife and walks The coast path along the cliff top leads on to Dodman Point; there is evidence of an Iron Age fort with a ditch and bank. At the point, a granite cross stands as a memorial to all the ships that have been wrecked around the point. There are superb views along much of the Cornish coast.

26 Lantic Bay, Polruan, Cornwall OS Ref: SX1451

A superb cove framed by high turf- and shrub-covered cliffs which can only be reached by a 10-minute walk from the nearest road. The shingle and sand beach shelves steeply. The undulating land approaches and the smooth-profiled cliffs give the area an impression of gentleness in comparison to the jagged outlines of the cliffs to the east. This is a fine bathing beach owned by the National Trust, but much care is needed when swimming due to a strong undertow.

Water quality No sewage is discharged in the vicinity of this beach. The beach was monitored by the NRA and found to meet the EC minimum coliform standards for bathing water in 1991; ★★★ in this year's listing section.

Litter A lot of plastic bottles, caps and rope are regularly washed up on to the beach which is cleaned by the National Trust.

Bathing safety Strong undertow.

Access From the car park off the Polruan to Polperro road there is a 10-minute walk along the coast path towards Pencarrow Head to reach a very steep path down to the cove. Be careful as this path can be dangerous when wet.

Parking There is a National Trust car park on the cliff-top road east of Polruan.

Toilets None.

Food None.

Seaside activities Swimming.

Wildlife and walks The 400 foot (120m) Pencarrow Head rises east of the beach and from its summit you can see from Devon to The Lizard on a clear day. The coast path that skirts the headland leads to the adjoining Lantivet Bay. West of Lantic Bay the coast path follows the cliffs to St Saviour's Point and Polruan at the mouth of the Fowey. Grey seals can often be seen in the bay.

27 Lansallos Bay, Cornwall   OS Ref: SX1651

This lovely small shingle and sand cove owned by the National Trust is completely unspoilt. This cove, shadowed by high cliffs, is reached by a 15-minute walk from Lansallos and this ensures that it remains relatively secluded even during high summer. The grass-topped cliffs slope gently to the rock-studded beach below. There are many rockpools full of interesting marine life, and seals are a common sight offshore.

Water quality No sewage is discharged in the vicinity of this beach. The NRA does not monitor this beach.

Bathing safety Safe bathing.

Access From the A387 north of Polperro there is a side road to Lansallos. It is approximately 15 minutes' walk from the village down the valley path to the cove.

Parking There is a National Trust car park in Lansallos village.

Toilets In Lansallos village.

Food Cream teas available in Lansallos Barton.

Seaside activities Swimming and fishing.

Wildlife and walks The coastal path west of the beach leads to Pencarrow Head, a 400 foot (120m) high headland which provides magnificent views of the Cornish coast. East of the beach the path leads along the cliffs to Polperro some 4 miles (6.4km) away.

28 Whitsand Bay, Freathy, Cornwall   OS Ref: SX4052

A 3 mile (5km) sweep of sand backed by 250 foot (75m) cliffs stretches from Portwrinkle south-east to Rame Head. The rugged slate cliffs slope gently down to the beach where rocky outcrops dot the pale grey sands. Portwrinkle, with its tiny harbour, overlooks the rocky shore at the western end of the bay. Once a pilchard fishing village, it is now given over to the holiday industry with holiday development ranging over the cliff top. Further east the beach remains unspoilt by development. Access points to this long stretch of beach are few; there are paths down the cliffs at Tregantle and Freathy, the former providing the easiest route down, but this part of the beach lies below the Tregantle Fort which is used as a firing range. There have also been reports that this section of beach suffers considerably from marine litter washed on to the shore. At Freathy the path is steeper but the reward is a superb clean and quiet beach. There are excellent views along the bay to Rame Head, its seaward-pointing finger ending in a knoll topped by a small chapel. On a calm day the water may look very inviting but beware of strong rip currents.

Water quality Portwrinkle monitored by the NRA and found to meet the EC minimum coliform standards for bathing water in 1991; ★★★ in this year's listing section. Three small outfalls discharge raw sewage at low water mark and one discharges treated sewage. A £900,000 scheme for a long sea outfall should be completed in 1995.

Litter There is a problem in some parts of the bay, with marine litter being washed on to the beach. There is a considerable amount of plastic including bottles, old buckets and packaging.

Bathing safety Bathing is unsafe; the beach is valleyed which causes a tidal race and undertow. Two life-saving clubs patrol the beach at weekends.

Access Whitsand is signposted from the B3247. There are paths down the cliffs at Portwrinkle, Tregonhawke, Tregantle and Freathy. The area around Tregantle Barracks is used by the army as a firing range and a red flag indicates when access is prohibited.

Parking There are clifftop car parks at the access points; there are 150 spaces at Freathy.

Toilets There are public toilets on the beach at Freathy.

Food At Freathy there is a café on the cliff top.

Seaside activities Swimming, surfing and fishing.

Wildlife and walks Tregantle Cliffs and Rame Head are owned by the National Trust and provide good walks over the scrub headland with fine sea views.

29 Cawsand Bay, Cawsand, Cornwall   OS Ref: SX4451

Cawsand Bay is at the approaches to Plymouth Sound, the largest of the series of rias (drowned river valleys) along the south coast. The bay overlooks the Plymouth breakwater, built in the 19th century to provide a safe and sheltered anchorage, and there is a continually changing scene of traffic, naval and civilian, plying in and out of the Sound. The bay curves 3 miles (5km) from Picklecombe Point to Penlee Point. The two villages of Cawsand and Kingsand fringe the southern end of the bay, their colourful houses overlooking the sand and shingle beach which is sheltered by the Rame Head Peninsula to the south. The beach is a series of moderately shelving sandy pockets between rocky outcrops. At either end of the beach the sand gives way to rocky foreshore backed by wooded slate cliffs.

Water quality Five raw outfalls discharge untreated sewage at low water mark, but they appear to be redundant or negligible in their discharges. The NRA does not monitor this beach.

Bathing safety Bathing is safe except when there are south-east winds.

Access A launching ramp leads from the village to the beach.

Parking There is a pay-and-display car park in the village with 100 spaces.

Toilets There are public toilets adjacent to the beach.

Food There is a beach shop and there are also hotels and cafés in the village.

Seaside activities Swimming, windsurfing, sailing, diving and fishing. There are boats available for hire.

Wet weather alternatives Cremyll and Rame Churches, Mount Edgcumbe House and Country Park.

Wildlife and walks 2 miles (3km) north along the coast path lies the Mount Edgcumbe Country Park, 800 acres (323 hectares) of wooded parkland with superb views of Drake Island and Plymouth Sound. The park contains the original Tudor house and a deer park. South of the beach the coastal path follows the wooded slopes to Penlee Point and continues westwards along the cliffs to Rame Head.

30 Wembury, Devon   OS Ref: SX5248

Wembury has been set up as a Marine Protected Area to maintain its diverse marine wildlife. It is a particularly attractive and unspoilt bay. A valley opens to the back of the beach where the only development is a car park and a small shop and café. Flanked on either side by low cliffs, a narrow strip of sand curves round the bay. Low tide reveals a series of sandy pockets between rocky reefs which contain numerous pools. This area is of significant marine biological interest and, while beach users should take the opportunity to investigate the shore life, a great deal of consideration is required so that the area remains unspoilt. The disturbance or collection of marine life should be avoided, as should littering, or any other type of damage to the beach and its surroundings. The view from the beach is dominated by the Great Mew Stone just off shore. There is excellent snorkelling in the area.

Water quality Beach monitored by the NRA and found to meet the EC minimum coliform standards for bathing water in 1991;*** in this year's listing section. One outfall serving 4,383 people discharges primary treated sewage 10 feet (3m) below low water mark west of the bay. A £100,000 scheme for a sewage treatment works is due for completion in 1992.

Litter A small amount of marine litter.

Bathing safety Safe bathing but beware of rocks off shore.

Access Wembury is signposted from the A379. A lane from the village leads down to the car park behind the beach, and a path approaches the beach about 33 yards (30m) away.

Parking National Trust car park behind the beach.

Toilets There are toilets at the car park.

Food National Trust café and shop adjacent to beach.

Seaside activities Swimming, windsurfing, diving, sailing and fishing.

Wildlife and walks The South-West Peninsula Coast Path skirts the bay, but the path to Wembury Point is frequently closed when the firing range around the point is in use.

31 Bigbury-on-Sea, Devon   OS Ref: SX6544

Bigbury-on-Sea is a pretty village with a sandy beach at the mouth of the South Devon Avon. Burgh Island, just off the beach, is connected by a causeway which is passable at low tide; at high tide there is a unique sea tractor which transports passengers to and from the island. The hotel on Burgh Island is reputed to have been the inspiration for Agatha Christie's 'Ten Little Indians'. Dogs are not banned from the beach but must be kept under control.

Water quality Beach monitored by the NRA and found to meet the EC minimum coliform standards for bathing water in 1991; ✳✳✳ (north) and ✳✳ (south) in this year's listing section. One outfall, serving 1,286 people, discharges primary treated sewage at low water mark.

Bathing safety Safe bathing except near river mouth. Lifeguards patrol between May and September.

Access From the village and car park.

Parking Car parking for 900 cars.

Toilets In the village and on the island.

Food Kiosk and café in the village, pub and hotel on the island.

Seaside activities Swimming, surfing, windsurfing, fishing, jetskiing.

Wildlife and walks Bigbury is on the South Devon Coast Path and leaflets are available describing the area. Between the rivers Avon and Erme, the path follows the undulating cliff-line passing Burgh Island and the beaches of Bigbury and Challaborough. It leads on through one of the most strenuous sections of the coast path: after rounding Beacon Point walking becomes easier as the path drops down to Wonwell Beach and the Erme estuary. The many wild flowers attract numerous butterflies in summer.

32 Slapton Sands, Devon   OS Ref: SX8445

A 2½ mile (4.5km) stretch of shingle beach extending from Pilchard Cove in the north to Torcross in the south. The main road from Dartmouth to Kingsbridge runs along the edge of the beach, with a large, reed-rimmed freshwater lake (Slapton Ley) on the other side. The village of Slapton itself is about a mile (1.6km) inland. The beach was used in 1943-44 as a practice area for the D-Day landings and all the local villagers were evacuated while the US army took over the area. A Sherman tank has been salvaged from the sea and is on display in Torcross as a memorial, and opposite the lane to Slapton there is a stone obelisk put up by the US army as a 'thank you' to the local people. As can be expected on such a long, open beach, it is often very windy but the views all round Start Bay are spectacular. At low tide it is possible to walk round the headland from Torcross to Beesands, the next cove along, but if you get cut off there is an arduous walk back on the cliff path.

Water quality Beach monitored by the NRA and found to meet the EC Guideline coliform standards for bathing water in 1991; ✳✳✳✳ in this year's listing section. One outfall serving 889 people discharges primary treated sewage 33 yards (30m) below low water mark.

Bathing safety Safe bathing but beach shelves steeply – beware of the undertow.

Access The A379 runs along the edge of the beach; access is easy.

Parking There are car parks at Strete Gate, Torcross and approximately half-way down the length of the beach.

Toilets In Torcross and at the car parks.

Food Shops, cafés and pubs in Torcross.

Seaside activities Swimming, fishing, and a children's play area at Strete Gate.

Wet weather alternatives Field Study Centre at Slapton Ley.

Wildlife and walks The area is rich in differing habitats and the Slapton Ley Field Centre organises guided walks throughout the summer. On the edges of the beach itself the unusual Yellow Horned Poppy can be found, which should be admired, not picked. Slapton Ley itself is the largest body of fresh water in the south-west of England and as a result is a mecca for many species of wildfowl and other animals. At Torcross there is a hide (with disabled access) to allow panoramic observation across the Ley and also a special corner where children can feed the many ducks and swans.

33 Blackpool Sands, Stoke Fleming, Devon   OS Ref: SY8747

Blackpool Sands is a complete contrast to its Lancashire cousin. The only development of this beach, an unspoilt cove at the northern end of Start Bay, comprises a car park, a building serving takeaway food and drink and a toilet block. A crescent of coarse golden sand ⅔ mile (1km) long is flanked by steep, wooded cliffs. On the southern side of the cove below Matthews Point a valley opens to the shore, from which a stream, Blackpool Lake, flows across the moderately shelving sands into a pool, very popular among families with small children. Easy access and safe bathing make it very popular. Dogs are banned from the beach between May and September.

Water quality Beach monitored by the NRA and found to meet the EC Guideline coliform standards for bathing water in 1991; ★★★★ in this year's listing section. No sewage is discharged in the vicinity of the beach.

Bathing safety Safe bathing, but care is required because the beach shelves steeply.

Access Signposted from Dartmouth on the A379. South of Stoke Fleming a side road leads to the car parks where there is a promenade to the sands.

Parking There are three car parks adjacent to the beach.

Toilets There are toilets at the car park.

Food Takeaway with off-licence and beach barbecue.

Seaside activities Swimming, windsurfing, sailing, fishing and diving. Toppers windsurf boards and canoes are available for hire. Sailing and windsurfing school with RYA instructors. Beach shop offers deckchairs, parasols etc for hire.

Wildlife and walks North of the beach the South Devon Coast Path can be followed, passing through Stoke Fleming to the entrance to the Dart Estuary. South, the footpath leads to Strete Gate and along the 5 mile (8km) sweep of Start Bay, fringed by shingle beaches, and on towards Start Point.

34 Torbay, Devon   OS Ref: SY9057-SX9366

Torquay, Paignton and the old fishing port of Brixham combine to make Torbay, one of Britain's most popular areas for seaside holidays and known as the English Riviera on account of the mild climate and abundant palm trees. The large bay has numerous beaches, all of which passed the EC minimum coliform standards for bathing water in 1991 (see listing section). There is a beach to suit every taste around Torbay, from the wide expanses of sand at Paignton and Goodrington to small sheltered coves on the north side of Torquay. As should be expected in a large holiday area, there are lots of things to do locally, and for trips inland, Dartmoor is not many miles away. Dogs are banned from most of the beaches between May and September.

Water quality All the beaches were monitored by the NRA and found to meet the EC minimum coliform standards for bathing water in 1991. See the listing section for details of sewage outlets in the area.

Litter All major beaches are cleaned daily during the summer season and as required in the winter.

Bathing safety Safe bathing generally. All beaches fly red flags when bathing is unsafe, and beach inspectors patrol with loud hailers.

Parking, toilets, food These facilities are not too far from any of the beaches in the area.

Seaside activities Swimming, fishing, sailing, pedalo and boat hire, boat trips. Beach cabin hire on main beaches.

Wet weather alternatives English Riviera Centre in Torquay. Kent's Cavern show caves, Paignton Zoo, Torbay Aircraft Museum, Compton Castle, Berry Pomeroy Castle, the Dart Valley Railway and the beautiful village of Cockington are all within easy reach. Leaflets are available from Beach Offices and Tourist Information Centres in Torquay, Paignton and Brixham, with details of activities and places to go.

Wildlife and walks The South Devon Coast Path extends round the bay and offers glorious views. More information may be obtained from Tourist Information Centres.

35 Teignmouth, Devon   OS Ref: SX9473

A 200 foot (60m) wide beach of red sand stretches for just over a mile (1.6km) from the Point at the mouth of the river Teign eastwards to the Parson and Clerk headland. The river mouth gives access to the busy harbour on the estuary side of the Point and provides an ever-changing boating scene. On the seaward side of the Point the steeply shelving beach is backed by a promenade and the Den Green Gardens. East of the Victorian pier, the promenade gives way to a sea wall with the British Rail Inter-City line, backed by steep cliffs, running parallel to it. Across the river mouth, reached by ferry from the Point, is Shaldon. Its strip of beach is unsafe for bathing but the Ness headland provides excellent views of Teignmouth and the estuary.

Water quality Beach monitored by the NRA and found to meet the EC minimum coliform standards for bathing water in 1991;★★★ in this year's listing section. Two outfalls serving 17,400 people discharge screened sewage through a tidal tank at low water mark.

Litter A very small amount of litter is reported on this beach, but the beach is cleaned daily.

Bathing safety Currents from the mouth of the river Teign affect bathing from the west end of the beach. Signs indicate the danger areas. The beach is patrolled by lifeguards from the end of May to September.

Access Links to the national rail and bus network. Local bus services from the Triangle on the promenade. Easy access to the beach with steps and ramps from the promenade.

Parking Car parks at the Point and at Eastcliff accommodate 350 and 200 cars respectively, and there are additional car parks within the town.

Toilets There are toilets at Eastfield promenade, near the pier, next to the children's paddling pool and at all the car parks.

Food There is a good selection of pubs, cafés, snack bars and ice-cream kiosks on or near the promenade.

Seaside activities Swimming and windsurfing from certain areas of the beach. Floats are available for hire during the summer. Facilities for playing tennis, bowls and crazy golf are provided at the Den. There is a botanical garden and children's zoo at Shaldon. There is an open bowls tournament in June and a regatta in August. Carnival week is in July and there is a fair during August.

Wet weather alternatives Pier amusements, local museum.

Wildlife and walks Set in beautiful countryside, cliff walks to the east and north provide excellent views seawards and over the town to the Ness. The wooded headland of the Ness also provides good views from the summit.

36 Budleigh Salterton, Devon   OS Ref: SY0782

The beach and sea wall have changed little since Millais painted *The Boyhood of Raleigh* here. The town remains a quiet resort. From the mouth of the River Otter, the wide red shingle beach extends 3 miles (5km) westwards past the promenade to the sandstone cliffs of West Down Beacon, known as the Floors. Small boats are winched up on to the flat pebbles, of which several hundred yards remain exposed at high tide. Dogs are banned from the beach between May and September.

Water quality Beach monitored by the NRA and found to meet the EC minimum coliform standards for bathing water in 1991; ** in this year's listing section. One outfall serving 5,066 people discharges untreated sewage 55 yards (50m) below high water mark.

Bathing safety Bathing safe. Beach patrolled at weekends by the Beach Rescue Club.

Access From the promenade.

Parking There is a large car park at the mouth of the river Otter (Lime Kiln) and a smaller one in the town centre 3 minutes' walk from the beach.

Toilets Blocks at each end of the promenade.

Food One refreshment kiosk with some chairs outside, by the Otter Mouth car park, and another at the Steamer steps at the west end of the beach. One small café on Marine Parade.

Seaside activities Swimming, diving, windsurfing and fishing from the beach. Indoor and outdoor bowling, East Devon golf course.

Wet weather alternatives Otterton mill – a water-powered mill still used to grind flour. Bicton Park 2 miles (3.3km) from Budleigh Salterton towards Otterton includes narrow gauge railway, countryside museum and other facilities.

Wildlife and walks Budleigh Salterton lies on the South Devon Coast Path. This can be followed west along the sandstone cliffs known as the Floors towards Exmouth. This route, offering excellent views, passes Littleham and Otter Coves before reaching Sandy Bay, which as the name suggests is a good sandy beach. East from Budleigh Salterton the coastal path leads to Ladram Bay. Here, the sandstone cliffs have been eroded into some spectacular shapes with huge blocks isolated by the waves. There are also several good walks in the Otter Valley, part of which is a conservation area with good bird life. A guide to 12 walks in the Otter Valley is available from the local tourist office.

37 Sidmouth, Devon   OS Ref: SY1287

An elegant Regency seaside resort overlooking Lyme Bay which has escaped over-commercialisation. Sidmouth has two beaches: the town beach and Jacob's Ladder beach to the west. There is great commitment from the local authority towards the maintenance of their beaches. The town sits in an open hollow between impressive sandstone cliffs facing a ⅔ mile (1km) long pebble beach. To the west are the Chit Rocks and the Connaught Gardens, which give access to the 1¼ mile (2km) shingle and sand beach of Jacob's Ladder backed by the 500 foot (160m) west cliff. Sidmouth has all the amenities one may require of a quiet resort and is an ideal place for relaxing on the beach or walking in the surrounding countryside, but not a spot for those seeking bright lights and amusements. However, the town comes alive during the first week of August when it hosts an International Folk Festival. Dogs are banned on the town beach between 1st May and 30th September.

Water quality Beach monitored by the NRA and found to meet the EC minimum coliform standards for bathing water in 1991 ; ★★ (Sidmouth) and ★★★ (Jacob's Ladder) in this year's listing section. One outfall serving 15,880 people discharges screened and macerated sewage through a tidal tank 440 yards (400m) offshore.

Litter Generally a clean and litter-free beach, cleaned by local authority.

Bathing safety Safe bathing. The beach is patrolled at weekends by the Sidmouth Inshore Rescue Club.

Access Steps and slope from the promenade lead on to the town beach; a sloping ramp gives access to Jacob's Ladder beach.

Parking Ham, Manor, and Bedford car parks close by in the town.

Toilets In the Connaught Gardens and Port Royal.

Food Cafés and kiosks at the town beach and a kiosk at Jacob's Ladder beach.

Seaside activities Swimming, windsurfing, sailing and fishing. There are paddle floats, windsurf boards and deck-chairs available for hire. Putting and golf courses.

Wet weather alternatives Sports centre, museum and theatre. New indoor swimming pool.

Wildlife and walks There are some excellent walks on the surrounding hills and cliffs; the views of Sidmouth and the Heritage Coast from Peak Hill, Fire Beacon and Salcombe Hill are excellent.

38 Branscombe, Devon   OS Ref: SY2188

A quiet, undeveloped 3 miles (5km) of pebble beach stretches from Beer Head to Weston Mouth. A wide valley opens to the coast at Branscombe Mouth with grassland stretching down to the edge of the beach. The cliffs and crags to the east are chalk, whereas to the west there are steep red sandstone cliffs. At Weston Mouth, a stream flows down a steep grassy valley to the beach which is more secluded due to the restricted access (pedestrian only).

Water quality No sewage is discharged in the vicinity of this beach. Beach monitored by the NRA and found to meet EC minimum coliform standards for bathing water in 1991; ★★★ in this year's listing section.

Litter A clean beach normally free of litter.

Bathing safety Safe bathing.

Access Branscombe is signposted off the A3052 between Sidmouth and Seaton. At Branscombe Mouth there is a short level walk from the car park to the beach.

Parking There is a car park adjacent to Branscombe beach with 400 spaces; limited parking in Weston village (20 spaces).

Toilets Public conveniences in the car park.

Food Café on beach.

Seaside activities Swimming, windsurfing, sailing, diving and fishing. Boats available for hire. Snorkelling and fishing competitions.

Wet weather alternatives Roman camp, pottery, forge and bakery all open to the public.

Wildlife and walks East of Branscombe, walks along the Hooken Cliffs take you to Beer Head. In the other direction the South West Way follows the cliffs to Weston, Sidmouth and beyond. The area is geologically very interesting with landslips, deep cut valleys and fossils. There is a varied and interesting flora and rock pools on the shore abound with marine life.

39 Seatown, Bridport, Dorset   OS Ref: SY4292

This is an undeveloped and completely unspoilt beach in a most attractive setting. The green and lush Winniford valley opens to the coast at Seatown, where a lovely shingle beach shelves steeply to some sand at low tide. Steep sandstone cliffs rise on either side of the valley, the mellow coloured sandstone making a pleasing contrast to the green grassland above. The cliffs show the distinctive signs of the sea's continual attack – sheer exposed rock at their summit with rock slumped at their base. To the west lies Golden Cap, the highest point on the southern coast, where the cliffs rise 626 feet (190m) above the shore. The beach is very popular with fishermen.

Water quality Beach monitored by the NRA and found to meet the EC minimum coliform standards for bathing water in 1991; ★★ in this year's listing section. No sewage is discharged in the vicinity of the beach.

Bathing safety The beach shelves steeply and great care is required when bathing.

Access A narrow lane from Chideock on the A35 leads to the shore.

Parking Car park behind the beach.

Toilets In the car park.

Food The pub overlooking the beach serves food.

Seaside activities Swimming and fishing.

Wildlife and walks On either side of the beach the rugged sandstone and shale cliffs rise and fall steeply where river valleys cut through to the sea. To the west of the beach the Dorset coast path climbs on to the Golden Cap and from its flat table summit there are terrific views along the coastline and inland over the undulating patchwork of fields. To the east is Thorncombe Beacon, where a fire used to be lit to warn of potential invasion.

40 Burton Bradstock, Dorset   OS Ref: SY4890

One of Dorset's four-star rated beaches, Chesil Beach officially begins here and runs the whole length of the coast as far as Portland. The shingle beach is backed by dramatic sandstone cliffs which are owned by the National Trust. At low tide a band of sand is revealed. The highly picturesque village of Burton Bradstock is worth exploring too, with its thatched, stone-built cottages set around a 15th-century church. Dogs (except guide dogs) are banned from the beach from June to September inclusive.

Water quality No sewage discharged in the vicinity of this beach, which was monitored by the NRA and found to meet the EC minimum coliform standards for bathing water in 1991; ★★★ in this year's listing section.

Bathing safety The beach shelves steeply and there is a strong undertow which can make bathing dangerous.

Access The beach is signposted off the B3157 in Burton Bradstock, 3 miles (5km) east of Bridport.

Parking There is a 500-space car park close to the beach.

Toilets Public toilets with facilities for the disabled.

Food Beach café.

Seaside activities Swimming.

Wildlife and walks The coast path follows the cliff with fine views over Lyme Bay. As with most stretches of the Dorset coast, there are good geological exposures to be admired.

41 Weymouth, Dorset   OS Ref: SY6779

The wide sweep of soft sand overlooked by the elegant Georgian houses of the Esplanade makes this a very popular beach. To the north of the town, the beach is backed by the Lodmoor Country Park which extends round the bay to Overcombe and Bowleaze Cove. To the south lies Weymouth harbour which combines the old and the new; tall ships, hydrofoils and luxury yachts contrast with the picturesque 17th-century fishing harbour. This is set in the old town which provides a pleasantly different atmosphere to the busy sea front. Through the lift-bridge in the old town lies a marina for 1,000 craft, beyond which lies Radipole Lake. There are views from the beach of the Isle of Portland and Portland Harbour. Weymouth has a reputation for sand highly suitable for building sand castles. Dogs are banned from the main beach areas but are permitted on a lead in a designated area near the Weymouth Pavilion Complex. Poop scoops are available free.

Water quality Beach monitored by the NRA and found to meet the EC minimum coliform standards for bathing water in 1991; *** (both beaches) in this year's listing section. No sewage is discharged in the vicinity of this beach.

Bathing safety Very safe swimming from all areas of the beach, which is patrolled by lifeguards throughout the holiday season, April to October. There is a lost children's hut on the beach near the King's Statue. From March to October there is a full-time beach supervisor and staff equipped with two-way radios. St John Ambulance post on the beach near the King's statue.

Access There are steps and ramps from the promenade to the sand. There is an hourly open-top bus service along the esplanade to Overcombe and Bowleaze Cove, and also to Portland.

Parking There are car parks at Swannery (800 spaces), Lodmoor (1000 spaces) and Pavilion (300 spaces).

Toilets Public conveniences with facilities for the disabled at three points along the beach.

Food Cafés all along the Esplanade.

Seaside activities Swimming and boating from the beach, with rowing and motor boats available for hire. There are organised sailing and windsurfing regattas throughout the season. Sand sculpture, Punch and Judy, merry-go-rounds, swings, bumper boats and a free children's beach club provide traditional entertainment. The Weymouth Country Park at Lodmoor offers a number of seaside attractions including mini golf, model world, miniature railway and leisure ranch.

Wet weather alternatives Pavilion Theatre and complex. Swimming pool, Diving and Shipwreck Centre, Nothe Fort museum, Sea Life Centre, butterfly farm, Portland Bill lighthouse and open days at the Portland navy base. Time walk at Hope Square in the Brewers Quay Complex.

Wildlife and walks Radipole Lake and swannery is a nature reserve with a wide variety of habitats from freshwater lagoon to grassland and scrub. There are many walks through the reserve where numerous types of birds can be seen, including the bearded tit and Cetti's warbler. There are conducted tours from the RSPB visitors' centre. The Lodmoor Country Park also contains a nature reserve with walks providing views across Weymouth Bay. There are cliff top walks on Portland which provide excellent views across the bay. Other paths allow access on to The Ridgeway and to the White Horse.

42 Ringstead Bay, Dorset   OS Ref: SY760814F

Chalk cliffs and undercliffs produced by chalk landslips surround Ringstead Bay and at their foot a pebble beach with scattered rockpools curves 1¼ miles

(2km) round the bay. 'Burning Cliff', to the east of the beach, is so named because oil shale smouldered for several years in the 19th century. There are magnificent views from White Nothe at the eastern side of the bay.

Water quality Beach monitored by the NRA and found to meet the EC minimum coliform standards for bathing water in 1991; ★★★ in this year's listing section. No sewage is discharged in the vicinity of this beach.

Bathing safety Care is required when swimming as the beach shelves steeply.

Access Ringstead is signposted off the A353, 3 miles (5km) east of Weymouth. The road leads to a National Trust car park on the crest of the down or, alternatively, a toll road can be taken to the car park in Ringstead.

Parking There are two car parks with approximately 400 spaces.

Toilets Public conveniences in the village.

Food Small café and shop.

Seaside activities Swimming, windsurfing, sailing, diving and fishing.

Wildlife and walks The area is of interest for its geology, fossils and the vegetation and wildlife of the undercliffs, particularly invertebrates. The White Nothe Undercliff Nature Reserve is run by the National Trust. The Dorset Coast Path skirts the cliff top. To the east, Durdle Door and Lulworth Cove are reached and westwards the path leads past the medieval village site towards Bowleaze and Weymouth, 5 miles (8km) away.

43 Durdle Door, Dorset   OS Ref: SY8280

This beach is famous for Durdle Door Arch, created by the great erosive power of the sea and probably the most photographed view along the Dorset coast. The eastern end of the beach (Durdle Door Cove) is protected by the arch while the rest of the beach is partially protected by a submerged offshore reef that dries in places along its length. The beach is a steep, narrow strand of mixed shingle, gravel and sand which makes a strenuous ⅔ mile (1km) walk to the western end where Bats Head, a chalk headland, forms an attractive boundary to the beach itself. All the cliffs backing the beach are steep and prone to occasional rockfalls – thus climbing or sheltering underneath them is not advised.

Water quality Beach monitored by the NRA and found to meet the EC Guideline standards for bathing water in 1991; ★★★★ (west) in this year's listing section. No sewage is discharged in the vicinity of this beach.

Litter A small amount of marine litter, including plastic, rope and wood, is washed up in Durdle Door Cove.

Bathing safety Care required as with most shingle and gravel beaches since there can be sudden steep slopes underwater. The western end of the beach may be cut off under certain tide and wave conditions.

Access Beach approached by steep ½ mile (800m) footpath from cliff top car park. Access on to the eastern end of the beach down a steep flight of steps cut into the bay cliff can be slippery in wet weather.

Parking Large cliff top car park at Durdle Door Caravan Camping Park (with excellent views across Weymouth Bay to the Isle of Portland).

Toilets At the caravan park.

Food Café and store in the caravan park.

Seaside activities Swimming, diving, snorkelling and fishing. The steep access to the beach means that heavy equipment, including picnic tables, should not be carried down.

Wildlife and walks The undulating cliffs form a challenging section of the Dorset Coast Path. To the east lies Lulworth Cove and the Isle of Purbeck, to the west White Nothe headland. However, the reward for tackling this stretch of Heritage Coast is a fine view across Weymouth Bay and to the glorious beaches below. The chalk habitat creates picturesque downland with its accompanying flora and fauna.

44 Lulworth Cove, West Lulworth, Dorset   OS Ref: SY8380

The spectacular scenery along the Dorset coast attracts large numbers of visitors and this is particularly true of Lulworth Cove. The dramatic cliffs and rock formations are famous among geologists. There is a series of layers of different rock types parallel to the shore; the band on the seaward edge is hard Purbeck Limestone which is very resistant to erosion. At Lulworth this hard rock has been breached and the invading sea has eroded the softer clay behind to form the impressive cove. A narrow shingle beach forms a margin to the round bay which is ringed by rugged cliffs. The eastern edge of the cove marks the edge of the Lulworth Army Firing Range. Access to the range is restricted to weekends and August. Local notices indicate when it is safe.

Water quality Beach monitored by the NRA and found to meet the EC minimum coliform standards for water in 1991; ★★★ in this year's listing section. One outfall serving 2,000 people discharges raw sewage several yards below low water mark just outside the cove. There have been reports that the waste is sometimes visible and is washed back into the cove. A £11.9 million improvement scheme should rectify the problem.

Bathing safety Bathing is only safe close inshore because of strong currents and rocks within the cove.

Access The road from West Lulworth leads down to the shore.

Parking There is a privately owned car park (Weld Estate) on the cliff top with about 1,300 spaces.

Toilets Public toilets including facilities for the disabled.

Food Beach café; several cafés, restaurants and hotels in West Lulworth.

Seaside activities Swimming, windsurfing, diving, sailing, canoeing, rowing and fishing. There are rowing boats available for hire and boat trips along the coast to Durdle Door.

Wildlife and walks Rockpools abound below the cliff and contain a wealth of marine life – between 20 and 30 different types of animals and plants can be seen. The surrounding area is also rich in wildlife, for a wide variety of flowers, butterflies and birds complement the unique geological features. There is a series of circular walks starting at the main car park. Clearly marked paths lead west over Hambury Tout to Durdle Door, a magnificent rock arch. There is a short walk from the car park to Stair Hoe, a second cove in the early stages of development. Waves break through a series of arches in the hard limestone and are eroding the softer rock lying behind. There are some excellent rock folds and faults exposed in the hole. When the Lulworth Army Range is open, marked paths can be followed east to Mupe Bay. It is worth stopping at Pepler Point to view the superb prospect across the cove from its narrow entrance. After entering the range a short detour leads to the remains of a fossil forest. Steps lead down the cliff where fossilised remains of trees can be seen in the cliff. On the range it is dangerous to leave the marked paths. Leaflets which describe the walks in detail are available at the information centre close to the beach.

45 Kimmeridge, Nr Wareham, Dorset   OS Ref: SY9078

The beach has no sand and is formed of cobbles, stones and smooth flat rocks sheltered below crumbling shale cliffs. It is a good spot for combining a coastal walk with exploration of the excellent rockpools. Better for older children than the young. The bay is part of the Purbeck Marine Wildlife Reserve, and a wealth of marine life abounds on the shore and in the shallow waters. On the eastern headland of this square bay stands the Clavell Tower, which was built as a folly and was for a time used as a coastguard look-out post. The tower now stands empty. The opposite side of the bay marks the edge of the army firing range, which covers the land between the bay and Lulworth Cove to the west. The shale cliffs around the bay are very unstable and beach users should not climb on the cliffs or sunbathe below them because of the danger of falling rocks. The bay provides some of the best conditions for windsurfing to be found in the south of England.

Water quality Beach monitored by the NRA and found to meet the EC minimum coliform standards for bathing water in 1991; ★★★ in this year's listing section. No sewage is discharged in the vicinity of this beach.

Litter A lot of plastic rubbish is frequently washed up on to the beach; it is cleaned occasionally.

Bathing safety Bathers must beware of submerged rocks that can make swimming dangerous. There are, however, no strong currents or dangerous tides. A coastguard's hut is manned by auxiliary coastguards at weekends and sometimes in rough weather during the summer.

Access A toll road from Kimmeridge village leads to the bay, and a track leads from the car park to the beach.

Parking There are two car parks on the cliff top with about 700 spaces.

Toilets There are two toilet blocks near the beach and a toilet for the disabled in Kimmeridge village, 1 mile (1.6km) from the beach.

Food Ice-cream kiosk. There is a shop/restaurant in Kimmeridge village.

Seaside activities Swimming, diving, windsurfing and fishing. There are two slipways for launching small boats from the beach.

Wildlife and walks There is an information centre at the eastern end of the bay run by the Dorset Trust for Nature Conservation which sponsors the Purbeck Marine Wildlife Reserve. The centre can provide information on the numerous animals and plants to be found around the bay. In addition, it produces a leaflet describing a nature trail which is laid out in the area. There are well-marked walks across the firing range to the west which are open at weekends, for a few days at Christmas, the two public holidays in May and for the whole of August. Information about opening days can be obtained by ringing the Range Office on Bindon Abbey 462721.

46 Swanage, Dorset   OS Ref: SZ0379

Swanage beach has consistently maintained a high standard of cleanliness and facilities. The safe sheltered bay is flanked by magnificent chalk headlands on either side: Ballard Point in the north and Peveril Point to the south of the bay. The gently sloping sands form a good 1¼ mile (2km) family beach with a promenade providing all the facilities of a small seaside resort. The development has not spoilt the sea front. Swanage is an ideal spot for a holiday combining days on the beach with explorations of the superb Dorset coastline. Dogs are banned from the beach between 1st May and 30th September.

Water quality Beach monitored by the NRA and found to meet the EC minimum coliform standards for bathing water in 1991; ★★(south) ★★★(central) and ★★★(north) in this year's listing section. One outfall serving 20,000 people discharges macerated sewage 110 yards (100m) below low water mark off Peveril Point.

Litter A clean beach with only a small amount of litter left by visitors; the beach is cleaned daily. There are reports that marine litter can be a problem after an east wind.

Bathing safety Safe bathing. No lifeguard, but a beach inspector patrols the beach during the summer. There is a first aid post on the promenade adjacent to the tourist information centre.

Access Steps and ramps from the promenade lead to the sand.

Parking There are car parks at Broad Road, De Moulham Road, Victoria Avenue and one in the town centre.

Toilets Public toilets with facilities for the disabled at several points along the promenade.

Food Numerous cafés, restaurants, and take-aways within easy reach of the beach.

Seaside activities Swimming, windsurfing, diving, sailing and fishing. There are pedalos and motor boats for hire. Fishing and boat trips are available from the quay, where there is also a diving school.

Wet weather alternatives Tithe Barn Museum and Arts Centre, Steam Railway rides, indoor bowling complex. The lifeboat house is open to visitors. Putlake Adventure Farm at Langton Matravers, Worth Matravers Craft Centre, Glen's Birds at Harmans Cross.

Wildlife and walks The Dorset Coast Path extends in both directions from Swanage Bay, passing through beautiful countryside along this section of coast. To the north of the beach Ballard Cliff rises on to Ballard Down, and the path follows the cliffs round to Handfast Point, which provides excellent views of Old Harry Rocks lying just off shore, and across Poole Bay. South of Peveril Point above Durlston Bay and Head is the Durlston Country Park. There is parking within the park and an information centre provides details of a series of walks in the area. The long-distance coast path follows the cliffs beyond Anvil Point Lighthouse, passing the Dancing Ledge, Seascombe cliff and continuing to St Aldhelm's Head and beyond. There is a series of shorter circular routes starting from the country park that explore both the coast and the beautiful scenery inland. A leaflet produced by the Dorset Heritage Coast Project describes the various walks.

47 Studland, Dorset   OS Ref: SZ0483

A lovely clean beach that is an Area of Outstanding Natural Beauty. 3 miles (5km) of excellent sandy beach are backed by unspoilt dunes. The beach sweeps south from the entrance to Poole harbour to the splendid chalk cliffs of Handfast Point, once connected to the Needles of the Isle of Wight, which are visible on the horizon most days. The beach can be divided into three areas – south beach, middle beach and the north or Knoll beach. Behind the Knoll beach there is a brackish lake and marsh area which forms the Studland Heath National Nature Reserve. Visitors should note that a section of the beach is used by naturists. By-laws require that dogs are kept on leads and all faeces must be removed by the owners from the beach. Jetskiing is banned.

Water quality Beach monitored by the NRA and found to meet the EC minimum coliform standards for bathing water in 1991; ★★★ in this year's listing section. No sewage is discharged in the vicinity of this beach.

Litter This is a very clean beach due to the excellent efforts of the National Trust. In summer 4-5 tons of litter are removed daily from the litter bins and sands.

Bathing safety Safe bathing off the main beach; strong currents at the entrance to Poole harbour make bathing at the northern end of the beach unsafe. The beach is patrolled by National Trust wardens from Easter to September.

Access Each section of the beach is signposted from Studland village. It is a short walk from the car parks to the sands. There is a wheelchair ramp at the Knoll beach.

Parking Four car parks provide space for 3,500 cars.

Toilets Five blocks. New toilets at Middle and Knoll beach have facilities for the disabled. There is also provision for nursing mothers at Knoll beach.

Food Cafés and kiosks.

Seaside activities Swimming, windsurfing, sailing and fishing. Windsurf boards are available for hire.

Wildlife and walks The Studland Heath National Nature Reserve containing a brackish lagoon, Little Sea, lies on the landward side of the beach. The reserve cannot be reached from the beach but must be entered from the road which bounds its western edge. There is a wide variety of wildlife including the rare smooth snake and adders. Walkers are advised to wear stout shoes and stick to the marked paths. A leaflet describing seven local walks is available from the National Trust Information Centre at Knoll beach. A leaflet which describes the local wildlife and guided walks in the area is produced by the Dorset Heritage Coast and Dorset Trust for Nature Conservation and is available locally. The Dorset Coast Path starts, or alternatively finishes, at the entrance to Poole Harbour. It follows the bay south and on to the Foreland. From the path there are splendid views of the cliffs and the chalk pillars, Old Harry and Old Harry's Wife, which are isolated from the adjacent headland by the ever-eroding waves. The path continues south towards Ballard Point where there are fine views of Swanage Bay.

48 Sandbanks, Poole, Dorset   OS Ref: SZ0487

An extremely well managed and popular beach with consistently good or excellent water qualty. From North Haven Point at the end of the Sandbank spit, the fringe of golden sand stretches 3 miles (5km) north-east to merge with the beaches of Bournemouth. The pedestrian promenade is backed by the steep pine- and shrub-covered Canford Cliffs. Flaghead Chine, Cranford Chine and Branksome Chine cut through the cliffs to the beach. South-west, the cliffs give way to the low-lying Sandbanks peninsula at the mouth of Poole Harbour. Here the beach is edged by dunes and overlooked by holiday development and the Sandbanks Pavilion and recreation area. The whole of Poole Harbour is a centre for sailing and water sports, and there is an ever-changing boating scene at the harbour entrance. There are excellent views across the harbour and of Brownsea Island from Evenning Hill off the western shore road. A removal of canine faeces by-law and dog ban between Sandbanks and Branksome Chine is in force from May to September, and dogs must be kept on a lead on the promenade.

Water quality Beach monitored by the NRA and found to meet the EC minimum coliform standards for bathing water in 1991; ★★★ in this year's listing section. No sewage is discharged in the vicinity of this beach.

Litter The beach is cleaned daily.

Bathing safety Safe bathing except at the extreme western end of the beach near the harbour entrance. Warning signs indicate where not to swim. Segregation of bathers and powered vessels is actively encouraged with a buoyed area in which boats must observe a strict speed limit. The beach is patrolled by lifeguards at weekends and on bank holidays from May to September and there is a first aid post manned by St John Ambulance at weekends.

Access There is easy access along the length of the beach; paths lead down the cliffs to the promenade. Disabled access is available to the promenade at Sandbanks, Branksome Chine and Branksome Dene Chine.

Parking There are seven car parks along the length of the beach with 1,400 spaces. There is also parking available on adjacent streets.

Toilets There are toilets (with facilities for the disabled) along the beach.

Food There are cafés, and kiosks close to the beach.

Seaside activities Swimming, windsurfing, sailing, and fishing. There are windsurf boards and boats for hire. Poole harbour has several windsurfing and sailing schools. There is also a putting green, crazy golf and a variety of children's amusements.

Wet weather alternatives Tower Park leisure complex incorporating Splashdown, Ice-Trax, Mega-Bowl, multi-screen cinema and sports centre; swimming pool, aquarium, Guildhall Museum, Archaeological Museum, Royal National Lifeboat Museum, Maritime Museum, Waterfront Museum, Arts Centre and Poole Pottery, Poole Park.

Wildlife and walks There is a car and pedestrian ferry from North Haven Point to Shell Bay, where the extensive Studland Heath National Nature Reserve backs an excellent beach. There is also a pedestrian ferry to Brownsea Island. 200 acres (80 hectares) of this 500 acre (202 hectare) National Trust-owned island is a nature reserve run by the Dorset Trust for Nature Conservation. There are many different types of habitat to be found on the island including heathland, woodland, freshwater lakes, salt marsh and the sea shore. There is a nature trail and guided walks are available during the summer. Further information is available from the National Trust shop on the island's landing quay.

49 Bournemouth, Dorset   OS Ref: SZ4109

Bournemouth is often referred to as 'the garden city by the sea' because of its many parks, including the upper and lower Bourne Gardens. These wind their way through the town centre following the Bourne Valley and emerge at the sea front. Bournemouth has an excellent family beach. Throughout the summer the wide promenade, which backs the golden sands, is traffic-free. The steeply sloping shrub-covered cliffs that rise above the promenade are bisected by a series of deep wooded glades, known as chines. These valleys all have their own individual characters and divide the long sea front into distinctive sections. This is not merely a seaside town, but truly a holiday centre. You may just want to enjoy the sun, sea and sand, but you can also take advantage of the resort's numerous facilities. There are two piers, amusements, and a beach club to entertain children. In addition there is a full programme of events staged throughout the summer including carnivals, regattas and competitions.

Water quality Beach monitored by the NRA and found to meet the EC minimum coliform standards for bathing water in 1991; all three beaches have ★★★ in this year's listing section. No sewage is discharged in the vicinity of this beach.

Litter Beach cleaned daily.

Bathing safety Hoisted red flags indicate when conditions are unsafe for swimming. Lifeguards, using inflatable safety boats, patrol the beach. All the deckchair attendants are qualified in life-saving. The Beach Leisure Department surveys the beach by closed circuit television during the season and all staff are first aid trained. There are two St John Ambulance first aid posts, and voluntary lifeguard stations at Southbourne and Durley Chine.

Access The promenade is reached by zig-zag pathways down the cliff. There is a cliff-lift to the east and west of the pier and at Fisherman's Walk.

Parking There are several car parks close to the beach and in the town, plus spaces along the roads.

Toilets There are 15 public conveniences along the promenade.

Food There are numerous catering outlets along the promenade.

Seaside activities Swimming, surfing, windsurfing, sailing and fishing. There are rowing boats and pedalo floats available for hire. There are boat trips from the pier. A land train operates along the promenade between Bournemouth and Boscombe Piers.

Wet weather alternatives Bournemouth International Conference Centre comprising leisure centre 110 yards (100m) from the beach with indoor swimming pool, exhibition and concert halls. Russel-Cotes Art Gallery and Museum, Transport Museum and the Shelley Museum. The Pier leisure centre and sea front amusements. The Littledown Centre with swimming pools, water slides, sports hall and gym. Two town centre cinemas (8 screens). Indoor bowling alley. Pier and Pavillion Theatres.

Wildlife and walks Stretching east from Bournemouth is the 1¼ mile (2km) long Hengistbury headland which separates Poole Bay and

Christchurch Bay, and encloses Christchurch Harbour on its landward side. Most of the headland remains undeveloped and has been designated as a Site of Special Scientific Interest because of the wide variety of plant and animal life it supports. The headland is a nature reserve owned by Bournemouth Borough Council. It contains a wide variety of habitats including grassland, heath, woods, salt marsh, freshwater marsh, dunes, rocky and shingle shore. There is a nature trail on the eastern slopes of the headland. The summit of Warren Hill on the landward end of the headland provides good views of Christchurch Bay, Poole Bay, the Solent and the Isle of Wight beyond. There is a south-facing 1 mile (1.6km) pebble and sand beach below the imposing sandstone cliffs. In sharp contrast to this undeveloped beach is the sandspit stretching north from the headland to the entrance of Christchurch harbour, where the groyne-ribbed sands are backed by beach huts. A small land train takes passengers from the Hengistbury Head car park to the tip of the headland.

50 Highcliffe Castle, Highcliffe, Dorset   OS Ref: SZ2093

From Highcliffe Castle (which resembles the ruins of an impressive cathedral rather than a castle), steps lead down the gently sloping shrub- and tree-covered cliffs directly on to the sand. A lovely, long beach of sand and pebble extends from Highcliffe Castle to Highcliffe Crow's Nest. This is a clean, unspoilt stretch of beach which is ideal for a day relaxing in the sunshine. Between 1st May and 30th September dogs are permitted on Highcliffe Castle beach but not on Highcliffe Crow's Nest. On the promenade, cliff paths and adjacent car park, dogs must be kept on a lead. Owners are asked to clean up after their dogs and receptacles are provided.

Water quality Beach monitored by the NRA and found to meet the EC minimum coliform standards for bathing water in 1991; ★★★ in this year's listing section. No sewage is discharged in the vicinity of this beach.

Litter During the summer the local authority employs a team of litter pickers to clean the beaches and surrounding area.

Bathing safety Safe bathing but care is required because the beach shelves quite quickly. A patrol boat operates daily from mid-July to early September. This stretch of coast has separate designated areas for swimming and windsurfing, which are signposted on the beach. There is a slight problem with weever fish.

Access From the A337 through Highcliffe a side road leads to Highcliffe Castle. There are steps and a path down the cliff. The steps are quite gentle but access may be difficult for the elderly and the disabled, particularly the walk back up.

Parking Car park at Highcliffe Castle with 100 spaces, 110 yards (100m) walk to beach. Car park at Steamer Point with 172 spaces, 330 yards (300m) walk to beach and car park at Highcliffe top with 600 spaces, 440 yards (400m) walk to the beach.

Toilets In Highcliffe Castle grounds and Highcliffe Crow's Nest.

Food During the summer there is often someone selling ices along the beach from a cool box.

Seaside activities Swimming and windsurfing; the latter is restricted to

Highcliffe Crows Nest; swimming is confined to Highcliffe Castle. Fishing.
Wildlife and walks There are woodland and nature walks on the cliffs
at Steamer Point, where an information centre can provide details of the
flora and fauna to be seen in the area.

51 Sandown Bay, Isle of Wight   OS Ref: SZ5984

The twin resorts of Sandown and Shanklin face Sandown Bay, the largest
bay on the Isle of Wight. From Shanklin Chine, a deep wooded cleft cutting through the cliffs, a safe and sandy beach curves gently northwards to
Sandown and the white cliffs of Culver Down beyond. Almost 2 miles
(3km) of unbroken sands separate these busy holiday resorts made popular
by the Victorians. Houses and hotels perch on the cliffs and downs which
ring the bay, sloping down to the esplanades which edge the beach. There
are pleasant walks at each end of the bay, and the old village of Shanklin
can be explored.
Water quality Beach monitored by the NRA and found to meet the EC
minimum coliform standards for bathing water in 1991; ★★★ in this year's
listing section. One outfall serving 50,000 people discharges secondary
treated effluent at Yaverland.
Litter The beach is cleaned by the local authority and licensed beach
operators.
Bathing safety Safe bathing.
Access Steps and ramps from the esplanade in both Sandown and
Shanklin. There is a lift down the cliff to the esplanade in Shanklin.
Parking In Shanklin two car parks off the esplanade. In Sandown sev-
eral car parks off the High Street.
Toilets At either end of the esplanade in both resorts.
Food Shops, cafés, pubs and restaurants along the esplanades.
Seaside activities Swimming, windsurfing and fishing. Beach huts,
boats and deck chairs for hire. Jetski hire at Shanklin.
Wet weather alternatives Pier and amusements, Sandown Leisure
Complex, zoo and museum. Putting and crazy golf, tennis courts. In Brad-
ing, just outside Sandown, a wax museum, dolls' museum, animal world
and Roman villa.
Wildlife and walks The Shanklin Chine provides a pleasantly contrasting walk away from the sea-front. A footpath south of Shanklin leads
along the cliffs to Luccombe. Here another chine gives access to Luccombe Bay – a small and undeveloped beach. North of Sandown the cliffs
can be followed on to Culver Down. There are excellent views back across
the bay.

South-East England

The south-east of England is rich in sharp coastal contrasts. There are long shingle banks, sand dunes, saltmarshes and the wide open skies of Norfolk. Low clay cliffs predominate in Suffolk, powerless to resist the forces of the invading sea. The creeks and mud flats of Essex and the Thames estuary provide yet another type of coastline, while the striking white cliffs of the south coast form an impressive backdrop to many busy holiday resorts and the ferry terminals that are the gateway to Europe. Long empty sands and crowded promenades are both to be found in this region.

The south-east has some of the most heavily developed coastal regions, and with people and popularity come problems. The heavy shipping traffic in the Channel creates a continual problem with marine litter and oil being washed up on to the beaches, despite international legislation to stop such pollution. Extensive stretches of the coastline suffer from pollution by sewage, although action is being taken at many sites in the south and Southern Water are applying innovative ideas to their sewage treatment responsibilities. Sewage sludge dumping off the Thames Estuary must end by 1998. Nuclear and industrial discharges are both still a cause for concern. The disturbance around Shakespeare Cliff from the construction of the Channel Tunnel will have a severe long-term impact on marine and coastal life. On a coastline under pressure from every type of human activity, tourism, industry, and residential development, continual effort is needed to ensure that those areas left unspoilt will remain so for future generations.

South-East England

13 Wells-next-the-Sea   Blakeney Point
                            Sheringham
        Hunstanton   Cromer
        Heacham   Holkham Bay   **12** Happisburgh
                  Brancaster   **11** Sea Palling
                            Mundesley

Kings Lynn

Great Yarmouth – North/Pier
Great Yarmouth – South **f**
– Power Station **f**

Norwich

f = failed to meet EC minimum coliform standards for
bathing water in 1991.
Numbered beaches appear in the detailed section.

10 Lowestoft

Kessingland
9 Southwold
8 Dunwich

Coastal walks

Saxon Shore Way
Gravesend to Rye 143 miles (230km).

7 Aldeburgh

Norfolk Coast Path
Hunstanton to Cromer (part of Peddar's Way and Norfolk
Coast Path).

Ipswich

Felixstowe
Dovercourt

South Downs Way, Sussex
(Starts at Eastborne)

Colchester

Walton-on-the-Naze
Frinton-on-Sea
Holland-on-Sea
Clacton-on-Sea **p/f**

Southend – Thorpe Bay   Jaywick
Southend – Westcliff **f**   Brightlingsea
Leigh-on-Sea

London

Shoeburyness

St Mildreds
Leysdown   Margate **f**
                  Joss Bay
Chatham   Broadstairs Beach **f**
        Minnis   Ramsgate **f**
Minster Leas   Sandwich Bay **f**
6 Whitstable (west beach)   Deal Castle **f**
Herne Bay **f**   St Margaret's Bay
                  Dover

Hythe   Folkestone **f**
Dymchurch **p/f**   Sandgate
Pagham   St Mary's Bay **f**
Bognor Regis **f**   Hove **f**   Littlestone **f**
Middleton-on-Sea   Brighton Palace Pier **f**
                  Saltdean
                  Newhaven **f**   Camber Sands **f**
on-the-Solent   Pett Level/Winchelsea
Stokes Bay   Brighton   **5** Bexhill-on-Sea
Southsea   Norman's Bay   Hastings **f**
        Southwick **f**   Pevensey Bay
Selsey   Lancing **f**   Eastbourne
Littlehampton Worthing   **4** Eastbourne
Bracklesham Bay   **3** Cuckmere Haven
Hayling West Wittering   Seaford

The South-East   See page 19 for further details

Beach No on Map	Rating. The more stars the better. f=failed	Resort	Pass/Fail track record	Sewage outlets	Population discharging from outlet	Type of treatment	Discharge point relative to low water mark, unless otherwise stated. Distance given in metres	Remarks
HAMPSHIRE								
	★★★	**Barton-on-Sea**	~~~PPP	1	17,400	Flow transfer	At LWM	Pebbles and shingle. Scheme under construction to provide secondary treatment by 1995.
	★★	**Milford-on-Sea**	PFFFPP					Pebbles. Improvements as above.
	★★	**Lepe**	PPPPPP					Sand and shingle. Only one sample failed Guideline standards.
	★★	**Calshot**	PFFPPP	1	448	Maceration/tidal tank		Mud. Improvement scheme.
	★★	Solent Breezes	~~~~~P					
	★★	**Hill Head**	~~~~~P					Dog fouling and sewage-related debris both a problem.
1	★★★	**Lee-on-the-Solent**	PPPPPP	1	200,000	Screens	5km below	Sand and shingle. New long sea outfall.
2	★★★	**Stokes Bay (Pier)**	PFPPPP					Improvements as above.
	★★	**Southsea (South Parade Pier)**	PFFPPP					Shingle.
	★★	**Eastney**	PPFPPP	1	200,000	Screens	5 km below	Shingle. New long sea outfall.
	★★★	**Eaststoke**	PPPPPP					Sandy.
	★★★	**West Hayling**	PPPPPP					Sandy.
WEST SUSSEX								
	★★	**West Wittering**	PPPPPP					Sandy. Safe bathing.
	★★	**East Wittering**	~~~~PP					
		Bracklesham Bay						Sandy. Water quality not monitored in 1991.
	★★	**Selsey Bill**	PFFPFP					Shingle. Bathing unsafe.
	★★★	**Pagham**	PPFPPP					Shingle.

Rating. The more stars the better. f=failed	Resort	Pass/Fail track record	Sewage outlets	Population discharging from outlet	Type of treatment	Discharge point relative to low water mark, unless otherwise stated. Distance given in metres	Remarks
f ★★	**Bognor Regis**	PPPPPF	1	71,500	Screens	3km below LWM	Sandy. Safe bathing. Some oil pollution of the beach in 1991.
f ★★	Felpham (Yacht Club)	~~~~~F					
★★	**Middleton-on-Sea**	PFFPPP					Sand and shingle.
★★★	**Littlehampton**	PFFPPP	1	53,000	Maceration/ screens	2.5km below LWM	Sandy. Safe bathing.
	Goring-by-Sea		1	45,000	Primary	At LWM	Sand and shingle. Safe bathing. Multi-million pound scheme planned for 1995. Water quality not monitored in 1991.
★★ ★★	**Worthing: East West**	FFFPPP	1	80,000	Primary	160 below LWM	Shingle and sand. Improvement scheme planned as above for 1995.
f ★★	**Lancing**	FFFFFF					Shingle and sand. Improvement scheme planned as above for 1995.
f ★★ ★★★	Shoreham (Kingston Beach) Shoreham-by-Sea Beach	F~~PPP	1	54,000	Screens	50 below	Commercial port. Improvement scheme planned as above by 1995.
EAST SUSSEX							
f ★★	Southwick	~FF~FF					Shingle. Improvement scheme planned for 1995 as above.
f ★★	**Hove**	FFFFFF					Pebbles and sand. Multi-million pound improvement scheme planned for end 1995 to manage storm water outfalls from Hove to Portobello.
★★ f ★★	**Brighton:** Kemp Town **Palace Pier**	PFFPFF	5		All storm water overflows		See above for planned improvements.
★★★	**Saltdean**	PPPPPP					Rocky with some sand.

Beach No on Map	Rating. The more stars the better. f=failed	Resort	Pass/Fail track record	Sewage outlets	Population discharging from outlet	Type of treatment	Discharge point relative to low water mark, unless otherwise stated. Distance given in metres	Remarks
		Portobello		1	300,000	Screens	1780 below	New long sea outfall. Also see above. Water quality not monitored in 1991.
	f ★★	**Newhaven**	PFFFFF		7,500	Primary	SSO	Sandy beach within breakwater. To be diverted to new long sea outfall at Seaford.
	★★	Seaford (east of outfall)		1	21,500	Screens	LSO	Shingle beach is steep. New long sea outfall.
	★★★	**Seaford (Dane Road)**	FFFFFP					
3		Cuckmere Haven						Pebbles. Water quality not monitored. Bathing not safe at the mouth of the river.
	★★★	Birling Gap						Steps down cliff to shingle beach. Many rock pools. Much marine litter in 1991.
4		**Eastbourne:**		1	90,000	Maceration/ screens	640 below	Multi-million pound improvement scheme planned for 1995. Shingle and sand.
	★★★	**Wish Tower**	PPPPP					
	★★	**East of Pier**						
	★★	**Pevensey Bay**	PFPPFP	1	9,590	Maceration/ tidal tank	360 below	Shingle with sand. Improvement scheme as above. Beach affected by sewage-related debris.
	★★	**Norman's Bay**	PPPPFP					Shingle with sand at low water.
		Cooden Beach		2			150 above	Shingle with sand at low tide. Storm water overflows. Water quality not monitored in 1991.
5	★★	**Bexhill** (Egerton Park)	PPPPPP	3	32,500	Maceration/ tidal tank	400 below	Sand and shingle. Beware sand holes. New long sea outfall.
	★★	Bulverhythe						Shingle.
	★★★	St Leonards Beach	~~~~PP	2	23,000	Maceration/ screens	2000 below	Shingle, sand and rocks. New long sea outfall.

Beach No on Map	Rating. The more stars the better. f=failed	Resort	Pass/Fail track record	Sewage outlets	Population discharging from outlet	Type of treatment	Discharge point relative to low water mark, unless otherwise stated. Distance given in metres	Remarks
	f **	**Hastings: Hastings (Queens Hotel)**		4	68,000	Screens/ maceration tank	140 below	Shingle and sand. New long sea outfall.
	f **	**Hastings Beach (Fairlight Glynn)**	PFFPPF					
	***	**Winchelsea**	PPPPPP					Shingle. Bathing only safe in calm weather.
	f **	**Camber Sands**	PFPPPF					Sand dunes. Ridges in sand can be a danger. Despite failing in 1991, won a Blue Flag in 1991 (based on 1990 results).
		Broomhill Sands		1	9,500	Secondary	300 above	Sandy and coarse shingle. Water quality not monitored in 1991.
KENT								
	***	Greatstone Beach	~~~~~P					
	f **	**Littlestone-on-Sea**	FFFFPF					Sandy.
	f **	**St Mary's Bay**	FFFPPF					Sandy.
	**	**Dymchurch: Dymchurch Hythe Road**		1	20,800	Secondary	Between HWM & LWM	Shingle and sand.
	f **	**Dymchurch Beach**	FFFFPF					
		Dymchurch Redoubt		1	3,000	Primary	At LWM	Pebbles and sand.
	**	**Hythe**	FFFPFP					Shingle and sand. New long sea outfall.
	***	**Sandgate: Sandgate Beach**	FFFPPP					Shingle. Multi-million pound improvement scheme to give primary treatment and long sea outfall in 1995.
	***	Sandgate Town Centre						
	f **	**Folkestone**	FFFFFF	1		Screens	At HWM	Shingle. Improvement scheme as above.

Beach No on Map	Rating. The more stars the better. f=failed	Resort	Pass/Fail track record	Sewage outlets	Population discharging from outlet	Type of treatment	Discharge point relative to low water mark, unless otherwise stated. Distance given in metres	Remarks
		The Warren		1	20,000	Raw	584 below	Danger from falling rocks. Improvement scheme as above. Water quality not monitored.
		Shakespeare Cliff		1	30,000	Maceration	635 below	Sand and shingle. Improvement scheme. Start of the tunnel. Water quality not monitored in 1991.
	**	Dover Harbour	~~~~~P					Windsurfing popular.
	***	**St Margaret's Bay**	FPPPPP					Shingle and rocks. Sewage-related debris a problem.
	f **	**Deal Castle**	FFFFFF	3	10,000	Screens/ maceration tank	731 below	Steep shingle. Multi-million pound scheme to give primary treatment and LSO in 1995.
	f *	**Sandwich Bay**	FFFFFF					Sandy. Improvement scheme as above.
	***	**Ramsgate:** Ramsgate Sands		3	20,000	Screens/ maceration	150 below	Sandy. Improvement scheme. Beach affected by sewage-related litter.
	f *	**Ramsgate Beach**	PFFFFF					
	***	Broadstairs		1	24,000	Screens	3.6 km	Sandy. Improvement scheme opened 1991. Sewage-related debris a problem.
	f **	**Broadstairs Beach**	FFFPFF					
	***	**Joss Bay**	FFPPPP					Sandy.
	***	Botany Bay	~~~~~P	1	60,000	Screens	1.9 km	Sandy. New LSO.
	***	Palm Bay	~~~~~P					Sandy. Watersports.
	f **	Walpole Bay						Sand, rocks.
	f **	**Margate**	PPPPPF					Sandy. Sewage-related debris a problem.
	***	Westbrook Bay	~~~~~P					Sandy.
	***	**St Mildred's Bay**	PFPPPP					Sandy.
	**	Westgate Bay	~~~~~P					Sandy.
	***	**Minnis Bay**	PPPPPP					Sand and rocks. Sewage-related debris a problem.

Rating. The more stars the better. f=failed	Resort	Pass/Fail track record	Sewage outlets	Population discharging from outlet	Type of treatment	Discharge point relative to low water mark, unless otherwise stated. Distance given in metres	Remarks
f ★★	**Herne Bay**	PFFFFF	1	10,000	Screens	460 below	Pebbles and sand. Improvement scheme planned for 1994.
★★★	**Whitstable**	PPPPPP	1	10,000	Screens/ maceration	1,500 below	Shingle.
★★★	Leysdown-on-Sea	FFPFPP					Sand, shingle and mud. Reported as badly littered in 1991.
	Minster Leas						Water quality not monitored in 1991.
★★★	Sheerness	~~~~~P					
SSEX							
★★★	Canvey Island	~~~~~P	1	45,500	Secondary	At LWM	Muddy sand.
★★★	Leigh-on-Sea	~~~~~P					Small sandy beach.
f ★★	**Westcliff-on-Sea**	FFFPPF					Sandy. Improvements planned for 1998.
★★	**Southend-on-Sea**	~~~PPP	1	210,000	Primary	500 below LWM	Sand, shingle and mud. Improvements as above.
★★★	**Thorpe Bay**	FFFPPP					Improvements as above.
★★★	**Shoeburyness East**						Sand and shingle. Improvements as above.
★★	Shoeburyness	~~~~~P					
f ★★	**West Mersea**		1	10,000	Secondary	To the colne	Muddy sand. Bathing dangerous. Improvements planned.
★★★	**Brightlingsea**	PFPPPP					
★★	**Jaywick**	PPPPPP	1	38,000	Maceration	650 below LWM	Sandy.
★★★	Clacton (off Coastguard Station)		2	300 below LWM		50 below LWM	Sandy. Stormwater outfalls only. Improvements planned for 1997.
f ★★	Clacton (Groyne 41)						
★★★	**Clacton (opposite Connaught Gardens)**	PFPPPP					
★★★	**Holland-on-Sea**	PFPPPP	1	70,000	Maceration	750 below LWM	Sandy. Safe bathing.

Beach No on Map	Rating. The more stars the better. f=failed	Resort	Pass/Fail track record	Sewage outlets	Population discharging from outlet	Type of treatment	Discharge point relative to low water mark, unless otherwise stated. Distance given in metres	Remarks
	★★★	**Frinton-on-Sea**	PPPPP	2			50 below	Sandy. Safe bathing. Storm overflows only. Treatment planned for 1998.
	★★★	**Walton-on-the-Naze**	PFPPPP	1	29,000	Secondary	50 below LWM	Sandy. Safe bathing. See above.
	★★★	**Dovercourt**	PFFPPP	1	11,000	Primary	At LWM	Sandy. Safe bathing. Outfall extension planned for 1997.
	★★	Harwich (Sailing Club)						
SUFFOLK								
		Felixstowe:		1	4,262	Maceration	630 below LWM	Red shingle and sand. Another outlet to docks serving 30,000. Improvement scheme for both beaches.
	★★	**South Beach**	FPPPP					
	★★★	**North Beach**	PPPPP					
7		Aldeburgh		1	4,000	Maceration	1,300 below LWM	Shingle.
8		Dunwich						Pebbles.
9	★★	Southwold (The Flats)						Sandy.
	★★★	**Southwold (The Denes)**						
		Kessingland		1	5,000	Secondary		Discharges to estuary mouth 2km south of beach. Water quality not monitored in 1991.
10		**Lowestoft:**		1	80,000	Maceration	1,000 below LWM	Sandy. Outfall improvements planned.
	★★★	**South beach**	PPPPP					
	★★	**North beach**	FPPPP					
	f ★★	**Gorleston Beach**						
		Great Yarmouth:		1	180,000 including screening discharge to river	Fine	1,050 below LWM	Sandy. Macerated sewage is discharged into the River Yare. Improvements to pumping and screens planned.
	f ★★	Power Station						
	f ★★	**Opposite Hospital**						
	★★	**Between Piers**						
	★★★	**Coastguard lookout**						
	★★★	**Caister Point**						

Beach No on Map	Rating. The more stars the better. f=failed	Resort	Pass/Fail track record	Sewage outlets	Population discharging from outlet	Type of treatment	Discharge point relative to low water mark, unless otherwise stated. Distance given in metres	Remarks
	★★★	California						
	★★★	**Hemsby**						
11		Sea Palling						Sandy.
12		Happisburgh						Sandy.
	★★★	**Mundesley**	PPPPPP	1	14,000	Secondary/ other	1,420 below LWM	Sandy.
	★★	Overstrand						Sand and shingle.
	★★	**Cromer**	PFFFPP	1	13,500	Tidal tank	100 below LWM	Sandy. Improvement scheme planned.
	f ★★	East Runton		1	1,400	Maceration	At LWM	Sandy. Improvement scheme planned.
	★★★	West Runton		1	1,400	Maceration	At LWM	Sand and pebbles. Improvement scheme planned.
	★★★	**Sheringham**	FFFFPP	1	10,000	Maceration	260 below LWM	Sand and shingle. Improvement scheme planned.
13	★★★	**Wells-next-the-Sea**	FFPPPP	1	3,700	Secondary	To inland drain	Sandy. Improvement scheme planned.
	★★★ ★★ ★★★ ★★★	**Hunstanton:** Old Hunstanton Beach North Beach Sailing Club **Main Beach Boat Ramp** South Beach Hunstanton Road	PPFPPP	1				Sand, stones and shingle. Storm overflow only. Sewage to Heacham STW.
	★★ ★★★ f ★★	**Heacham** North Beach South Beach South Beach (near River)		1	24,000	Secondary/ tertiary	To river	Gravel. New STW completed 1990. Private beach.
	★★★	Snettisham Beach						˙Near RSPB Reserve

1 Lee-on-the-Solent, Hampshire   OS Ref: SU5700

A long, gently curving ribbon of groyne-ribbed shingle with sand at low tide faces the Solent, with views of Southampton Water and across to the Isle of Wight. The residential development along Marine Parade overlooks this uncommercialised beach. Marine Parade West is separated from the beach by the Solent Gardens, which slope down to a promenade on two levels edging the shingle. Another promenade and flat lawns separate Marine Parade East from the beach. The steep shingle may not be the most comfortable for sunbathing on but it is popular with the more active beach user. There is a designated area for water skiing, and recommended launching areas for windsurfers. There is always something to watch off shore, whether it is the water sports or the continual shipping traffic plying the Solent. Dogs are banned from the central section of the beach from May to September inclusive. Dogs on the promenade must always be kept on a lead and must not foul either the footpaths or the adjoining grass verges.

Water quality Beach monitored by the NRA and found to meet the EC minimum coliform standards for bathing water in 1991; ★★★ in this year's listing section. One outfall serving 200,000 people discharges primary treated sewage ⅔ mile (1km) below low water mark from Peel Common, to the north of Lee. There is a £600,000 sewerage improvement scheme under construction.

Litter The beach is cleaned regularly by the local authority. Heavy usage of the Solent leads to problems on the beaches, with marine debris and oil being washed ashore.

Bathing safety Safe bathing. Water skiers must use the area buoyed near the Daedalus slipway and windsurf boards should be launched from the Hill Head end of the beach.

Access Lee-on-the-Solent is signposted from the A32; the B3385 leads to Marine Parade running parallel with the shore. There is level access and ramps to the promenade from which there are steps and ramps to the shingle.

Parking Two car parks with approximately 250 spaces are signposted off Marine Parade; two other car parks with approximately 150 spaces are located at the Hill Head end of the beach.

Toilets At the Solent Gardens and the Daedalus slipway (Marine Parade East and Marine Parade West).

Food There are shops and cafés on Marine Parade opposite the Solent Gardens. There is a café and sheltered terrace garden off the promenade and a pub at Hill Head.

Seaside activities Swimming, water skiing and windsurfing.

Wet weather alternatives In Gosport there is a local museum, Fort Brockhurst and the submarine museum.

Wildlife and walks The Solent Way coastal footpath can be followed in either direction from the beach. To the north it skirts the Titchfield Haven Nature Reserve and continues along the shore to the River Hamble, an extremely popular yachting centre. To the south it can be followed to Stokes Bay. A section of the grassland adjacent to the Daedalus slipway has been set aside as a conservation area.

2 Stokes Bay, Gosport, Hampshire OS Ref: SZ5998

The arc of Stokes Bay, with its almost manicured shingle, curves from the No 2 Battery Fort south to Fort Gilkicker, fortifications built in 1860 to protect the western approaches to Portsmouth docks. The narrow band of shingle, which shelves quite steeply to some sand at low tide, widens landward towards the south-east of the bay; the long shore drift currents continually move the shingle in this direction and this has led to the build-up of a wide area of flat shingle stretching towards Fort Gilkicker. The beach, overlooking Ryde on the Isle of Wight, has a wide-open feel about it. The promenade is level with the shingle and is backed by flat grassed recreational areas which are in turn bordered by the trees and shrubs of the adjacent park and school. Popular for water sports; windsurfers can be seen throughout the year. Dogs are banned from certain areas of the beach. Dogs on the promenade must be kept on a lead and should not be allowed to foul.

Water quality Beach monitored by the NRA and found to meet the EC minimum coliform standards for bathing water in 1991; ★★★ in this year's listing section. One outfall serving 200,000 people discharges primary treated sewage ⅔ mile (1km) below low water mark from Peel Common, to the north of Lee-on-the-Solent.

Litter The beach is cleaned regularly by the local authority. Heavy use of the Solent by shipping leads to problems on the beaches; marine debris is frequently washed ashore.

Bathing safety Safe bathing. Swimming and windsurfing is restricted to specific areas of the beach which are signposted. First aid post near sailing club. Inshore rescue boat station at southern end of the bay.

Access Stokes Bay is signposted from the B3333 between Lee-on-the-Solent and Gosport. There is easy parking off the road behind the beach and level access on to the shingle.

Parking Car parks are signposted at each end of the beach and at its centre, with over 300 spaces. There is also some parking along the promenade.

Toilets At the car park adjacent to the No 2 Battery Fort, on the promenade near the sailing club and at Gilkicker.

Food Café on the promenade.

Seaside activities Swimming, windsurfing, sailing, canoeing and diving. Two public slipways. Children's paddling pool, miniature golf and tennis courts behind the beach.

Wet weather alternatives In Gosport there is a local museum, the submarine museum and Fort Brockhurst.

Wildlife and walks The Solent Way footpath can be followed southeast past Fort Gilkicker towards Portsmouth Harbour or north-west to Lee-on-the-Solent and beyond.

3 Cuckmere Haven, Westdean, East Sussex OS Ref: TV5298

A path from the Seven Sisters Country Park Centre leads through the lovely Cuckmere valley to this quiet pebble beach. The river, which meanders through the valley, disappears below the pebbles. The impressive white chalk cliffs of the Seven Sisters stretch away east to Beachy Head. Below them there are numerous rockpools which abound with marine life. This is an ideal spot for those who want to combine sun bathing with exploring the shore and surrounds. The nature trail starting from the superbly restored flint barn which houses the Country Park Interpretative Centre is well worth following.

Water quality No sewage is discharged in the vicinity of this beach. The NRA does not monitor this beach.

Litter A lot of plastic and metal cans and bottles both washed up and left by visitors.

Bathing safety The swiftness of the incoming tide and the associated currents can cause problems. Bathing is not safe at the mouth of the river.

Access Pedestrian access only; a 1 mile (1.6km) walk on a marked path through the Cuckmere Valley from the Country Park Centre at Exceat on A259 leads to the beach.

Parking Car park at Country Park Centre.

Toilets At Country Park Centre.

Food Golden Galleon Pub at Exceat Bridge provides superb food.

Seaside activities Swimming and diving.

Wet weather alternatives The Country Park Centre and The Living World exhibition of animals from the countryside and seashore.

Wildlife and walks A 1½ mile (2.5km) or 3 mile (5km) circular trail through the country park covers a selection of wildlife habitats, saltmarsh, river meadows and the chalk grassland above the cliffs. Leaflets which describe the route are available at the Country Park Centre. The South Downs Way follows the cliffs and cuts through the valley. Survey work by the Marine Conservation Society showed that the shallow seas of this stretch of coast are particularly rich in marine life and the area has been designated as a Voluntary Marine Nature Reserve.

4 Eastbourne, East Sussex   OS Ref: TV6199

This shingle beach is at the centre of 3 miles (5km) of accessible beach and 2 miles (3km) of promenades with splendid gardens backed by a parade of elegant hotels and houses. Access to the beach is by steps and ramps. Wooden groynes hold the pebbles at the high tide level and give way to sand at low tide. The promenades provide easy walking from the foot of the white chalk cliffs of Beachy Head at the western boundary via the Martello Tower, bandstand, pier, Redoubt Fortress, Treasure Island and the Butterfly Centre to the fishing and boating beaches at the eastern end. Ample seating on all promenade levels. Dogs are banned from the central beach area between 1st May and 30th September, with lead restrictions and poop scoop regulations elsewhere. Eastbourne Borough Council take great pride in the resort's spotless image.

Water quality Beach monitored by the NRA and found to meet the EC minimum coliform standards for bathing water in 1991; ✶✶ (east of Pier) and ✶✶✶ (Wish Tower) in this year's listing section. One outfall serving 87,000 people discharges macerated and screened sewage 710 yards (650m) below low water off Langney Point. Macerated sewage has been observed off the beach and there have been complaints about smell. A new £17 million long sea outfall may rectify the problem. Prevailing winds, currents and tides take the sewage effluent towards Pevensey Bay.

Bathing safety Restricted bathing west of the Wish Tower because of rocks. Mixed bathing and boating east of the Redoubt requires extra care. The central area, Wish Tower to Redoubt, provides safe bathing unless the red warning flags are flying. Seasonal lifeguard cover is based at the Wish Tower from June to September.

Access Steps and ramps lead down from the esplanade to the beach. There are beach wheelchairs available from the bathing station on the lower esplanade.

Parking Pay-and-display car parks at the fishing station, Prince's Park and Wish Tower. Free parking on the promenade, in some areas restricted between 20th May and 20th September to four hours. Multi-storey car park in Trinity Place off the sea-front and Ashford Road in the town centre.

Toilets Adjacent to the bandstand, pier, Wish Tower, Holywell, Redoubt and the fishing station.

Food Ice cream and refreshment kiosks on promenades and cafés at Holywell, Wish Tower and the Redoubt. Also cafés on the Pier and in town.

Seaside activities Swimming, sailing, windsurfing and angling. Sailing and canoeing lessons at the sailing clubs. Two pleasure boats cruise from the beach west of the pier to Beachy Head and the Lighthouse with fine views of the Seven Sisters. The pier provides amusements, dances, boat trips and angling. Beach cabins and canoes for hire at the Wish Tower. Military bands and entertainments at the bandstand. Children's entertainment at Treasure Island, the Fort Fun playgrounds and at the Wish Tower. Putting and mini-golf at Holywell, Prince's Park and Treasure Island. Boating lake at Prince's Park. Dotto rail-less train runs from the Wish Tower to Holywell.

Wet weather alternatives Sovereign Centre all-weather 'beach' recreation centre, Redoubt Fortress Military Museum and Aquarium, Butterfly Centre, pier amusements and dances, Winter Garden dances. The town provides theatres, cinemas, local history museums and art gallery.

Wildlife and walks To the west of the town rises Beachy Head and the South Downs. The view is of rolling chalk hills and cliffs and there is a Visitors' Centre at Beachy Head. The Downs also offer fine views across the town to the east where lie the Crumbles, Pevensey Marshes and the Sussex Weald.

5 Bexhill-on-Sea, East Sussex   OS Ref: TQ7407

Bexhill has 2 miles (4.2km) of beach, meticulously maintained and groomed.The beach consists of shingle between recently replaced sea-defence groynes with safe exposed sands at low tide. There are excellent facilities for recreation and very tight control over graffiti, vandalism and litter. Behind the beach lie wide, clean promenades with cafés, shelters and amusements. The De La Warr Pavilion on the sea front caters for all tastes, with plays, concerts and exhibitions. Old Bexhill is slightly inland from the sea and nearby are the Manor Gardens. Dogs are banned from the beach during the summer although reports suggest this may not always be effective.

Water quality Beach monitored by the NRA and found to meet the EC minimum coliform standards for bathing water in 1991;★★ in this year's listing section. A new long sea outfall deals with the sewage from Bexhill, St Leonard's and Hastings.

Litter The beach is cleaned regularly.

Bathing safety Safe bathing. Lifeguards at weekends in the summer.

Access Easy access to the beach from the promenade.

Parking Extensive parking on the sea-front.

Toilets Two blocks on the promenade and at the De La Warr Pavilion.

Food Cafés, restaurants and kiosks.

Seaside activities Swimming, fishing, sailing, windsurfing.

Wet weather alternatives De La Warr Pavilion, museum, amusement arcades, nearby shops.

Wildlife and walks The local authority have erected interpretation boards on local wildlife and fossils to be found in the area. Galley Hill, at the eastern end of the town, offers splendid views. From the small car park it is a short walk down the hill to a secluded shingle beach at Glyne Gap.

6 Whitstable, Kent   OS Ref: TR1166

This is a quiet resort that retains much of its traditional seafaring atmosphere around the harbour and in the old town with its narrow streets, alleyways and weather-boarded cottages. Whitstable was famous for its oysters which are still produced and celebrated annually with an oyster week in July. There is also a carnival in August. Whitstable's main beach lies to the east of the harbour. Undulating grassy slopes lead gently down from Marine Parade to the promenade and sea wall which edge the pebble beach. A long bank of shingle known as the Street extends seawards from the west end of the beach. ⅔ mile (1km) of the bank is exposed at low water and is a good spot for collecting shells, but is dangerous to swim from. From the slopes at Tankerton there are good views east along the curving beach to Swalecliffe and Herne Bay, with excellent sunsets. Swalecliffe at the eastern end of the Tankerton slopes is used by water skiers as a launching area. The sport is very popular in the bay and the World Water Skiing Championships have been held here.

Water quality Beach monitored by the NRA and found to meet the EC minimum coliform standards for bathing water in 1991; ★★★ in this year's listing section. One outfall serving 10,000 people discharges screened and macerated sewage 1 mile (1.6km) below low water mark.

Bathing safety Bathing is safe except near the Street where there are unpredictable currents. Warning notices indicate where it is unsafe. There is a mobile coastguard lookout.

Access Steps and ramps from promenade.

Parking Free car parking on Marine Parade and in Gorrell Tank car park opposite harbour.

Toilets At Priest and Sow Corner (near the sailing club), Beach Walk at the end of Tankerton Slopes, the Harbour and Island Wall.

Food A wide variety of cafés, restaurants, ice-cream kiosks and snack bars in the town within easy reach of the beach.

Seaside activities Swimming, windsurfing, sailing, water skiing and fishing. Bowling green, tennis courts and golf course.

Wet weather alternatives Whitstable Museum, Ethnic Doll and Toy Museum, Sherwood Armoury Museum, sports centre, bowling (ten pin and indoor).

Wildlife and walks The Saxon Shore Way follows the banks of the Swale passing through the South Swale Local Nature Reserve on the edge of Graveney Marshes, just west of Whitstable. It continues through the town, along the shore to Herne Bay and the Bishopstone mud cliffs beyond.

7 Aldeburgh, Suffolk   OS Ref: TM4757

The long strip of unspoilt shingle beach falls within the Suffolk Coast and Heath Area of Outstanding Natural Beauty and the Suffolk Heritage Coast. A wide sea wall protects the charming town from the continual attack of the North Sea. Colour-washed houses and hotels face this 'working' beach from which a considerable number of boats fish, selling most of their catch of crabs, lobster and a variety of fish from sea-front huts. The local lifeboat can also be seen drawn up on the shingle. The beach has steep shingle ridges with some sand at low tide and stretches 2 miles (3km) north to Thorpeness. This Edwardian holiday village built around a man-made lake, The Meare, is a mixture of traditional weather-boarding combined with mock Tudor elegance. The working windmill standing on the heathland behind the beach is also the Heritage Coast visitors' centre and it is well worth a visit to find out more about this curious village and adjacent stretch of unspoilt coast.

Water quality One outfall serving 4,000 people discharges macerated sewage ¾ mile (1.3km) below low water mark. The NRA does not monitor this beach.

Litter The beach is generally very clean, but subject to occasional spotting with tar and oil from passing ships. It is cleaned by the local authority.

Bathing safety The beach shelves quite steeply but evenly except at Thorpeness, where some ridges and pits in the sea bed can be dangerous. It is dangerous to swim near the groynes.

Access Level access from the road on to the promenade and across the shingle to the north.

Parking Car parks at each end of town adjacent to the beach. Car parks in Thorpeness can be busy on summer weekends.

Toilets Public toilets at the Moot Hall and by the coastguard station at the southern end of the promenade.

Food Several cafés, pubs and hotels overlook the beach. Ice-cream vendor on the promenade. Tea shop and inn at Thorpeness.

Seaside activities Swimming, diving, windsurfing, sailing and fishing.

Wet weather alternatives Moot Hall Museum, Thorpeness Windmill, Heritage Coast Visitors' Centre. Snape Maltings Concert Hall on the banks of the River Alde, a short distance inland, is the home of the Aldeburgh Festival. Gallery, craft centre, shops and restaurants at the Maltings.

Wildlife and walks A very good map is available from tourist information which details the network of paths that covers Aldeburgh and its surrounding area. Aldeburgh lies on the Suffolk Coastal Path which runs from Felixstowe to Lowestoft. From the village of Snape the route follows the banks of the River Alde and joins the Sailors' Path. This crosses Snape Warren and the marshes north of the town to reach Aldeburgh beach, where shingle plants such as sea holly and the sea pea abound. The path continues north along the beach to Thorpeness and beyond. The Meare at Thorpeness, the remnant heath, with dry reedbeds, scrub and birch woodland support a wide variety of birdlife.

8 Dunwich, Saxmundham, Suffolk   OS Ref: TM4770

This stretch of pebble beach forms part of a long coastal strip that is continually under attack from the waves. Dunwich village, for example, was once a sizeable town but it is progressively falling into the sea. Between Dunwich village and Minsmere, the RSPB reserve to the south, the shingle-ridged beach is backed by low sand cliffs and heathland owned by the National Trust. The heather and heath plants that thrive on the cliffs provide an attractive splash of colour when in full bloom. The steep banks of shingle which give way to sand at low tide curve northwards, protecting the low-lying meadows behind. Great care is needed to ensure that these coastal defences remain undamaged. This is a very quiet beach in an area frequented for the wildlife interest rather than for any holiday beach atmosphere.

Water quality No sewage is discharged to the beach. The NRA does not monitor this beach.

Litter Some flotsam is washed up on to the beach.

Bathing safety War remains between low and high tide can be dangerous for swimmers.

Access The beach car park is signposted from the village; there is direct access on to the shingle from the car park.

Parking There is a public car park adjacent to the beach, plus National Trust and RSPB car parks at Dunwich Heath and Minsmere Reserve respectively.

Toilets In the public car park, Dunwich Heath and Minsmere.

Food Beach café at the car park.

Seaside activities Swimming, windsurfing and fishing.

Wet weather alternatives Museum of local history in Dunwich. Two bird hides on the beach edge of the Minsmere Reserve are open to the public free of charge; others require permits. The Coastguard cottages at Dunwich Heath have an exhibition area along with shop, tearooms and toilets.

Wildlife and walks There is a marked footpath around the edge of Dunwich Heath which gives the visitor a tour of all the various habitats that the 214 acre (86.6 hectare) site contains. South of the heathland the near 2,000 acre (800 hectare) RSPB reserve includes reedbeds, lagoons, heath and woodland. Over 100 different bird species have been recorded breeding within the reserve which makes it one of the most important reserves in Great Britain. There is a car park, shop and information centre on the reserve.

9 Southwold, Suffolk   OS Ref: TM5076

Southwold once had a pier but all that remains is a short skeleton and the buildings on the promenade. Nevertheless, it is still the focal point for this 3 mile (5km) long beach of sand and shingle. To the north rainbow-coloured beach huts line the sea wall which edges the groyne-ribbed beach of soft sand. The beach curves northwards below sand cliffs rising to replace the sea wall. South of the pier the groyne-ribbed beach of sand and shingle stretches to the harbour at the mouth of the River Blyth. Wheeled changing huts line the promenade below scrub-covered slopes. The attractive town of Southwold sits aloft, built around seven greens and shadowed by its lighthouse.

Water quality Beach monitored by the NRA and found to meet the EC minimum coliform standards for bathing water in 1991; ★★★ in this year's listing section. No outfalls discharge in the vicinity of the beach.

Bathing safety Safe bathing except near the groynes and at the river mouth. Life-saving equipment provided.

Access The sea front is signposted within the town; car parks adjacent to the promenade/sea wall. There are steps and a steep ramp on to the beach.

Parking Three car parks with a total of 300 spaces adjacent to the pier and harbour.

Toilets On the promenade, including facilities for the disabled.

Food Café, bar, shop and takeaway at the pier.

Seaside activities Swimming, surfing, windsurfing, sailing and fishing. Amusement arcade. Boating lake.

Wet weather alternatives St Edmund's Hall and museum.

Wildlife and walks There are walks along the river and across the meadows. The climb to the summit of Gun Hill is well worth the effort for the reward of some good views. The Suffolk Coastal Path runs north towards Lowestoft and south to Dunwich Forest and Minsmere, approximately 3 miles (5km) from Southwold.

10 South Beach, Lowestoft, Suffolk   OS Ref: TM5491

Lowestoft is a popular resort and a busy port which is split in half by the narrow strip of Lake Lothing. The two sides are linked by a bridge which is occasionally raised to admit large merchant ships into the heart of town. South beach is a 3 mile (5km) long pleasure beach, offering golden sand and all the normal paraphernalia of piers, stalls and amusements. Cleaned every day by the local authority.

Water quality Beach monitored by the NRA and found to meet the EC minimum coliform standards for bathing water in 1991; ★★★ in this year's listing section. One outfall serving 80,000 people discharges screened and macerated sewage 1,500 yards (1,200m) below low water mark.

Bathing safety Safe bathing except near the harbour entrance. The beach is patrolled by lifeguards during the summer months.

Access Direct from the promenade.

Parking There are four car parks near the beach with approximately 800 spaces.

Toilets Four sets of toilets including one with facilities for the disabled. Another set has showers and a baby changing area.

Food There is a full range of catering outlets at a variety of prices.

Seaside activities Swimming, surfing, fishing, windsurfing, sailing. Punch and Judy shows, two piers.

Wet weather alternatives Multi-sports centre, large central library, Maritime Museum, two cinemas and theatres.

Wildlife and walks Guided walking tours of the fishing harbour start from the Tourist Information Centre on the Esplanade. Lowestoft marks the northern end of the Suffolk Coastal Path which runs for 50 miles (90km) south to Felixstowe. Lowestoft Ness is Britain's easternmost point.

11 Sea Palling, Norfolk   OS Ref: TG4327

Ten miles (16km) of coastline that is undeveloped and not readily accessible. From Sea Palling the fine stretch of sandy beach to Waxham can be reached. A beautiful unspoilt beach, the gentle sloping sands are fringed by substantial marram-covered dunes. The beach is ideal for a quiet day by the sea; no facilities, no razzmatazz, just sand, sea and sky. 3 miles (5km) south, the Broads come within a couple of miles of the dunes, the only protection that the flat, low-lying land has against the sea. The beach is cleaned daily during the season. Oil on the sand has been observed in winter.

Water quality No outfalls in the vicinity of this beach. The NRA does not monitor this beach.

Bathing safety Bathing can be dangerous on the ebb tide because of undertow currents.

Access From the village of Sea Palling, on the B1159, a road leads to an access point over the dunes.

Parking Car park behind dunes provides spaces for 100 cars.

Toilets In Sea Palling village.

Food A tea shop and two pubs in the village serve food.

Seaside activities Swimming, windsurfing and fishing.

Wildlife and walks Fossils have sometimes been found in the area of the beach, also jet and amber. The more remote parts of the beach are popular for birdwatching.

12 Happisburgh, Norfolk   OS Ref: TG3831

The stretch of coastline from Happisburgh (pronounced Hapsboro) east to Winterton is one of the cleanest in Norfolk. There is a continuous gently sloping sandy beach backed by clay cliffs and sand dunes. This attractive stretch of coastline remains undeveloped. Happisburgh, dominated by its red and white lighthouse and the 110 foot (33m) spire of St Mary's Church, is a good family beach, offering safe swimming for children between the groynes that hold the sands in place. The village is set back from the beach on the 50 foot (15m) clay cliffs, an advantage in an area where the ravages of the sea are much in evidence.

Water quality No outfalls in the vicinity of this beach. The NRA does not monitor this beach.

Bathing safety Safe bathing. Inshore lifeboat. Coastguard's lookout.

Access From the village on the B1159 a side road leads to parking above the beach. A concrete ramp leads past the inshore lifeboat hut to the beach.

Parking Two car parks with 100 spaces.

Toilets On cliff top, includes facilities for the disabled.

Food Ice-cream van.

Seaside activities Swimming, windsurfing, diving, sailing and fishing.

13 Wells-next-the-Sea, Norfolk   OS Ref: TF9146

This beach lies approximately 1 mile (1.6km) north of Wells-next-the-Sea, a quaint Norfolk port. Although popular, its extensive sands mean that you can always find a quiet position on the beach. The adjacent pinewoods give it a beautiful backdrop as well as providing cover for walks. The surrounding marsh countryside is famous for its birds. By-laws are now in force banning dogs from part of the beach. The small town of Wells has an assortment of shops, cafés and amusements.

Water quality Beach monitored by the NRA and found to meet the EC minimum coliform standards for bathing water in 1991, ★★★ in this year's listing section. No outfalls in the vicinity of this beach.

Bathing safety Care is required in certain tidal conditions: a siren is sounded when it is dangerous. The safe and dangerous areas are marked on a large plan at the entrance to the beach. The beach is patrolled by lifeguards at weekends from May to September, with full-time cover in the summer school holidays.

Access Either by road, on foot along the sea wall or by miniature railway.

Parking Car park behind the dunes provides space for 300 cars: there is an overflow car park when that is full.

Toilets By the car park and in the pinewoods.

Food Kiosk on beach, small takeaway adjacent to car park.

Seaside activities Swimming, windsurfing, sailing. Miles of walks, good birdwatching, two steam railways.

Wet weather alternatives Wells is full of Norfolk charm and worth exploring. Holkham Hall (home of the Earl of Leicester) has magnificently decorated rooms and a bygones section. Also close by is Walsingham with its famous Christian shrine and medieval buildings.

Wildlife and walks Wells is on the Norfolk Coastal Path. The beach is incorporated into an SSSI, adjoins a national nature reserve and is part of a designated area of outstanding natural beauty and heritage coast. Inland, Pensthorpe Waterfowl Park is a fascinating place to visit.

The East Coast

Fabulous, spectacular, dramatic, remote, wild and mysterious have all been used to describe the east coast. The beautiful sweeping bays of golden sand, unspoilt fishing villages and clifftop castle ruins of Northumberland; the rugged cliffs and sandy crescents of Yorkshire; the magnificent chalk cliffs of Flamborough with mile upon mile of sand stretching south, backed by the fast-retreating mud cliffs of Humberside; the ever-changing sand banks of Lincolnshire. Unfortunately, less complimentary terms have also been used to describe parts of this coastline. Industry comes to the shore, with steel works, power stations, oil and chemical works. They discharge a cocktail of toxic chemicals, polluting the coastal waters and their wildlife.

Millions of tonnes of dredged spoil, sewage sludge and fly ash dumped offshore add to the problem, although the dumping of fly ash and sewage sludge is to ended in the next few years. Waste from coal mines still blackens the beaches of Tyne and Wear, Durham and Cleveland, although the practice is diminishing. Sadly the damage is enormous – dive surveys carried out by the Marine Conservation Society at Seaham in 1991 revealed the awful truth.

Sewage pollution contaminates many of the bathing waters, particularly around the Tyne and Tees. None of the beaches in the region escapes the problem of marine litter.

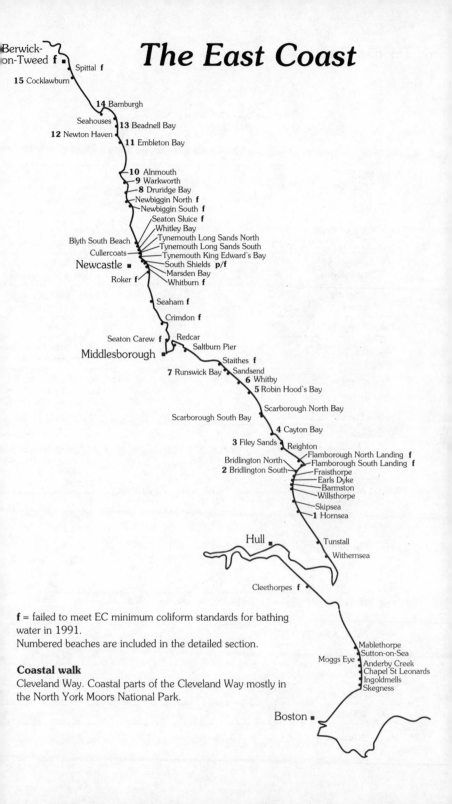

The East Coast

Berwick-on-Tweed **f**
Spittal **f**
15 Cocklawburn
14 Bamburgh
Seahouses
13 Beadnell Bay
12 Newton Haven
11 Embleton Bay
10 Alnmouth
9 Warkworth
8 Druridge Bay
Newbiggin North **f**
Newbiggin South **f**
Seaton Sluice **f**
Whitley Bay
Tynemouth Long Sands North
Tynemouth Long Sands South
Tynemouth King Edward's Bay
Blyth South Beach
Cullercoats
South Shields **p/f**
Newcastle ■
Marsden Bay
Roker **f**
Whitburn **f**
Seaham **f**
Crimdon **f**
Seaton Carew **f**
Redcar
Saltburn Pier
Middlesborough ■
Staithes **f**
7 Runswick Bay
Sandsend
6 Whitby
5 Robin Hood's Bay
Scarborough North Bay
Scarborough South Bay
4 Cayton Bay
3 Filey Sands
Reighton
Flamborough North Landing **f**
Flamborough South Landing **f**
Bridlington North
2 Bridlington South
Fraisthorpe
Earls Dyke
Barmston
Willsthorpe
Skipsea
1 Hornsea
Hull ■
Tunstall
Withernsea
Cleethorpes **f**
Mablethorpe
Sutton-on-Sea
Moggs Eye
Anderby Creek
Chapel St Leonards
Ingoldmells
Skegness
Boston ■

f = failed to meet EC minimum coliform standards for bathing water in 1991.
Numbered beaches are included in the detailed section.

Coastal walk

Cleveland Way. Coastal parts of the Cleveland Way mostly in the North York Moors National Park.

The East Coast

See page 19 for further details

Beach No on Map	Rating. The more stars the better. f=failed	Resort	Pass/Fail track record	Sewage outlets	Population discharging from outlet	Type of treatment	Discharge point relative to low water mark, unless otherwise stated. Distance given in metres	Remarks
LINCOLNSHIRE								
	★★★	**Skegness**	PPPPPP					Sandy. Bathing safe. Lindsey Coast improvement scheme.
	★★★	**Ingoldmells**	PFPPPP	1	122,000	Maceration/ screens	1420 below	Sandy. Bathing safe. Improvements as above.
	★★★	**Chapel St Leonards**	PFPPPP					Sandy. Bathing safe. Improvements as above.
	★★★	**Anderby Creek**	PPPPPP					Sandy. Bathing safe. Improvements as above.
	★★★	**Moggs Eye**	PPPPPP					Improvements as above.
	★★★	**Sutton-on-Sea**	FFFPPP					Sandy. Bathing safe. See improvements below.
	★★★	**Mablethorpe**	PFPFPP	1	37,000	Secondary	To inland drain	Sandy. Bathing safe. Improvements to existing full treatment plant planned in 1995.
HUMBERSIDE								
	f ★	**Cleethorpes**	FFFFFF	1	66,000	Maceration/ screens	At LWM	Sandy. Safe bathing at high tide. Improvements planned in 1995 to give secondary treatment.
	★★	**Withernsea**	FFPPFP	1	12,000	Primary	At LWM	Sand and shingle. £8m improvement scheme to be completed 1992.
	★★★	**Tunstall**	PPPPPP					Sand and pebbles. Safe bathing, but not at low tide. Improvement scheme as above.
1	★★★	**Hornsea**	PPPPPP	2	16,000	Screens/ maceration	1,000 below LWM	Sandy.
	★★★	**Skipsea Sands**	PPPPFP					Sandy.
	★★	**Barmston**	PPPPPP					Sand and shingle.
	★★★	**Earls Dyke**	PPPPPP					Sandy.
	★★	**Fraisthorpe**	PPPPPP					Sandy.
	★★★	**Willsthorpe**	PPPPPP					Sandy.
	★★	**Bridlington South**	PPPPPP	1	56,000	Screens	1,600 below	Sandy.

Beach No on Map	Rating. The more stars the better. **f**=failed	Resort	Pass/Fail track record	Sewage outlets	Population discharging from outlet	Type of treatment	Discharge point relative to low water mark, unless otherwise stated. Distance given in metres	Remarks
2	★★★	**Bridlington North**	PPPPPP	2			At LWM	Sandy. Storm water overflows.
	f ★	**Flamborough South Landing**	FPFFFF	1	200			Sandy. Sewage works discharges to a stream which reaches the sea. Bathing dangerous. £4m improvement scheme to be completed 1994 to give primary treatment and a long sea outfall.
	f ★★	**Flamborough North Landing**	PPPPPF					
		Thornwick Bay		1	300	Primary	At LWM	Rocky. Bathing very dangerous. Water quality not monitored in 1991.
YORKSHIRE								
	★★★	**Reighton Sands**	PPPPPP					Sand and boulders.
3	★★★	**Filey**	PPPPPP	2	13,800	Maceration	200 below	Red sand. 1 storm water overflow.
4	★★	**Cayton Bay**	PPPPPP					Sandy. Bathing safe.
		Scarborough:		1	93,750	Screened	1.5 km LSO	Sandy. £31m long sea outfall completed early 1991. Sludge contaminated with faecal micro-organisms found on North Beach in 1991. Much local debate.
	★★★	**South Beach**	FFPFP					
	★★	**North Beach**	PFPFPP					
5	★★	**Robin Hood's Bay**	PPPPPP	1	5,500			Rocky. Swimming dangerous. £5m improvement scheme to be completed 1994.
6	★★★	**Whitby**	PPPPPP	1	20,000	Raw	At LWM	Sandy. Bathing safe.
	★★★	**Sandsend**	PPPFPP	1	450	Raw	At LWM	Sand and shingle. Major incident involving raw sewage on the beach in 1991, involving children contracting serious illnesses.
7	★★	**Runswick Bay**	PPPPPP	1	480	Raw	At LWM	Sand and shingle.
	f ★	**Staithes**	~PPFFF	1	4,000	Raw	At LWM	Sand and rocks.

Beach No on Map	Rating. The more stars the better. f=failed	Resort	Pass/Fail track record	Sewage outlets	Population discharging from outlet	Type of treatment	Discharge point relative to low water mark, unless otherwise stated. Distance given in metres	Remarks
CLEVELAND								
	f ★	Skinningrove	~~~~~F	1	7,700	Raw	At LWM	Sandy.
	★★	**Saltburn-by-the-Sea (Pier)**	FFFPPP	2	13,850 6,800	Raw Raw	At LWM At LWM	Sand and pebbles. Improvements planned to give long sea outfall by 1996, primary treatment in 1998 and secondary treatment by 2000.
	f ★	Saltburn Gill						
	f ★★	Saltburn East (Sea at the Ship)						
	f ★	Skelton Beck (Beach)						Transfer of flow from Guisborough STW, which discharges into the Beck, to Marske STW and long sea outfall in 1992.
	f ★	Skelton Beck (Footbridge)						
	f ★★	Marske-by-the-Sea	~~~~~F	1	12,800	Raw	LSO	Sandy. Storm water outfall.
	★★★	**Redcar (Stray)**		1	35,000	Screened.	1599 below	Sand and rocks.
	★★	**Redcar (Granville)**						
	f ★★	**Redcar (lifeboat station)**						
	★★	**Redcar (Coatham Sands)**		1	1,200	Raw	25 below	Sandy. Storm water outfall only.
	f ★★	**Seaton Carew North Gare**		2	31,300	Maceration	At LWM	Sandy. £11.4m improvement scheme provided new LSO in 1991. Primary treatment is planned for 1994, secondary for 2000.
	f ★	**Seaton Carew Centre**	FFFFFF		28,500	Maceration	25 below	
	f ★★	**Seaton Carew North**						
		Hartlepool		5	22,800	4 Raw 1 Screened/ maceration	2x25 below 3xLWM	Sandy.
	f ★	The Stell						
DURHAM								
	f ★★	**Crimdon Park**	FFF~FF	1	4,000	Screened/ tidal tank	At LWM	Sandy. Improvements planned to provide screens in 1993, extended outfall in 1996, primary treatment in 1998 and secondary treatment in 2000.
	f ★★	Crimdon South						

Beach no. on map	Rating. The more stars the better. f=failed	Resort	Pass/Fail track record	Sewage outlets	Population discharging from outlet	Type of treatment	Discharge point relative to low water mark, unless otherwise stated. Distance given in metres	Remarks
		Blackhall		1	10,500	Raw	At LWM	Sand and pebbles. Water quality not monitored in 1991.
	f ★★ ★★	Lime Kiln South Lime Kiln North						
	f ★ f ★	Denemouth North Denemouth South		1	31,500	Screened/ tidal tank	At LWM	Sand with stones and coal waste.
		Horden		2	6,900 8,100	Raw Raw	Above LWM Above LWM	Sand with coal waste. Water quality not monitored in 1991.
		Easington		1	8,500	Raw	At LMW	Sand with coal waste. Badly polluted coastline. Water quality not monitored in 1991.
	f ★	Dalton Burn						
	f ★★	**Seaham Remand Home**		4	36,600	Raw	25 below	Improvement scheme to reduce storm water outfall use and to provide primary treatment in 1995, secondary treatment by 2000. Badly polluted coastline.
	f ★★	**Seaham Beach** FFFFFF						Sand.
	f ★★	Featherbed Rocks						
	f ★	Ice House Burn						

TYNE AND WEAR

Beach no. on map	Rating. The more stars the better. f=failed	Resort	Pass/Fail track record	Sewage outlets	Population discharging from outlet	Type of treatment	Discharge point relative to low water mark, unless otherwise stated. Distance given in metres	Remarks
	f ★	Ryhope South		2		Raw	At LWM	Sandy. Storm sewage overflows only.
	f ★	Hendon South						
		Sunderland		2	500 175,000	Tidal tank Screened	At LWM 300 below LWM	Rocky outfalls situated south of Wear Estuary.
	★★★ f ★★	**Roker/ Whitburn South** Roker/ Blockhouse	PFFFPP	1		Raw	25 below	Sandy. Storm sewage overflows subject to extension and screening in 1994.

Beach No on Map	Rating. The more stars the better. f=failed	Resort	Pass/Fail track record	Sewage outlets	Population discharging from outlet	Type of treatment	Discharge point relative to low water mark, unless otherwise stated. Distance given in metres	Remarks
		Seaburn		1		Raw	At LWM	Sandy. Storm sewage overflow. Water quality not monitored in 1991.
	f ★★	**Whitburn**	~~~PFF	1		Raw	At LWM	Sandy. Storm sewage overflow.
	★★	**Marsden Bay**	PFFPPP					Sandy.
	★★★	**South Shields (Sandhaven)**	FFPPFP	2		Raw	At LWM	Sandy. Storm sewage overflows only.
	f ★	South Shields (Inner Harbour)						
	f ★	North Shields						
	f ★	Tynemouth (Haven)		2		Raw	At LWM	Sandy. Storm water overflow only.
	★★★	**Tynemouth (King Edward's Bay)**						
	★★★	**Tynemouth (Long Sands South)**						
	★★★	**Tynemouth (Long Sands North)**						
	★★★	**Tynemouth (Cullercoats)**	~~~FPP	1		Raw	At LWM	Sandy. Storm water outfall only. Staff maintain beach facilities well.
	★★	**Whitley Bay**	PPFFPP	10		Raw	At LWM	Sandy. Storm water outfall only. Improvement scheme to extend outfalls being considered for 1995.
	f ★★	**Seaton Sluice**	FPFFPF	1	43,000	Tidal tank	60 below	Sandy. Improvement scheme to divert sewage to Howdon STW in 1992. Storm water will be screened and discharged down existing outfall.

NORTHUMBERLAND

Beach No on Map	Rating. The more stars the better. f=failed	Resort	Pass/Fail track record	Sewage outlets	Population discharging from outlet	Type of treatment	Discharge point relative to low water mark, unless otherwise stated. Distance given in metres	Remarks
	★★	**Blyth: South Beach**	~~~PPP	1	28,500	Maceration	30 below	Sandy.
		North Beach						Sandy.
	f ★★	Cambois South						
	f ★	Cambois North						

Beach no on map	Rating. The more stars the better. f=failed	Resort	Pass/Fail track record	Sewage outlets	Population discharging from outlet	Type of treatment	Discharge point relative to low water mark, unless otherwise stated. Distance given in metres	Remarks
	f ★★	**Newbiggin South**	FFFFFF	2	29,000	Maceration	At LWM	Sandy. Improvement scheme to provide primary treatment in 1995.
	f ★	**Newbiggin North**			5,000	Raw	At LWM	
		Cresswell		1	1,800 summer (200 winter)	Other	At LWM	Sandy. Water quality not monitored in 1991.
8	★★★	**Druridge Bay**	PPPPPP	1	5,500	Screened/ maceration	At LWM	Sandy.
	★★★	**Amble (Links)**		1	8,000	Screens/ maceration	250 below	Rocky.
9	★★★	**Warkworth**	PPPPPP					Sandy.
10	★★★	**Alnmouth**	PFPPPP					Sandy.
	f ★★	River Aln Estuary						
		Longhoughton Steel		1	3,000	Screened/ Raw	At LWM	Sandy cove. Water quality not monitored in 1991.
		Craster		2	400	Maceration	30 below	Water quality not monitored in 1991.
11		Embleton Bay						Sandy.
12	★★★	**Low Newton (Newton Haven)**	PPPPPP					Sandy.
13	★★★	**Beadnell Bay**	PPPPPP	1	2,000 summer (1,200 winter)	Maceration	At LWM	Sandy.
	★★★	**Seahouses (North)**	PPPPPP	1	6,000	Screens/ maceration/ tidal tank	100 below	Sandy.
14	★★★	**Bamburgh**	PPPPPP	2	1,000 summer (700 winter)	Maceration/ tidal tank	At LWM	Sandy.
					100	Raw	At LWM	
		Holy Island		1	500 summer (200 winter)	Maceration/ tidal tank	At LWM	Pebbles. Water quality not monitored in 1991.

Beach No on Map	Rating. The more stars the better. **f**=failed	Resort	Pass/Fail track record	Sewage outlets	Population discharging from outlet	Type of treatment	Discharge point relative to low water mark, unless otherwise stated. Distance given in metres	Remarks
15		Cocklawburn Beach		1	300	Raw	20 above	Sand and rocks. Emergency outfall only.
	f ★★	**Spittal**	FFFPFF					Improvement scheme to install fine screens planned.
	f ★	Spittal Quay						Improvement scheme.
		Berwick-upon-Tweed:		1		Raw	At LWM	Sandy.
	f ★	Upstream of STW						
	f ★	Downstream of STW						

1 Hornsea, North Humberside   OS Ref: TA2047

From Barmston just south of Bridlington to the shingle of Spurn Point is the fastest eroding section of coastline in Britain. Tens of feet of the clay cliffs are lost annually. This makes access to the coastline difficult with the erosion of roads, paths and steps. Hornsea is one of the few places where there is a break in the cliffs and sea defences attempt to stop the advancing sea. A sea wall and promenade face the mile (1.6km) long beach of sand and pebbles which virtually disappears when the tide rises. A park and various seaside amusements line the promenade. The quiet town of Hornsea is set back from the sea.

Water quality Beach monitored by the NRA and found to meet the EC minimum coliform standards for bathing water in 1991, ★★★ in this year's listing section. One outfall serving 16,000 people discharges screened and macerated sewage ⅔ mile (1km) below low water mark. One storm sewage overflow.

Bathing safety Due to strong currents off shore, bathing is only safe close inshore. The central section of the beach is patrolled by lifeguards at weekends.

Access Steps and ramp from promenade to sands.

Parking Several car parks adjacent to the promenade.

Toilets Several on promenade, all with facilities for the disabled.

Food Six cafés at central section of beach, several more in the town centre.

Seaside activities Swimming, windsurfing, sailing, jetskiing and fishing. Golf course nearby.

Wet weather alternatives Hornsea Pottery is situated to the south of the town and has shops selling bargains in pottery, clothing and shoes. There is also a birds of prey collection, butterfly world and children's adventure playground.

Wildlife and walks Hornsea Mere lies just south of the town. This 2 mile (3km) long lake is part of an RSPB reserve whose 5 acres (2 hectares) are an important wintering ground for wildfowl. There is a large population of reed warblers in the reed swamps. A public footpath along the south shore, through woods and open fields, provides good views of the area. There are boat launching facilities on the Mere.

2 Bridlington, North Humberside   OS Ref: TA1866

Bridlington is a bustling holiday resort which has won a whole variety of awards in the past, including the Blue Flag. With its two beaches, it combines the traditional seaside holiday entertainments with new up-to-date facilities, and there is easy access to the natural beauty of the adjacent Flamborough Headland Heritage Coast. The safe, sandy beaches are separated by Bridlington harbour; stone quays enclose a tidal harbour which is a continually changing scene of fishing and pleasure craft. The south beach extends for 5 miles (8km) with the busy promenade giving way to steep cliffs south of town. North beach is popular for watersports, being sheltered by the cliffs that sweep north to Flamborough Head.

Water quality Beach monitored by the NRA and found to meet the EC minimum coliform standards for bathing water in 1991, ★★ (south) and ★★★ (north) on this year's listing section. One outfall at Bridlington South serving 56,000 people discharges screened sewage 1 mile (1.6km) below low water mark. Two storm water outfalls discharge storm overflow to the north beach at low water; however, this only occurs at infrequent intervals following heavy rainfall.

Litter The beach is cleaned by the local council. By-laws banning dogs from the beach were successfully introduced in 1990.

Bathing safety Safe bathing.

Access Steps and ramps from the promenade.

Parking Sea-front and adequate spaces within town.

Toilets On promenade.

Food Selection of cafés and restaurants along promenade.

Seaside activities Swimming, windsurfing, diving, fishing, sailing, water skiing and paragliding. Windsurfing and sailing facilities are available for hire. Fishing tackle is also for hire and there are fishing trips daily from the harbour. Bridlington is the venue for the UK windsurfing championship.

Wet weather alternatives Leisure World, Fun Parks, Sewerby Hall and Park, Portminian Model Village, Park Rose Pottery, John Bull World of Rock, Harbour Museum, Historic Old Town and the picturesque Yorkshire Wolds, including Burton Agnes Hall and Sledmere House.

Wildlife and walks To the north lies Flamborough Head, 300 feet (90m) of towering chalk cliff. The area is rich in magnificent scenery, with natural arches, stacks and caves to be admired or explored. Several guided walks and special events are on offer and details can be obtained from the Heritage Coast Information Centre, South Landing, Flamborough. The RSPB bird sanctuary is situated to the north at Bempton.

3 Filey Sands, Filey, North Yorkshire   OS Ref. TA1180

Five miles (8km) of wide flat golden sands at Filey are sheltered by Filey Brigg, a rocky promontory that extends 1 mile (1.6km) out to sea. From the headland you can enjoy good views north to Scarborough and south to Flamborough Head. Below the gently sloping grass-covered cliffs, the beach curves to the coble landing at the north end of the town. Traditional coble fishing boats are drawn up behind the protective wall and the fishermen are often seen busy mending their nets. South of the landing a promenade and gardens face the beach which all but disappears at high tide. The Georgian residences of this elegant resort overlook the bay. The beach is cleaned daily and dogs are banned from the central part of the beach between May and September.

Water quality Beach monitored by the NRA and found to meet the EC minimum coliform standards for bathing water in 1991, ★★★ in this year's listing section. Two outfalls serving 13,800 people discharge macerated sewage 220 yards (200m) below low water mark.

Bathing safety Bathing requires caution as there are strong cross-currents. Warning flag system. Inshore rescue boat and coastguard lookout.

Access Ramps at the southern end of the promenade and the coble landing lead on to the sand.

Parking There are three pay-and-display car parks at West Avenue (880 spaces), Station Avenue (280) and Country Park (3,000). There is street parking on the promenade and on Church Hill.

Toilets 'Superloo' at Cargate, toilets at coble landing and Royal Parade.
Food Various kiosks and pub at coble landing, Margate Hill and Royal Parade.
Seaside activities Swimming (beware currents), surfing, windsurfing, sailing, diving and fishing (very good off Filey Brigg, boats available for hire). Boating, putting and amusements. An Edwardian Festival is held in June.
Wet weather alternatives Amusement arcades at coble landing, museum.
Wildlife and walks The area is renowned for its bird life and interesting geology. A nature trail along Filey Brigg starts at the foot of the cliff below Filey Country Park. The Brigg should be avoided in rough weather when heavy seas can crash over the rocks, making them dangerous for walkers and anglers.

4 Cayton Bay, North Yorkshire   OS Ref: TA0685

Steep, wooded cliffs surround the small arc of this bay and many of the boulders fringing it bear the imprints of fossil ammonites and belemnites. The National Trust owns the northern half of the bay. At low tide, sandbanks are revealed which may trap the unwary if the incoming tide is not watched. It is also dangerous to cross the rocks at the southern end of the bay. The rockpools abound with marine life and will keep the amateur naturalist engrossed for hours.
Water quality Beach monitored by the NRA and found to meet the EC minimum coliform standards for bathing water in 1991, ★★ in this year's listing section. No sewage is discharged in the vicinity of the beach.
Bathing safety Safest at high water; at other times beware of incoming tide.
Access Signposted off the A165, path down from the holiday camp at the top of the cliffs.
Parking Car park with 50 spaces approximately 1 mile (1.6km) from beach.
Toilets By the car park, open between Spring Bank Holiday and the end of October.
Food None.
Seaside activities Swimming, surfing, fishing.
Wet weather alternatives The woods at the top of the cliff will at least provide some shelter; for the less hardy the resort of Scarborough is less than 3 miles (5km) away.
Wildlife and walks The Cleveland Way runs close by the beach; it can be followed north through Scarborough and into the North York Moors National Park.

5 Robin Hood's Bay, North Yorkshire   OS Ref: NZ9505

A wide sweeping bay framed by crumbling red cliffs stretches from Ness Point and the village of Robin Hood's Bay south to the 600 foot (180m) headland of Old Peak with its scattered housing of Ravenscar. Magnificent views of the bay can be obtained from the undulating farmland on the cliff

top. There is a remnant cliff line inland. A 40 foot (12m) high sea wall protects the cluster of fishing cottages that make up Robin Hood's Bay village.
Vehicle access to the older parts of the village is restricted and to get to the
beach you have to park at the top of the hill and walk down through the
village. Elsewhere there is limited access to the shore of this huge bay.
Boggle Hole, where Mill Beck cuts through the cliffs, is a sheltered shingle
and rock cove. Stoupe Beck Sands is an 880 yard (800m) stretch of sand
in the middle of the bay. This area of the bay is very isolated with no facilities; the beach is reached down a paved track through a wooded valley.
The headland at Ravenscar and the rocky shore below are owned by the
National Trust and offer excellent views north along the coast. All have a
wild feel to them and mats of washed-up seaweed are commonplace,
which some may find unpleasant. The National Trust Coastal Centre at
Ravenscar features displays including a marine aquarium with specimens
borrowed from the rocky shore.

Water quality   Beach monitored by the NRA and found to meet the EC
minimum coliform standards for bathing water in 1991, ★★ in this year's
listing section. There is one outfall serving 5,500 people: a £5 million
improvement scheme will be completed in 1994.

Bathing safety   Safe bathing but beware of sharp rocks.

Access   The main access to the beach is from Robin Hood's Bay village,
signposted off the A171 south of Whitby. There is a regular bus service to
the village and parking above.

Parking   Pay-and-display car park at the top of the hill (267 spaces).

Toilets   By the beach.

Food   Various cafés, kiosks and pubs.

Seaside activities   Swimming, diving and fishing.

Wildlife and walks   The area is famed for its geology and fossils – there
is a geological trail from Ravenscar. The Cleveland Way follows the bay
and there is a network of paths on the cliffs. There is much to interest the
beachcomber with rockpools full of life.

6 Whitby, North Yorkshire   OS Ref: NZ88901175

Built on a steep wooded inlet of the River Esk, Whitby is crowned by its
ancient Abbey dominating the headland. It is situated in the middle of one
of Britain's most delightful stretches of coast, with cliffs and fine bays inter-
spersed with picturesque fishing villages. A vast stretch of sand is comple-
mented by a number of beach chalets. Whitby was the home of Captain
Cook and an important whaling port, and was primarily a fishing port until
1979 when a marina- type development to accommodate some 200 craft
and land adjacent for car parking was completed. Superb views of the
unspoilt coastline can be seen from the Abbey and also from the whale-
bone arch just above the pier.

Water quality   Beach monitored by the NRA and found to meet the EC
minimum coliform standards for bathing water in 1991, ★★★ in this year's
listing section. One sea outfall on East Cliff.

Bathing safety   Safe bathing.

Access   A171 coastal road to Whitby town, then follow signs to beach.

Parking   Pay-and-display parking at marina (460 spaces), street parking and
other car parks.

Toilets In car parks.

Food A variety of cafés, pubs and fast food outlets.

Seaside activities Swimming, rock angling, fishing trips, pleasure boats.

Wildlife and walks Nature walks along Cleveland Way and the Falling Foss Forest Trail near Whitby.

7 Runswick Bay, Runswick, North Yorkshire   OS Ref: NZ8016

From the picturesque hillside village of Runswick, the broad sandy beach, backed by steeply sloping clay cliffs, curves south-east to the rocky headland that bounds the bay. The crescent of sand gives way to rocky shore at either end. The old village of Runswick nestles at the base of the cliffs with the new one perched above. There is easy access to the beach and the area is not over-commercialised. There are beach huts and chalets on the scrub-covered cliffs. Good views across the bay are to be had from the village of Kettleness on the southern headland.

Water quality Beach monitored by the NRA and found to meet the EC minimum coliform standards for bathing water in 1991, ★★ in this year's listing section. One outfall serving 480 people discharges raw sewage at low water mark. Complaints received in 1991 about possible sewage odour.

Bathing safety Safe bathing.

Access A road off the A174 north of Whitby leads down to Runswick village. There is a ramp to the beach.

Parking Pay-and-display at the bottom of the hill with 104 spaces.

Toilets By car park.

Food Cafés and shops in village.

Seaside activities Swimming, sailing and fishing.

Wildlife and walks The area is excellent for walking with the Cleveland Way skirting the bay. Following the route north for 2 miles (3km) you reach the tiny harbour of Mulgrave, now falling into disrepair below the cliffs. Further north at the mouth of a tiny rocky inlet is Staithes Harbour. The village, with its closely packed houses and network of alleyways, nestles in the steep valley.

8 Druridge Bay, Cresswell, Northumberland   OS Ref: NZ2993

A 5 mile (8km) curving sweep of golden sand is fringed by dunes with rocky outcrops at either end, at Cresswell and Hadston Carrs. Cresswell is the easiest point of access and may be busy on a sunny afternoon, but a short walk along the shore will bring you to miles of quiet sand. There are views north along the bay to Coquet Island and its lighthouse.

Water quality Beach monitored by the NRA and found to meet the EC minimum coliform standards for bathing water in 1991, ★★★ in this year's listing section. One outfall serving 5,500 people discharges untreated sewage at low water mark.

Bathing safety Swim with extreme caution as the tides and currents are strong and unpredictable.

Access The A1068 leads to Cresswell and the Druridge Bay Country Park. It is a short walk from the car parks across the dunes.

Parking Near Cresswell there is a car park with 100 spaces; at Cresswell Ponds there is space for 10 cars, and on Druridge Links a National Trust car park has 150 spaces. Druridge Bay Country Park has parking for 200 cars and also coaches.

Toilets In Cresswell village and at Druridge Bay Country Park at the northern end of the bay.

Food Café and tea room in village, mobile ice-cream vans.

Seaside activities Swimming (beware currents), sailing and fishing.

Wildlife and walks At the northern end of the beach is the Druridge Bay Country Park. There are also nature reserves at Druridge and Hauxley. Cresswell Ponds have been designated as a Site of Special Scientific Interest. It is a superb area for birdwatching; the Northumberland Wildlife Trust has recently opened its Druridge Pools Reserve to the public and hide facilities are available. The Trust also runs the Blakemoor Visitor Centre where details of bird numbers and species can be found. South of the bay, beyond the smaller Broadsands beach and the rocky outcrops of Snab Point, there is the sharply contrasting Lynemouth beach, blackened by coal dust washed from waste tips that line the beach.

9 Warkworth, Northumberland   OS Ref: NU2606

Between Warkworth Harbour at the mouth of the Coquet Estuary and the Aln Estuary lie 3 miles (5km) of fabulous sandy beach. The beach, edged by sand dunes, extends northwards for 2 miles (3km) to merge with Alnmouth Links. The town of Amble lies on the southern banks of the estuary and here fishing cobles may be seen in the harbour and yachts moored in the river or at the Braid Marina – winner four times in the past of the European Blue Flag for ports, awarded for environmental quality and good facilities. Coquet Island lies 1 mile (1.6km) off shore, sheltering the harbour entrance. The island is an RSPB reserve and boat trips are available from the harbour. The views back across the estuary with the backdrop of Warkworth Castle are most impressive. The near-perfect mediaeval village of Warkworth, an idyllic spot with dramatic castle, hermitage and unique fortified bridge is set a mile (1.6km) inland, almost enclosed by a meander of the river Coquet. Warkworth beach is signposted from here. The picnic site by the beach has panoramic views of the Coquet Estuary. There is access to Alnmouth Links south of Bilton on the A1068 but there is very limited parking behind the dunes.

Water quality Beach monitored by the NRA and found to meet the EC minimum coliform standards for bathing water in 1991, ★★ in this year's listing section. One outfall serving 8,000 people discharges screened and macerated sewage at Amble.

Litter Some marine litter and fishing debris is washed on to the beach.

Bathing safety Bathing is dangerous at high tide. There is an inshore and offshore rescue boat and coastguard station at Amble.

Access North of Warkworth a turning off the A1068 is signposted.

Parking Car park at picnic site with space for 50 cars.

Toilets In car park.

Food None. Tea rooms in village a mile (1.6km) away.

Seaside activities Swimming, golf course (Warkworth), river and sea fishing from Amble.

Wildlife and walks The picnic site and surrounding area at Warkworth beach is managed by the Northumberland National Park and the National Trust owns the land to the north. A coastal path stretches the 3 miles (6km) from Warkworth to Alnmouth and is described in a leaflet available locally. A walk to the south takes you through dunes to the long break-water serving Warkworth harbour and some interesting salt marshes which were designated as a Site of Special Scientific Interest in 1988. Coquet Island with its prominent lighthouse is frequented by colonies of breeding seabirds – puffins, terns, eider. These may be viewed from boat trips around the island organised by the RSPB and information can be obtained at Amble Tourist Information Office.

10 Alnmouth, Northumberland   OS Ref: NU2410

A 1 mile (1.6km) expanse of sand stretches from the picturesque village of Alnmouth north to the Marsden Rocks. At low tide over 440 yards (400m) of excellent sand is exposed. The beach is bordered by a large car park and golf course, behind which lies the village. Alnmouth was a port of some importance during the 18th century, but due to a change in the course of the river little can be seen of the old harbour; however the old granaries have been carefully converted into pubs, shops, eating places and accommodation, retaining its unspoilt character.

Water quality Beach monitored by the NRA and found to meet the EC minimum coliform standards for bathing water in 1991, ✦✦✦ in this year's listing section. No sewage is discharged in the vicinity of the beach.

Bathing safety There are dangerous currents at some states of the tide.

Access Alnmouth is signposted off the A1068 south of Alnwick. A road through the golf course to the north of the village leads to the beach car park.

Parking Parking for 150 cars adjacent to beach.

Toilets In the village.

Food Numerous cafés and restaurants in the village.

Seaside activities Swimming, surfing, windsurfing, fishing and sailing in estuary. Two links golf courses north of village.

Wildlife and walks There is an excellent coastal walk north from Aln-mouth along the rocky shore with its series of small sandy bays to explore. Fulmars glide effortlessly along these cliffs where a wide range of seabirds can be seen. At Howick Haven you can either continue north along the low cliffs to the fishing village of Craster or turn inland following the wooded valley for 1 mile (1.6km) to the grounds of Howick Hall, where the gardens are open in summer.

11 Embleton Bay, Northumberland   OS Ref: NU2329

This scenically outstanding bay is bounded to the south by the craggy headland on which stand the dramatic ruins of Dunstanburgh Castle. The steep basalt cliffs are known as Gull Crag because of the numerous nesting seabirds, especially kittiwakes and fulmars. The excellent sandy Embleton beach, bordered by sand dunes and a golf course, stretches north from the boulder-strewn shore below the Crag to merge with the Newton Haven beach at the northern end of the bay.

Water quality No sewage is discharged on to the beach. The NRA does not monitor this beach.

Litter A clean beach but with some marine debris washed up, especially in winter.

Bathing safety Safe bathing on the incoming tide; there are undercurrents on the ebbing tide.

Access From Embleton village on the B1339 follow the road leading to the golf course or Dunstan Steads Farm. A path leads directly on to the beach and connects with the coastal footpath.

Parking Roadside parking for approximately 100 cars.

Toilets In the village.

Food In the village.

Seaside activities Swimming.

Wildlife and walks This stretch of coastline is owned by the National Trust. There are excellent views across the bay from the Heritage Coast path to the south; the path continues along the rocky foreshore to Craster, a classic fishing village with miniature harbour, rows of neat cottages and the stone sheds where the world famous Craster kippers are smoked.

12 Newton Haven, Northumberland   OS Ref: NU2525

Newton Haven's ⅔ mile (1km) crescent of sand lies at the northern end of Embleton Bay. Low tide exposes a wide beach which is fringed by dunes. Sheltered by a grass headland to the north and an offshore reef, the beach is popular for watersports. It is overlooked by the village of Low Newton, an attractive square of fishermen's cottages and pub now owned by the National Trust. Behind the dunes lies Newton Pool, a freshwater lagoon which is a nature reserve.

Water quality Beach monitored by the NRA and found to meet the EC minimum coliform standards for bathing water in 1991, ★★★ in this year's listing section. There is no sewage discharged in the vicinity of this beach.

Litter Some oil drums and fishing debris are washed up, particularly in winter.

Bathing safety Bathing is safe on the incoming tide; there are undercurrents on the ebbing tide.

Access From the car park on the approach road to Low Newton, signposted off the B1339 from High Newton. It is a short walk down to the village with direct access to the beach. A path leads along Low Newton beach to Embleton Bay.

Parking There is a car park 330 yards (300m) from Low Newton and on the road sides with space for about 100 cars. Parking in the village is for residents and disabled badge holders only.

Toilets Adjacent to beach.

Food Pub with snacks and tea room in High Newton ⅔ mile (1km) away.

Seaside activities Swimming, windsurfing, sailing, diving, canoeing and fishing.

Wildlife and walks There are bird hides at Newton Pool (one with disabled access) and a wide variety of species can seen, particularly in winter. The Heritage Coast Path stretches south round Embleton Bay to Dunstanburgh Castle and north around Newton Point to the wide sweep of Newton Links and Beadnell Bay.

13 Beadnell Bay, Beadnell, Northumberland   OS Ref: NU2229

The golden sands of this superb beach sweep south on a 2 mile (3km) long curve to the rocky outcrop of Snook Point. A stream meanders across the sands in the centre of the bay and to the south is a good area for collecting shells. At the northern end of the beach is the tiny harbour of Beadnell, still used by the traditional east coast fishing cobles. It has the distinction of being the only east coast harbour to actually face west! Standing on the quay are some huge 18th-century limestone kilns. These impressive structures have been restored and are owned by the National Trust. Golden Starfish winner for the second year running.

Water quality Beach monitored by the NRA and found to meet the EC minimum coliform standards for bathing water in 1991, ✱✱✱ in this year's listing section. One outfall serving approximately 2,000 people discharges macerated and screened sewage at low water mark.

Litter A very clean beach: two wardens are employed to oversee the maintenance of the beach.

Bathing safety Bathing is safe on the incoming tide; there are dangerous undercurrents on the ebb.

Access A road from the B1340 in Beadnell village leads to the harbour. Short walk from car park to sand.

Parking Large car park at north end of bay near harbour with 200 spaces. Small car park at Newton Links at south end of bay with space for 30 cars.

Toilets In Beadnell car park.

Food Ice-cream van at car park.

Seaside activities Swimming, windsurfing, sailing, diving, water skiing and canoeing. Outdoor sports hire centre at car park.

Wildlife and walks This stretch of coastline provides some splendid walking. South, a path around the edge of the bay leads to Newton Haven, the lovely Embleton Bay and the romantic ruins of Dunstanburgh Castle. To the north, the rocky shore gives way to sand that stretches to Seahouses.

14 Bamburgh and Seahouses, Northumberland   OS Ref: NU1834

A 150 foot (45m) rock outcrop towers above beautiful long sandy beaches and provides the magnificent setting for Bamburgh Castle. From the castle rock there are spectacular views of the sandy beaches stretching north to Holy Island and south to Seahouses. Seaward lies the panorama of the Farne Islands, their rocky cliffs falling steeply to the water below. It was from the Longstone lighthouse on Outer Farne that Grace Darling set off to rescue the crew of the Forfarshire. The row that made her a national heroine is remembered in the Grace Darling Museum in Bamburgh. Today the trip to the Islands is made from the little harbour at Seahouses. Inland,

Bamburgh village nestles below the castle among undulating fields. Between Bamburgh and Seahouses there are 4 miles (6.5km) of superb beach with sand which squeaks when walked over. Backed by the St Aidan's and Shoreston Dunes, the sands give way to rocky shore at Seahouses where the rockpools are full of marine life.

Water quality Both Bamburgh and Seahouses were monitored by the NRA and found to meet the EC minimum coliform standards for bathing water in 1991, both ★★★ in this year's listing section. There are two outfalls at Bamburgh; one, serving approximately 1,000 people, discharges macerated sewage through a tidal tank at low water mark; the other serves 100 people and discharges untreated sewage at low water mark. One outfall at Seahouses serving 6,000 people discharges screened and macerated sewage through a tidal tank 110 yards (100m) below low water mark.

Litter A little wood, plastic and fishing debris is washed on to the beach. Litter left by visitors is cleared by the National Trust.

Bathing safety Bathing is safe only on the incoming tide due to undercurrents as the tide ebbs; beware of off shore winds. Life belts are available at Seahouses. Inshore rescue boat and lifeboat.

Access There is access from both Bamburgh and Seahouses which lie on the B1340, with easy access to the beach across dunes.

Parking Bamburgh: large car park in Bamburgh has over 200 spaces. Three dune car parks with approximately 25 spaces in each, plus space for about 50 cars along the road above dunes.

Seahouses: car park in village has 500 spaces. Space for 30 cars parking on verge of B1340 north of Seahouses.

Bamburgh:

Toilets In village.

Food Café and hotel in village, and ice-cream vans on or near beach.

Seaside activities Swimming, surfing, windsurfing, diving, sailing and fishing.

Wet weather alternatives Castle, Grace Darling Museum and her grave in village.

Seahouses:

Toilets In village.

Food In village.

Seaside activities Swimming, golf course, amusements.

Wet weather alternatives Marine Life Centre.

Wildlife and walks This fantastic section of coastline falls within the Northumberland Heritage Coast and is also designated as an Area of Outstanding Natural Beauty. Below the lofty position of Bamburgh Castle, a walk north along the shore leads to Budle Bay. The salt marsh, mud and sand flats are part of the Lindisfarne Nature Reserve which covers the whole of the Fenham Flats, Holy Island Sands and most of the island itself. The area provides feeding for thousands of waders and wildfowl. It is dangerous to cross the sands; access to the island is by the causeway which is covered for at least 11 hours each day. With its Castle and Priory, the Island is steeped in history and its distinctive conical shape leaves a lasting impression on the memory. The beaches around the island are wide and sandy but unsafe for swimming because of strong currents. The Farne Islands to the south of Holy Island are of international importance for their large colonies of seabirds and grey seals. The 30 islands that make up the

Farnes are a National Trust Nature Reserve and landing is permitted on Inner Farne and Staple Island. Boats make the hour-long trip from the harbour at Seahouses in good weather. Further information about the service is available from the National Trust shop in Seahouses. Access is restricted during the bird breeding season from mid-May until mid-July.

15 Cocklawburn, Scremerston, Northumberland   OS Ref: NU0349

The retreating tide exposes rockpools in the rocks which bound this ⅔ mile (1km) long section of sandy beach. This is the accessible end of an extensive sandy beach, which stretches south as Cheswick Sands towards Holy Island. The further south-east you venture along the beach, the quieter the beach becomes. Wide flat sands revealed at low tide join the island with the mainland. They should not be crossed by foot – use the causeway road from Beal. The influence of man is much in evidence at the Cocklawburn beach with the remains of lime kilns and waste heaps on the edge of the beach. The modern activity of man imposes on the beach at times too, with the sound of trains on the railway line to Edinburgh which runs parallel with the shore.

Water quality One outfall serving 300 people discharges untreated sewage 22 yards (20m) above low water mark. The NRA does not monitor this beach.

Bathing safety Safe bathing on the incoming tide; undercurrents on the ebb tide make swimming dangerous; beware also of off shore winds.

Access Turning east from the village of Scremerston, a lane leads down to and then runs parallel with the shore. The beach is reached by a short walk through the dunes.

Parking Cars can be parked at several places along the lane on grassland behind the dunes. There is space for approximately 200 cars.

Toilets None.

Food None.

Seaside activities Swimming, surfing, windsurfing and fishing.

Wildlife and walks The dunes that edge the beach support very good flora and an area at the southern end of the beach is a Northumberland Wildlife Trust Nature Reserve. The limestone outcrops are favoured by cowslips, cranesbills and vetches which add to the variety of plants to be found. A path north along the rocky shore leads to the mouth of the river Tweed where fishermen netting salmon can often be seen.

North-West England

For the region which pioneered the concept of the seaside resort, it's rather sad there are no 'good beaches' from the north-west in a guide such as this. The north-west does have some lovely stretches of coastline; birdwatching on Morecambe Bay with the Lake District as a backdrop, or the Victorian elegance of Southport are but two regional attractions.

However, the whole region suffers from major pollution problems which affect nearly all its shores. The Irish Sea is heavily polluted; it is the most radioactive sea in the world and it is more chemically contaminated than the North Sea. The Mersey Estuary and Liverpool Bay have suffered particularly. For example, unacceptable amounts of mercury, cadmium and lead are released into the bay each day, mostly from industrial and contaminated sewage discharges to the Mersey and its tributaries. In addition at least 1.5 million tons of sewage sludge (destined to end by 1998) and 3.5 million tons of dredged spoil (sediments dredged from the estuary usually contaminated with heavy metals and other persistent toxic chemicals) are dumped into Liverpool Bay each year. Blackpool, the most famous and still one of the most popular seaside resorts of them all, looks out on to this toxic mess. As a result, its beaches remain some of the most grossly polluted in the whole of the UK.

Thus, visitors to the beaches in this region must, unhappily, expect to see strands of foam resulting from excessive algal growth triggered by the very high nutrient inputs from sewage. They will also come across the refuse dumped illegally from the boats and ships which continually use the waterway, and a variety of sewage-related debris on the beaches. Despite the plans for considerable investment in sewage treatment over the next few years, a legacy of terrible under-investment means that in 1991 the water quality at north-west beaches was worse than in the previous year. Sadly, it will be many years before it will be advisable to go into the water at most of the region's beaches. This is certainly the worst region in the UK for polluted beaches.

North West England

Carlisle

Silloth **f**

Allonby **f**
Allonby South **f**

Whitehaven

St Bees

Seascale **f**

Silecroft

Askam-in-Furness **f**
Aldingham **f**

Haverigg **f**
Roan Head

Bardsea

Barrow-in-Furness

Newbiggin **f**

Walney Westshore
Walney Sandy Gap
Walney Biggar Bank

Morecambe **f**

Heysham **f**

Fleetwood **f**

Cleveleys **f**

Blackpool **f**

Lytham St Annes **f**
Lytham St Annes South **f**

Southport **f**

Ainsdale **f**

Formby **f**

New Brighton **f**
Moreton
Moels **f**

Liverpool

Birkenhead

f = failed to meet EC minimum coliform standards for bathing water in 1991.

North-West England   *See page 19 for further details*

Beach No on Map	Rating. The more stars the better. f=failed	Resort	Pass/Fail track record	Sewage outlets	Population discharging from outlet	Type of treatment	Discharge point relative to low water mark, unless otherwise stated. Distance given in metres	Remarks
	f ★★	**Skinburness (Silloth)**	~FF~FF					
	f ★★	**Silloth (Lees Scar)**	FPFPFF	1	3,000	Screened	60 below	Sand and shingle. Sewage treatment works planned for 1995 providing secondary treatment.
	f ★	**Allonby South**	~FFFFF	1	300	Screened/ Tidal tank	50 below after high tide	Sand and rock, slightly muddy. Popular beach. Primary treatment planned for 1994 for base flows only.
	f ★★	**Allonby West Winds**	FFFPPF					
		Maryport		1	11,500	Raw	Above LWM	Sand, shingle. Fishing port. Improvements planned. Water quality not monitored.
		Flimby		3	100 1,500 50	Raw Raw Raw	150 above 150 above 150 above	Sand and shingle. Improvements planned. Water quality not monitored.
		Siddick		2	3,500 50	Raw Raw	Above LWM 200 below	Improvements planned. Water quality not monitored.
		Workington		4	2,500 6,000 12,000 5,500	Raw Raw Raw Raw	At LWM 10 above 20 above Below HWM	Shingle/slag. Low amenity. Improvements planned for all four outfalls. Water quality not monitored.
		Harrington		1	3,500 + industry	Raw	At LWM	Shingle/slag. Popular beach. Improvements planned. Water quality not monitored.
		Parton		1	200 + industry	Screened/ maceration	800 below	Shingle/sand. Low amenity. Improvements planned. Water quality not monitored.

Beach No on Map	Rating. The more stars the better. f=failed	Resort	Pass/Fail track record	Sewage outlets	Population discharging from outlet	Type of treatment	Discharge point relative to low water mark, unless otherwise stated. Distance given in metres	Remarks
		Whitehaven		3	500	Raw	Above HWM	Shingle and black sand.
					1,000	Raw	Above LWM	Cliffs. Little used.
					25,500	Raw	At LWM	Industrial pollution from nearby works. Water quality not monitored.
	***	**St Bees**	F~~PPP	1	2,000	Primary/ tidal tank	At LWM	Sand/shingle. Strong tank currents. Proposed long sea outfall and stormwater management for 1995.
		Nethertown		1	500	Raw	At LWM	Sand/shingle. Water quality not monitored.
		Braystones		1	9,000	Raw	50 below	Sand/shingle. Improvements planned. Water quality not monitored.
	f **	**Seascale**	FFFFFF	1	2,200	Raw	Below LWM	Sand/shingle and rocks. Improvements being considered for 1995. Nearby radioactive discharges from Sellafield (Windscale).
		Ravenglass		1	250 + heavy tourist trade	Primary	To Esk at LWM	Shingle and mud. Water quality not monitored.
	**	**Silecroft**	FPPPPP					Sand and shingle.
	f **	**Haverigg**	FFFFFF					Sand dunes. High amenity. Improvement scheme at Millom to ensure Haverigg compliance.
		Millom		1	7,500	Primary	At LWM	Sand and shingle. Water quality not monitored.
	f **	**Askam-in-Furness**	F~~FFF	1	2,350	Secondary	To Duddon Channel	Sand. Bathing safe inshore. Pollution in Duddon Estuary. Improvement scheme planned.

Beach No on Map	Rating. The more stars the better. f=failed	Resort	Pass/Fail track record	Sewage outlets	Population discharging from outlet	Type of treatment	Discharge point relative to low water mark, unless otherwise stated. Distance given in metres	Remarks
		Barrow-in-Furness		32	73,000	Raw/other		All discharge to Walney Channel. Secondary treatment planned for 1996. Water quality not monitored.
	★★	**Roan Head**	FFFPFP					Beaches to the west of the island have sand dunes and normal bathing facilities. Walney Channel is badly polluted and used by boats only.
	★★★	**Walney Island: West Shore**	FFFPFP					
	★★★	**Walney Island: Biggar Bank**	PPPFPP					
	★★	**Walney Island: Sandy Gap**	PFPFPP					
	f ★★	**Newbiggin**	~FF~FF					Sandy. UV disinfection of secondary STW effluent planned for late 1992.
	f ★★	**Aldingham**	~FF~FF					Sandy.
	f ★★	**Bardsea**	FFFPPF					Sandy. Country park. Improvement scheme to transfer flows to Ulverston STW.
		Grange-Over-Sands & Kents Bank		3	11,500	Secondary		Discharges to Wyke Beck. Mud, shingle and sand. New sewage treatment works. Water quality not monitored.
		Arnside		1	2,000	Tidal tank		Mud, shingle and sand. New pumping station has reduced the number of occasions when overflow operates. Water quality not monitored.
		Hest Bank		2	2,850	Secondary	One above HWM and one below	Mud flats, sea retreats 4 miles (6.4km). No bathing. Water quality not monitored.

Beach No on Map	Rating. The more stars the better. f=failed	Resort	Pass/Fail track record	Sewage outlets	Population discharging from outlet	Type of treatment	Discharge point relative to low water mark, unless otherwise stated. Distance given in metres	Remarks
f ★		**Morecambe:** **Morecambe North**	F~FFFF	1	31,000	Raw	At LWM	North beach mud and shingle. South beach sandy with safe bathing. £20 million improvement scheme planned for 1997.
f ★		**Morecambe South**	F~FFFF					
f ★★		**Heysham**	FFFPFF	1	3,500	Primary	At LWM	Sand. Popular beach. Linked to Morecambe scheme.
		Pilling Sands		1	1,000	Tidal tank	To Broadfleet	Mud flats/salt marsh. Outfall has been moved. Water quality not monitored.
		Knott End-on-Sea		1	1,100	Raw	To Wyre Estuary	Sand/mud flats Water quality not monitored.
f ★★		**Fleetwood (Pier)**	FFFFFF	1	31,000	Tidal tank	At LWM	Sand. Stormwater overflow at HWM which often overflows on to the beach. Linked to Fylde Coast scheme. Long sea outfall planned from new Fleetwood secondary STW by 1996.
f ★		Rossall	~~~~~F					
f ★		**Cleveleys**	FFFFFF	1	81,000			To be linked to Fylde Coast scheme for 1996.
f ★★		**Bispham**	~FF~FF					
f ★		**Blackpool:** **Blackpool North**	FFFFFF	2	105,000	Screened	Below LWM	Sand. Discharges of storm water directly on to the beach occur once or twice a year. Improvement scheme planned (the Fylde Coast scheme) due for completion by 1996, secondary treatment envisaged. Until then, remains badly polluted and unsuitable for bathing.
f ★★		**Blackpool Lost Children's Post**	FFFFFF					
f ★		**Blackpool South**	FFFFFF					
f ★		Blackpool Squire's Gate						
f ★		Blackpool Manchester Square						
f ★★		Blackpool Coral Island						
f ★★		Blackpool Anchorsholme						

Beach No on Map	Rating. The more stars the better. f=failed	Resort	Pass/Fail track record	Sewage outlets	Population discharging from outlet	Type of treatment	Discharge point relative to low water mark, unless otherwise stated. Distance given in metres	Remarks
	f ★★	**St Anne's North**	FFFFFF	1	42,000	Screened	At LWM	Sand. Outfall discharges into channel of the Ribble Estuary. Will be diverted to Preston STW.
	f ★	St Anne's Granny's Bay						
	f ★	Lytham Jetty						
	f ★★	**Lytham St Anne's**	FFFFFF					
	f ★	**Southport**	FFFFFF	4	91,500	Primary	To Crossens Pool	Sandy beaches. 3 storm water overflows, which are to be abandoned when the Southport STW is extended.
	f ★★	Birkdale	~~~~F					
	f ★★	**Ainsdale**	FFFPPF	0	12,000	Secondary		To inland waterway.
	f ★★	**Formby**	PPFPPF	0	18,000	Secondary		To River Alt.
		Hightown						Sand and some muddy areas around Alt estuary. Emergency overflow into Alt Estuary. Sewage is treated at Formby sewage treatment works. Water quality is not monitored.
		Blundell Sands		2	48,100			An £8 million scheme commmences in 1992 to shut these two outfalls. Water quality not monitored.
		Brighton-le-Sands						Water quality not monitored.
	f ★	**Crosby**	~~~~~F					
		Waterloo						Water quality not monitored.
	f ★	New Brighton, Victoria Road						All flows diverted to Wallasey screening plant.
	f ★	New Brighton, Dalmorton Road						All flows diverted to Wallasey screening plant.
	★★	**New Brighton, Harrison Drive**	FPPFPP					All flows now diverted to Wallasey screening plant.

Beach No on Map	Rating. The more stars the better. **f**=failed	Resort	Pass/Fail track record	Sewage outlets	Population discharging from outlet	Type of treatment	Discharge point relative to low water mark, unless otherwise stated. Distance given in metres	Remarks
	★★★	Wallasey (Leasowe Bay)	~~~~~P					
	★★	**Moreton**	PPPPPP	1	65,000	Maceration	3000 below	A long sea outfall discharges the macerated effluent through diffusers.
	★★★	Hoylake Red Rocks	~~~~~P					
	★★★	Hoylake Baths	~~~~~P					
	f ★★	Meols	FFPFFF					

THERE ARE NO BEACHES IN THE NORTH WEST REGION CURRENTLY CONSIDERED TO WARRANT FURTHER DETAILED INFORMATION AS ONE OF BRITAIN'S BEST BEACHES.

Scotland

If you are looking for a clean beach in the UK you are most likely to find one in Scotland. That is not to say that Scotland does not have problems around the coast. There are Scottish beaches that have failed to meet the minimum EC bathing water quality standard. Sea-borne rubbish is washed up on to the shore. Sewage sludge and dredged spoil are dumped off the Clyde, Forth and Tay estuaries. Industrial waste is discharged into the coastal water, particularly the Clyde and Forth. Nuclear installations at Chapelcross, Hunterston, Torness and Dounreay contribute to pollution of the sea. There is development of the coastline detrimental to scenic value. The west coast lochs are studded with the floating cages of the troubled fish farming industry. The offshore structures of the North Sea oil and gas industry that dot the horizon have resulted in the growth of onshore terminals and the view along the Cromarty Firth is dominated by a string of massive platforms.

By contrast there is probably some of the most spectacular coastal scenery in the country, including the long sand dunes of the east coast, and the rocky shore of Fife with its series of picturesque fishing villages. There are also the cliffs and stacks of Caithness, and of course the west coast, Highlands and Islands, sea lochs, towering mountains and fantastic sunsets. There are hundreds (if not thousands) of beaches and tiny sandy bays, mostly remote, deserted and beautiful. Many can only be reached by the keen walker but without a doubt the effort is well worthwhile. The beaches that follow are those which are relatively easily accessible for a day at the sea or as a starting point to explore the delights of this coastline further. The sands of the Western Isles have not been included in the section; if you take the boat to the outer islands, beaches abound and every one is a good beach. If you are looking for peace and solitude combined with traditional hospitality, then try Scotland.

14 Sandside Bay
Dunnet Bay
Thurso
16 Balnakeil Bay
Farr Bay
13 Duncansby Head
17 Sandwood
Sinclair's Bay
15 Coldbackie
Wick
18 Scourie
20 Clachtoll **19** Clashnessie Bay
21 Achmelvich
22 Achnahaird
23 Achiltibuie
Ullapool
12 Dornoch
Lossiemouth Silversands
Lossiemouth East **f**
Inverboyndie Bay
24 Gruinard Bay
Invergordon
Fraserburgh
e Coral Beaches
25 Gairloch
Banff **f**
9 Sandend
8 Strathbeg
Nairn
11 Burghead
10 Cullen
Peterhead
Inverness
Cruden Bay
26 Applecross
Balmedie
Aberdeen Ballroom
Aberdeen
Aberdeen Footdee
Scotland
7 Muchalls
28 Morar
6 Stonehaven
29 Camusdarrach
30 Traigh, Arisaig
St Cyrus **f**
1 Sanna Bay
5 Montrose
Calgary Bay
Arbroath **f**
Carnoustie **f**
Oban
4 Tentsmuir Point
33 Erraid
St Andrews West
St Andrews East
2 Thorntonloch
Dunglass
1 Pease Sands
Coldingham
Glasgow
Edinburgh
White Sands
Eyemouth **f**
Saltcoats
35 Brodick
Bay
Irvine **f**
34 Machrihanish
36 Blackwaterfoot
37 Troon
Prestwick **f**
Ayr **f**
Turnberry **f**
Girvan
Southerness
Stranraer **f**
Sandyhills

failed to meet EC minimum coliform standards
bathing water in 1991.
mbered beaches appear in the detailed section.

astal walk
th Road Bridge to Newburgh 94 miles (152km).

Shell Bay
f Largo
Crail
Lower Largo **f**
Anstruther
Lundin Links
Pittenweem **f**
Elie/Earlsferry
Kinghorn **f**
Kirkcaldy
North Berwick **f**
Burnt Island
3 Gullane
Milsey Bay
Aberdour Silversands **f**
Pettycur
Seacliff
Dunbar East **f**
Cramond
Belhaven
f Silverknowes
Peffer Sands
Edinburgh
Portobello
Broad Sands
f
Gosford
Seton Sands

Scotland   *See page 19 for further details*

Beach No on Map	Rating. The more stars the better. f=failed	Resort	Pass/Fail track record	Sewage outlets	Population discharging from outlet	Type of treatment	Discharge point relative to low water mark, unless otherwise stated. Distance given in metres	Remarks
BORDERS								
	f ★★	Eyemouth	PPPFPF	2	4,500	Other	Above LWM	Rocks and sand.
					1,000	Raw	Above LWM	Bathing can be unsafe.
	★★★	Coldingham Bay	PPPFPP	1	200	Raw	Above LWM	Sandy. Safe bathing.
1	★★★	**Pease Sands**	PPPPPP	1	1,000	Secondary	Above LWM	Red cliffs and sand.
LOTHIAN								
	★★★★	Dunglass	~~~~~P					Coarse sand and rocks.
2	★★★	Thorntonloch	PPPPPP					Mostly sandy.
	★★★★	Whitesands Bay	PPPPPP					Sandy.
	f ★★	Dunbar East	~~~~~F					Sand and rocks.
	★★	**Belhaven Beach**	PPPPPP	1	4,200	Screens/ maceration	At LWM	Sandy. Beware undertow when swimming. New long sea outfall for 1992.
	★★★	Peffersands	PPPPPP					Sandy.
	★★★	Seacliff	~~~~~P					
	★★	**Milsey Bay**	PPFPPP	2	2,100	Raw	At LWM	Sandy and rock outcrops
	f ★★	North Berwick Bay	PPFFFF	2	2,800	Raw	At LWM	Sandy and rock outcrops.
	★★	**Yellowcraig (Broad Sands Bay)**	PPPPFP	1	300	Raw	At LWM	Sandy, some rocks.
3	★★★	**Gullane Bay**	PPPPPP					Sand and dunes.
	★★★	Gosford Sands	PPPFFP	1		Raw	At LWM	Sand with rocky upper shore.
	★★★	Longniddry		1		Secondary	At LWM	Sand and rocks. Popular with windsurfers.
	★★★	Seton Sands	FFP~FP	1	3,700	Primary	At LWM	Sand and rocks.
	f ★★	Fisherrow	~~~~~F					
	f ★	Portobello	FFFFPF	1	4,500	Screened	At LWM	Mostly sand.
	f ★★	Silverknowes						Sand and mud.
	★★★	Cramond	~~~~~P					Sand, very low tide.
FIFE								
	★★★	Dalgety	~~~~~P	1		Secondary	At LWM	Sand and rocks.

Rating. The more stars the better. f=failed	Resort	Pass/Fail track record	Sewage outlets	Population discharging from outlet	Type of treatment	Discharge point relative to low water mark, unless otherwise stated. Distance given in metres	Remarks
★★★	Aberdour Harbour	~~~~~P					Sand and rocks.
f ★★	**Aberdour Silversands**	PPPPFF	1	2,500	Primary	At LWM	Sandy.
★★★	Burntisland	PPP~~P	2	2,200	Screens	At LWM	Sandy.
f ★★	**Pettycur**	FFP~PF	1	1,120	Primary	At LWM	Sandy.
f ★★	Kinghorn	FFFFFF	1	2,400	Primary	50 below	Sandy. Localised problems in 1991.
f ★★	**Kirkcaldy Linktown**	FF~~FF	2 1	50,000	Screens Screens	At LWM Via LSO	Sandy.
★★★	**Pathhead Sands**	~~~~~P					Sand/coal spoil.
f ★	Leven West	~~~~~F	1	110,000	Screens	LSO	Sandy.
f ★★	Leven East	PPP~FF	1	< 100	Septic tank	At LWM	Wide sands.
★★★	Lundin Links	PPPPFP	1	1,090	Primary	200 below	Sandy to west.
f ★★	Lower Largo	FFFFFF	1	1,400	Screens	At LWM	Rocky with some sand.
f ★★	Upper Largo						
★★★	Shell Bay	PPFFPP	1	100	Primary	At LWM	Sandy.
★★★	Elie/Earlsferry	PPPFFP	1	1,200	Raw	Via LSO	Muddy sand.
f ★★	Pittenweem	PPP~FF	1	500	Screens	At LWM	Rocky. Fishing port.
★★★	Anstruther	PPPPPP	7	3,115	Screens	At LWM	Sand and rocks.
★★★	Roome Bay, Crail	PPPPPP	4	1,200	Screens	At LWM	Sand and rocks.
★★★	St Andrews East	PPFFFP					
★★★	**St Andrews West**	PPPPPP	1	16,000	Primary	At LWM	Sandy.
★★★	Tentsmuir Point	~~~~PP					Sand and dunes. Presence of substantial amounts of tidal rubbish reported in 1991.
f ★★	Tayport	~~~~~F					
f ★★	Broughty Ferry	FFF~~F					
f ★★	Monifieth	FFF~~F					
f ★★	**Carnoustie**	PPPFFF	1	10,000	Raw	Above LWM.	Sandy.

Beach No on Map	Rating. The more stars the better. f=failed	Resort	Pass/Fail track record	Sewage outlets	Population discharging from outlet	Type of treatment	Discharge point relative to low water mark, unless otherwise stated. Distance given in metres	Remarks
	f ★★	**Arbroath**	PPFFFF	2	9,000 / 21,000	Raw / Screened	At LWM / 900 below	Red sands. Diversion of flow to Inchcape late 1992.
	f ★★	Arbroath Victoria Park	~~~~~F					
	★★★	Lunan Bay	~~~~FP					Sandy. Safe bathing except at river mouth.
5	★★	**Montrose**	PPPPPP	2	8,000 / 6,000	Maceration / Raw	Below LWM / Below LWM	Sandy. Safe bathing except at river mouth.
	★★★	Westhaven	~~~~~P					
GRAMPIAN								
	f ★★	St Cyrus	~~~PFF	1	820	Maceration	At LWM	Sand/saltmarsh.
6	★★★	Stonehaven	PPPPPP	2	9,000	Maceration/ primary	At LWM	
7		Muchalls						Pebbles/rock. Bathing unsafe.
	★★★	**Aberdeen/ Ballroom**	PPPPPP	2	269,450	Screens/ maceration	2,500 below LWM	Sand. New LSO soon.
	★★★	Aberdeen/ Footdee						
	★★★	Balmedie	~~PPPP					10 miles of sand and dunes. Sewage-related debris and dog-fouling o the beach reported in 1991.
	★★★	Collieston	~~~~PP	1	200	Maceration	At LWM	Old fishing port.
	★★	Cruden Bay	~~PPFP	1	2,200	Maceration	At LWM	Sand and dunes.
	★★★	Lido Peterhead	~~PPPP	1	20,450	Screened	Via LSO	Storm water receives primary treatment. San
8		Strathbeg Bay						Sand and dunes. Water quality not monitored.
	★★	St Combs	~~~~FP					Small fishing port.
	★★★	**Fraserburgh**	PPFPPP	12	15,690	Raw	Variable	Sand and dunes. Improvement scheme under way. Sewage-related debris reported the beach.
	★★★	Rosehearty	~~~~PP	1	1,250	Raw		Old fishing port. Golf course.

Rating. The more stars the better. f=failed	Resort	Pass/Fail track record	Sewage outlets	Population discharging from outlet	Type of treatment	Discharge point relative to low water mark, unless otherwise stated. Distance given in metres	Remarks
f ★★	Banff Links	~~FFFF	2	4,420	Raw	Variable	Sand. Improvement scheme under way.
★★★	Inverboyndie	~~~~~P					Panoramic bay. Coastal rangers.
★★★	Sandend Bay	~~~~PP	1	280	Settlement		Sandy. Disabled parking. Good facilities.
0 ★★★	**Cullen**	PPPPPP	2	1,500	Raw	At LWM	Sandy.
	Findochty		2	1,050	1 raw, 1 macerated	1 at and 1 below LWM	Sand. 2 raw outfalls closed. Water quality not monitored in 1991.
	Strathlene, Buckie		12	15,000	Raw	Variable	Sand. Water quality not monitored in 1991.
f ★★	Lossiemouth East	FFFPPF	1	42,700	Screens	Via LSO	Sandy
★★★	Lossiemouth Silversands	PPPPPP	2		Raw/ maceration	SSOs	
	Hopeman		1	1,663	Raw	At LWM	Water sports. Water quality not monitored in 1991.
1	Burghead		1		Raw	Via LSO east of harbour	Sandy. Bathing not recommended. Much litter.
HIGHLAND							
★★★/ ★★★	Nairn East/ Central	PPFP~P	3		2 raw, 1 primary		Sandy. Improvement scheme.
	Rosemarkie						Sand/gravel and shingle. Very popular in summer. Water quality not monitored.
	Cromarty				Raw		Untreated sewage discharges to beach. Water quality not monitored.
	Nigg Bay						Popular beach in summer. Water quality not monitored.

Beach No on Map	Rating. The more stars the better. **f**=failed	Resort	Pass/Fail track record	Sewage outlets	Population discharging from outlet	Type of treatment	Discharge point relative to low water mark, unless otherwise stated. Distance given in metres	Remarks
		Portmahomack						Sand/dunes. Fishing, sailing and windsurfing popular. Water quality not monitored.
12		Dornoch						Sandy.
		Sinclair's Bay Wick		3	700	2 raw 1 primary	1 tank 2 at LWM	Sandy. Water quality no monitored.
13		Duncansby Head						Small, sandy.
		Dunnet Bay/ Murkle Bay		2	200 1000	Maceration Primary	Above LWM Below LWM	Sand and dunes. Water quality not monitored.
		Thurso		1	9,000	Maceration	450 below	Sandy. Water quality nc monitored.
14		Sandside Bay						Dunes, rocky outcrops.
15		Coldbackie						Sand/dunes.
16		Sango Bay/ Balnakeil Bay		1	200	Primary	At LWM	Sand/dunes.
17		Sandwood Bay						Sand/dunes.
18		Scourie		2	300	Primary	At LWM	Sandy.
19		Clashnessie Bay						Sandy.
20		Clachtoll						Sandy.
21		Achmelvich						Sandy.
22		Achnahaird						Sandy. Dunes becoming badly eroded due to visitor pressure.
23		Achiltibuie						Shingle.
24		Gruinard Bay						Sandy.
25		Gairloch		3		Primary		Sandy. Safe bathing.
26		Applecross						Sandy.
27		Coral Beaches						Sand/shells.
28		Morar						Sandy.
29		Camusdarrach						Sand/dunes.
30		Traigh, Arisaig						Sand/dunes.
31		Sanna Bay						Sandy.

Beach No on Map	Rating. The more stars the better. f=failed	Resort	Pass/Fail track record	Sewage outlets	Population discharging from outlet	Type of treatment	Discharge point relative to low water mark, unless otherwise stated. Distance given in metres	Remarks
32		Calgary Bay						Sand/dunes.
33		Erraid						Sand/dunes.
STRATHCLYDE								
		Kilchattan Bay		1	170	Raw	At LWM	Water quality not monitored.
		Kames Bay		several	550	Raw		Sand and pebbles. Water quality not monitored.
		Dunoon (West Bay)		1	not known	Raw	Below LWM	Sand and pebbles. Some water quality monitoring in 1991.
		Ganavan		1	100	Septic tank	Below LWM	Sand and rocky outcrops. Some water quality monitoring in 1991.
34		Machrihanish		1	200	Raw	At LWM	Sandy.
		Carradale		2	480	Raw	At LWM	Water quality not monitored.
		Helensburgh		1	13,200	Maceration		Sand and pebbles. Some water quality monitoring in 1991.
		Portkil/ Meiklecross		1 1	< 100 < 100	Raw Raw	Below LWM Above LWM	Sand and rocks. Water quality not monitored.
		Gourock (West Bay)		4	2,600	Raw	Below LWM	Shingle and rocks. Some water quality monitoring in 1991.
		Lunderston Bay		1	not known	Septic tank	Above LWM	Shingle and sand. Some water quality monitoring in 1991.
		Wemyss Bay		3	100 100 11,000	Other Other Maceration	Above LWM Above LWM Below LWM	Shingle and sand. Some water quality monitoring in 1991.
		Largs		1	12,000	Other	Below LWM	Sand and rocks. Some water quality monitoring in 1991.
		Fairlie		2	700 800	Raw Raw	Below LWM At LWM	Sand and rocks. Water quality not monitored.
		Millport		11	2,700	Primary	At LWM	Sand and rocks. Some water quality monitoring in 1991.

Beach No on Map	Rating. The more stars the better. f=failed	Resort	Pass/Fail track record	Sewage outlets	Population discharging from outlet	Type of treatment	Discharge point relative to low water mark, unless otherwise stated. Distance given in metres	Remarks
		Seamill		3	4,500	Raw	All at LWM	Sand and rocks. Improvements planned. Some water quality monitoring in 1991.
		Boydston		1	4,000	Maceration	At LWM	Sand and rocks. Improvement scheme planned. Water quality not monitored.
	**	**Saltcoats**	PPFFFP	2	13,500	Raw	Both below LWM	Sandy. Improvement scheme under construction.
		Stevenston		1	41,000	Screens	⅔ mile (1km) below LWM	Sandy. Some water quality monitoring in 1991.
	f **	**Irvine (Beach Park)**	FFFFFF					Sandy. Improvement scheme completed in 1991.
		Gailes		1	100,000	Screens	1 mile (1.5km) beyond LWM	Sandy. Water quality not monitored.
35		Brodick Bay		2	700	Both raw	1 beyond LWM, 1 above LWM	Rocks and sand.
		Lamlash Bay		6	950	Raw	All at LWM	Rocks and sand. Water quality not monitored.
		Whiting Bay		2	800	Raw	Below LWM	Sand and shingle. Water quality not monitored.
36		Blackwaterfoot						Sand and shingle.
		Troon (North)		1	6,300	Raw	At LWM	Sandy. Improvement scheme planned. Some water quality monitoring in 1991.
37 ★★★		**Troon (South)**	PPPPPP					Sandy.
	f ★★	**Prestwick**	PPPFFF					Sandy.
	f ★★	**Ayr**	FFFFFF	1	16,200	Screens	140 below LWM	Sandy. Improvements planned.
		Doonfoot		1	8,000	Maceration	220 below LWM	Sand/rocks. Improvements planned. Some water quality monitoring in 1991.

Beach No on Map	Rating. The more stars the better. **f**=failed	Resort	Pass/Fail track record	Sewage outlets	Population discharging from outlet	Type of treatment	Discharge point relative to low water mark, unless otherwise stated. Distance given in metres	Remarks
		Butlins (Heads of Ayr)		1	10,000	Secondary	Below LWM	Sandy. Water quality not monitored.
		Maidens		1	600	Primary	At LWM	Sandy and rocks. Improvement scheme planned. Some water quality monitoring in 1991.
f ★★		**Turnberry**	PPF~FF	1		Primary	Beyond LWM	Sand and rocks. Improvement scheme under consideration.
★★★		**Girvan**	FFFPFP	3	4,000	Screens/ maceration	10 below	Sandy. Improvement scheme in preparation.
					500	Tidal tank	At LWM	
					2,500	Tidal tank	At LWM	

DUMFRIES AND GALLOWAY

f ★★		Stranraer Marine Lake	~~~~~F					
f ★★		Stranraer Cockle Shore	~~~~~F					
★★★		Portpatrick Outer Harbour	~~~~~P					
		Portlogan Bay		1	75	Primary	200 below HWM	Sandy. Water quality not monitored.
★★★		Drunmore	~~~~~P					
		Ardwell Bay		1	75	Primary	75 below HWM	Sand/shingle. Water quality not monitored.
f ★★		Sandhead	~~~~~F					Failure possibly due to contamination by animal faeces.
★★★		Monreith	~~~~~~P					Affected by sea-borne litter, especially after winter storms, although cleared for holiday season.
★★★		Mossyard	~~~~~P					
★★★		Carrick Shore	~~~~~P					
★★★		Brighouse Bay	~~~~~P	1	400	Secondary	30 below	Sandy.
★★★		Dhoon	~~~~~P					
f ★★		Rockcliffe	~~~~~F					

Beach No on Map	Rating. The more stars the better. **f**=failed	Resort	Pass/Fail track record	Sewage outlets	Population discharging from outlet	Type of treatment	Discharge point relative to low water mark, unless otherwise stated. Distance given in metres	Remarks
	★★★	**Sandyhills**	PPPPFP	1	200	Secondary	To tidal watercourse	Sandy. Sometimes affected by livestock faeces from inland.
		Southerness		1	3,500	Primary	500 above	Sand/rock. Water quality not monitored in 1991.
	★★★	Powfoot	~~~~~P					
	f ★	Annan Waterfoot	~~~~~F					Unsuitable for bathing, due to deep channel and nearby Annan sewage outfall. There will be no more monitoring in 1992.

1 Pease Sands, Cockburns Path, Berwickshire   OS Ref: NT7971

The deep wooded valley of Pease Burn opens out on to the sandy cove of Pease Bay, which gained a Heinz Good Beach Guide four-star grading in 1991. Framed by red cliffs, a shrub- and grass-covered bank fringes the landward side of the sands beyond which is a large caravan and mobile home park. ¾ mile (1.2km) of good sandy beach is very much dominated by the caravan site that rings the bay.

Water quality Beach monitored by the local River Purification Board and found to meet the EC Mandatory coliform standards for bathing water; ★★★ in this year's listed section. One outfall serving 1,000 people discharges secondary treated sewage.

Bathing safety Safe bathing.

Access A steep road from the A1107, just south of its junction with A1.

Parking Car park with 100 spaces directly off beach.

Toilets At car park.

Food Small shop adjacent to beach.

Seaside activities Swimming and fishing.

Wildlife and walks Good walks are available in Pease Dean. A cliff path can be followed north of the beach passing the tiny village and harbour of Cove and leading to the Dunglass Gorge.

2 Thorntonloch, Lothian   OS Ref: NT752744

Shallow dunes back on to this beautiful sandy beach which is about ¼ mile (400m) long. To the south there are beautiful views of the Berwickshire cliffs, while to the north is the Torness nuclear power station. There is a caravan site near the beach. The water at this beach gained a Heinz Good Beach Guide four-star grading in 1991.

Water quality Not a designated EC bathing water, but the water quality was monitored by the River Purification Board and found to meet the EC Mandatory coliform standards for bathing water; ★★★ in this year's listed section.

Bathing safety There is a fairly strong undertow and swimmers should use extreme caution.

Access The beach is a short walk from the car park.

Parking Car park for approximately 40 cars.

Toilets At the caravan site.

Food There is a small shop at the caravan site.

Seaside activities Swimming, fishing, windsurfing.

Wildlife and walks This is a good birdwatching area.

3 Gullane, East Lothian   OS Ref: NT4882

This is an absolutely beautiful and completely unspoilt 1½ mile (2.5km) sweeping sandy bay. The extensive flat sands exposed at low tide are backed by Gullane Bents, a series of 15 foot (5m) high dune ridges behind which scrubland slopes up 68 feet (20m) to flat grassland. Here there is parking and a picnic area, overlooked by the houses of Gullane village. The curve of sand is bounded at either end by rocky outcrops of black pillow lava. To the east there is a series of tiny sandy bays only accessible by foot along the coast path. Muirfield golf course overlooks this lovely bay and the view across the beach is frequently seen as a backdrop to televised tournaments.

Water quality Beach monitored by the River Purification Board and found to meet the EC Mandatory coliform standards for clean bathing water; ★★★ in this year's listed section. No sewage is discharged in the vicinity of the beach.

Litter All litter is cleared daily in summer.

Bathing safety Bathing is safe from this beach.

Access The beach is signposted from Gullane village on the A198, there is a 110 yard (100m) walk down through the dunes to the beach.

Parking Car park with 500 places on grassland behind Gullane Bents.

Toilets Block at centre of beach signposted 110 yards (100m) from the beach.

Food Refreshment stand. Also in Gullane village.

Seaside activities Swimming and windsurfing. Riding track around the bay and three golf courses. Children's play area off path through the dunes.

Wet weather alternatives Golf museum adjacent to the shop owned by golf professional J. Hume (open by arrangement) and Myreton motor museum near Aberlady.

Wildlife and walks The beach has a large lug worm population as evidenced by the casts left on the sand. Rock outcrops at each end of the beach contain pools rich in marine life including mussels, crabs, anemones and numerous snails. The rocks at the west end of the beach are covered in barnacles but very little seaweed. Inland the dunes are stabilised by marram grass and the dune slacks (areas between the sand ridges) have a rich and diverse vegetation.

4 Tentsmuir Point, Tayport, Fife   OS Ref: NO5024

A large area of the extensive sand dunes north of the Eden Estuary dunes has been stabilised by the conifers planted in the 1920s by the Forestry Commission. The coastline can still be reached along roads cut through the forest giving access to parking and picnic areas beyond the forest. A wild and remote spot with a wide flat sandy beach backed by high sand dunes which are continually moving seawards.

Water quality No sewage is discharged in the vicinity of this beach. The water was monitored by the local River Purification Board and found to meet the EC Mandatory coliform standards for bathing water; ★★★ in this year's listed section.

Bathing safety Beware of offshore currents.

Access From Leuchars, take the unclassified public road and head north east until signposted. Alternatively, from Tayport, take the B945 until signposted Kinshaldy Beach.

Parking Forestry Commission car park behind dunes.

Toilets At the car park.

Food   None.

Seaside activities   Swimming.

Wildlife and walks   A large area of the shore, including dunes and developing scrub woodland, is a National Nature Reserve. Earlshall Muir and Eden Estuary are both SSSI's. The area is a feeding ground for numerous waders and wildfowl. This is an excellent spot for walking with views across the offshore sand and north across to the Tayside coast. The adjacent forest provides walks of varying duration and distance, cycle tracks, picnic and barbecue facilities. The site has much archaeological interest and is of high conservation value containing ponds, lochs and bird hides.

5 Montrose Links, Montrose, Tayside   OS Ref: NO7358

From the mouth of the South Esk 4 miles (6.5km) of magnificent beach stretch north to the mouth of the North Esk. At low tide there are 220 yards (200m) of firm clean sands backed by a 30 foot (9m) high dune ridge. Access is from the southern end of the beach where the delightful little town of Montrose is separated from the beach by two links golf courses. At the entrance a stretch of seawall edges the beach, protecting the car park and facilities above. A beach with so much space there should never be an overcrowding problem and the further north you walk along it, the quieter it should be.

Water quality   Beach monitored by the River Purification Board and found to meet the EC Mandatory coliform standard for bathing water; ★★ in this year's listed section. An outfall serving 8,000 people discharges macerated sewage below low water mark, another serving 6,000 people discharges untreated sewage below low water mark. Despite this the water has passed the EC Mandatory coliform standards for the last six years.

Litter   The beach is cleaned regularly by the local authority.

Bathing safety   Safe bathing except near the river mouths at each end of the beach. Beach wardens patrol a clearly designated area of the beach.

Access   The beach is signposted from the A92. A road through the golf course leads to car parks at the south end of the beach. Steps lead down on to the sands.

Parking   Two car parks adjacent to the beach with approximately 350 spaces.

Toilets   At the car park.

Food   Café at the car park.

Seaside activities   Swimming, windsurfing and fishing. Children's amusement play area. Small amusement arcade.

Wet weather alternatives   Museum, amusement arcade and indoor swimming pool.

Wildlife and walks   The tidal basin to the west is a nature reserve. Low tide reveals extensive mud flats which are an important feeding ground for wintering birds.

6 Stonehaven, Grampian   OS Ref: NO8786

At a break in the rugged sandstone cliffs the waters of Cowie and Carron flow to the sea at Stonehaven. Nestling between the Downie and Garron headlands is Stonehaven itself, which retains the atmosphere of a traditional fishing village, its quaysides busy with boats. The fishing has declined but the twin basin harbour is used by pleasure craft in summer. A ⅔ mile (1km) sand and pebble beach curves away north of the harbour below the rolling farmland which rises beyond the town. The beach is not popular for swimming but is often busy with people taking advantage of the promenade facilities. Steep 200 foot (60m) cliffs rise on either side of the bay and offer excellent walking with splendid views along the cliffs and over Stonehaven bay.

Water quality Beach monitored by the River Purification Board and found to meet the EC Mandatory coliform standards for bathing water; ★★★ in this year's listed section. Two outfalls serving 9,000 people discharge macerated and primary treated sewage 10 yards (9m) below and 1 yard (1m) above low water mark.

Bathing safety Some currents can make swimming dangerous. Inshore rescue boat and lifeboat station.

Access From promenade.

Parking Ample on sea-front and adjacent to the leisure centre.

Toilets On sea-front.

Food Café.

Seaside activities Swimming and windsurfing. Sailing, diving and fishing trips from the adjacent harbour. Cliff top golf course. Open air heated swimming pool and leisure centre.

Wet weather alternatives Dunnottar castle, Tolbooth museum of local history, indoor pool and leisure centre, amusement arcades.

Wildlife and walks The promenade leads north to the fishing village of Cowie. North from Cowie a grass cliff path beside the golf course provides glorious sea views across Stonehaven Bay. 2 miles (3km) along the cliff top path there is a steep valley which leads down to two secluded pebbly coves at Skatie Shore. South from Stonehaven, a mile (1.6km) walk along the cliffs leads to the War Memorial from which there are panoramic views of the coast and inland. Continuing south for 2 miles (3km), the path leads to Dunnottar Castle. This impressive castle stands on an isolated sandstone cliff 170 feet (50m) above the sea. The connection between the castle rock and mainland was cut to allow easier defence. A further 4 miles (6.5km) south lies the Fowlsheugh Bird Reserve, one of the largest bird colonies in the UK, with 2 miles (3km) of cliff providing a home to thousands of seabirds. Parking at Crawton village provides easy access to the reserve.

7 Muchalls, Nr Stonehaven, Grampian   OS Ref: NO9292

This is a spectacular stretch of coastline whose rock formations include stacks, arches, and caves with an underground waterfall. There are several rock and pebble coves below the steep cliffs but take care as some are cut off at high tide with no escape routes. Swimming is out of the question due to dangerous rocks off shore but the cliff top scenery and the interesting coves with their numerous rockpools make the area worth a visit.

Water quality No outfalls discharge in the vicinity of the beach. The RPB does not monitor this beach. Crude sewage discharges into a small

stream entering the nearby beach but this is due for improvement in 1992.
Bathing safety There are unsafe rocks off shore.
Access From Muchalls village, just off the A92, there are two access
routes – a very steep path and a road under the railway lead to the shore.
Parking In village.
Toilets None.
Food Pub and hotel in village.
Seaside activities Fishing.
Wet weather alternatives Muchalls Castle (check opening times as
only open on occasional days in summer).
Wildlife and walks A cliff top path gives fine views of the cliff forma-
tions to the north and the numerous nesting seabirds that frequent the
rocky ledges. Rock pools on the shore contain a wealth of interest for the
beach walker but remember to keep an eye on the tide.

8 Strathbeg Bay, Grampian   OS Ref: NK0663

This little-frequented beach has 3½ miles (6km) of sand and substantial
dunes stretching from the rocky Cairnbulg Point south, past the fishing villages of Inverallochy and St Combs to Rattray Head. The beach is not particularly scenic but if you seek solitude on a remote and peaceful beach the
wind-swept sands of Rattray should meet your requirements. The lighthouse off the headland indicates the presence of a reef which causes swift
currents and makes swimming dangerous. South of Rattray Head a further
7 miles (11km) of deserted sandy beach stretches to Peterhead, but the
shore is dominated by the St Fergus gas terminal.
Water quality No sewage is discharged in the vicinity of this beach.
The RPB does not monitor this beach.
Litter Marine litter is a frequent problem along these shores.
Bathing safety Care is required as the currents off Rattray Head are
dangerous.
Access There is a path through the dunes at St Combs, off the B9033
south-east of Fraserburgh, and another at Rattray Head, reached via a
road off the A952 south of Crimond.
Parking There is a car park at St Combs and very limited parking at
Rattray Head.
Toilets None.
Food None.
Seaside activities Swimming (beware currents), sailing, diving and
fishing.
Wildlife and walks The Loch of Strathbeg RSPB reserve, with its visi-
tor centre and observation hides, lies just behind the dunes. It is the largest
dune slack pool in Britain and is an important site for wintering wildfowl.
Admission is by permit only, available from the warden, Jim Dunbar (Lon-
may 2522).

9 Sandend, Grampian   OS Ref: NJ5566

From Fraserburgh to Inverness is a stretch of coast known as the Banff-
shire Riviera. It is characterised by towering cliffs, small sheltered sandy

bays and fishing villages. Clear waters wash this most attractive sandy beach. ⅔ mile (1km) of dunes fringe the beach landwards and the bay is framed by high cliffs.

Water quality There is one outfall serving 280 people, discharging primary treated sewage. The water was monitored and found to meet EC Mandatory coliform standards ; ★★★ in this year's listed section.

Bathing safety Heavy surf on occasions.

Access Sandend is signposted off the A98; it is a short walk from the car park to the beach. Telephone nearby.

Parking Car park with 100 spaces including disabled parking.

Toilets Public conveniences in village.

Food Small shop and restaurant.

Seaside activities Swimming, surfing, windsurfing, sailing, diving and fishing.

Wildlife and walks East of the bay the coast path climbs over the cliffs on to the headland which offers excellent sea and coastal views. The path continues to Portsoy, a charming fishing village with a small harbour which has won awards for its architectural restoration. West of Sandend the cliff path can be followed to the ruins of Findlater Castle with its impressive position 165 feet (50m) above the waves. However, the ruins are not safe to enter. Below the ruins is the lovely secluded Sunnyside beach, its sweep of golden sand nestling below the steep cliffs.

10 Cullen Sands, Cullen, Grampian   OS Ref: NJ5167

The dipping Cullen quartzites form a spectacular rocky coastline and create the extremely scenic Cullen Bay. From the curving quays of the harbour, sheltering below the cliffs at the eastern end of the bay, an arc of rock-studded sand sweeps west past the isolated stacks known as the Three Kings. Beyond, the Boar's Craig rises and the sands give way to rocks below the cliffs of Portknockie headland. Here there are caves, known as the Preacher's and the Whale's Mouth, to explore and numerous rockpools to investigate. Relax on the sands (but watch the tide), or stretch your legs to enjoy the wonderful scenery around the bay. The railway once passed through Cullen but all that remains is a series of graceful viaducts. They separate the narrow streets of Seatown that cluster around the harbour from the upper town with its open square and wider streets.

Water quality Beach monitored by the River Purification Board and found to meet the EC Mandatory standards for bathing water; ★★★ in this year's listed section. Two outfalls serving 1,500 people discharge raw sewage at low water mark.

Bathing safety There are strong cross tides so care is required.

Access From Seatown and from the road to the golf course.

Parking Car park close to harbour. Large car park beside beach next to golf course.

Toilets Public toilets at the harbour are open all year.

Food Tea room at beach in summer. Two hotels in Seatown. Cafés and hotels in upper town.

Seaside activities Swimming, putting, bowls and a golf course. Sea-angling and boat trips from the harbour.

Wet weather alternatives Maritime Museum and swimming pool at Buckie, about 5 miles (9km) away.

Wildlife and walks From the harbour a path leads east along the shore to the excellent sandy cove of Sunnyside Bay. The path climbs to the cliff top and continues to Findlater Castle, a 15th-century ruined castle sitting on a rocky promontory 165 feet (50m) above the sea, but beware: the ruin is not safe to enter. A return journey can be made along the cliff top, giving excellent views along the coast and across to Sutherland and Caithness. Alternatively you may head east to Sandend Bay, another of the lovely coves along this coastline complete with its own small harbour. West from Cullen there is a well-marked path alongside the golf course. The path leads up from the rocky shore to Portknockie on the cliff top. There are superb views of this magnificent rocky coast; just off shore lies the Bow Fiddle rock, where erosion of the dipping rock strata has produced an arch resembling the tip of a violinist's bow. Further west from Portknockie the cliff path leads to Findochty with its sheltered sandy cove and harbour; there are superb views of the Moray Firth, which is home to between 150 and 200 bottle-nosed dolphins, and Black Isle.

11 Burghead Bay, Burghead, Grampian   OS Ref: NJ1169

The solid fishing cottages that make up Burghead stand on a low rocky promontory overlooking the 6 mile (10km) curve of Burghead Bay. At the western end of these long flat sands is Findhorn, situated at the mouth of the large, tidal Findhorn Bay. The quiet but somewhat windswept beach of fine sand and pebbles is rimmed by dunes, on which there is a Forestry Commission conifer plantation. A road has been made through the mature pines at Roseisle and there are parking and picnic facilities. The beach can be reached along paths through the trees. Wartime concrete defences once stood on grassland well back from the beach but the retreating sand means that they now stand on the tidal sands.

Water quality Sewage is discharged from a long sea outfall east of the harbour. The RPB does not monitor this beach.

Litter Reports of large amounts of litter on the beach have been received in 1991.

Bathing safety There are strong currents at the western end where the River Findhorn flows out of Findhorn Bay. Bathing is not recommended in Findhorn Bay but is safe from the beach at Findhorn, Roseisle and Burghead.

Access At either end of the bay at Findhorn or Burghead and also by paths from Roseisle Forest.

Parking At Findhorn dunes and picnic site, Roseisle Forest picnic site and at Burghead.

Toilets At Findhorn and Roseisle picnic sites (including facilities for the disabled). Public toilets at the harbour in Burghead.

Food Pubs, hotels and fish and chips available in Findhorn and Burghead. Wholefood café at Findhorn Bay Caravan Park.

Seaside activities Swimming (but not in the bay), diving, fishing, windsurfing and water-skiing. Findhorn Bay is a sailing centre with racing throughout the summer. Rowing, sailing and motor boats are available for hire at Findhorn. Sea-angling trips from Burghead harbour.

Wet weather alternatives Burghead Well. Findhorn Foundation (a spiritual community based east of Findhorn village which runs a craft shop and takes conducted tours during the summer). Swimming pool and museum at Forres.

Wildlife and walks There is a walk from Burghead to Findhorn along the shore, where rock and sand pools contain a variety of marine life. 2 miles (3km) south-west of Burghead is the Forestry Commission Roseisle Forest. Pathways from the beach lead to glades in the Corsican and Scots pines planted in the 1930s. Continuing along the shore the walk leads on to the Findhorn peninsula where the extensive tidal Findhorn Bay provides excellent birdwatching.

12 Dornoch, Highland   OS Ref: NH7989

The excellent Royal Dornoch links golf course attracts many visiting players but the lovely sandy beach remains quiet and uncommercialised. The approach to the beach from Dornoch is unassuming; the low-lying lands do not permit any view of the beach until you cross the dunes. To the south of the beach is the entrance to the Dornoch Firth which stretches almost 20 miles (32km) inland. The wide sands stretch 3 miles (5km) north narrowing towards Loch Fleet, a small sea-loch. There is access to the beach from the village of Dornoch, and at the northern end at Embo. Further north in Sutherland the main A9 hugs the shore which is only a ribbon of sand.

Water quality Sewage is treated by septic tank and discharged at Blackburn away from the beach. The RPB does not monitor this beach.

Bathing safety There are currents at the northern and southern ends of the beach; safe bathing in the main bay at Dornoch.

Access From the square in Dornoch a road leads to the shore and golf courses, another takes you to Embo; there is a short walk across dunes to the sand.

Parking Dornoch: two car parks, one overlooking the sea with spaces for 20 cars, the other close by has a further 20 spaces. Embo: car park with 25 spaces.

Toilets New toilet block at caravan site backing beach.

Food None (At Embo: Grannie's Heilan Hame Café and fish and chip shop – seasonal).

Seaside activities Swimming (in the main bay). Royal Dornoch Golf Course, local pipe band parade during the summer and Highland Games during August.

Wet weather alternatives Dornoch Cathedral. Local social club is open for supervised games during the season.

Wildlife and walks Loch Fleet, a sea-loch at the northern end of the beach, is the last of the Firth indents into this coastline heading north. The loch and the alderwoods behind the mound embankment are nature reserves which contain a wide variety of wildlife. The Scottish Wildlife Trust Reserve Warden runs a series of guided walks during the summer. These include an exploration of the woodland and estuary or the sand dunes and sea shore. Otherwise, access to the reserves is restricted. In the nearby Skelbo Wood, the Forestry Commission has laid out several forest trails; the walks start from the Commission's car park off the B1698.

13 Duncansby Head, John o'Groats, Highland   OS Ref: ND4173

Travellers taking the A9 north beyond Inverness are normally heading for John o'Groats as the most northerly point of Scotland. Not to be missed is Duncansby Head, without a doubt one of the finest pieces of coastline in Britain. The road from John o'Groats takes you to the Duncansby lighthouse. From the small car park the view to the islands is hard to beat. On a clear day the panorama laid out before you can be breathtaking. Just off shore beyond the white foaming tidal races are the Pentland Skerries and Stroma, on which you can see many abandoned dwellings. Beyond, Swona, South Ronaldsay, Hoy and the mainland of Orkney complete the picture. Tucked below the headland, just off the lighthouse approach road, is a tiny beach. A mere 110 yards (100m) in length, the narrow strip of sand is shadowed by the red sandstone of the headland. A delightful spot, this may not be the beach to seek out for a day by the sea, but after enjoying a stroll on the headland, relax awhile and watch the seals that bob around off shore. This is one of many little beaches along the north coast between the Duncansby and Dunnet Headlands, although most are difficult to get to and are not as attractive, lacking the backdrop of sheer red cliffs.

Water quality No sewage is discharged in the vicinity of this beach. The RPB does not monitor this beach.

Bathing safety The sandy beach shelves steeply and swimming is dangerous.

Access Duncansby Head is signposted from the A9 south of John o'Groats. A short walk from the parking area down the hill across turf leads on to the sands.

Parking Car park at Duncansby lighthouse with approximately 25 spaces.

Toilets None.

Food None.

Wildlife and walks A short walk over the headland passes a narrow inlet or geo whose cliff walls rise nearly 200 feet (60m) above the waves. A short distance further and you are rewarded with the marvellous view of Duncansby Stacks, their steeple-like outlines pointing skywards. These are also known as Muckle Stack. Boat trips around this stretch of coast are available from John o'Groats.

14 Sandside Bay, Reay, Highland   OS Ref: NC9774

This area has some of the best exposed rocky coastline in Britain. Low cliffs, rocky outcrops and dunes bound this long flat sandy beach. At the western end of the bay is the tiny harbour of Fresgoe: a tranquil old-world air prevails around the little-used harbour. A sharp contrast to the view along the coast east to the Dounreay Fast Reactor. A remote and quiet beach.

Water quality No sewage is discharged in the vicinity of the beach. The RPB does not monitor this beach.

Bathing safety Safe bathing.

Access The road to Fresgoe runs alongside the bay, and it is a short walk from the road down a track between dunes to the beach.

Parking Parking in area along the side road.

Toilets Toilet block on road close to the car parking area.

Food None. The closest shop is in Reay village 2 miles (3.5km) away.

Seaside activities Swimming.

Wet weather alternatives Dounreay Exhibition Centre.

Wildlife and walks There is a short cliff walk from the beach.

15 Coldbackie, Tongue, Highland   OS Ref: NC6160

The half-moon of Coldbackie Sands faces Tongue Bay at the mouth of the Kyle of Tongue, one of the three deep indents into the north coast. The undulating turf-covered moorland which dominates this corner of Scotland slopes down to the grass-covered dunes which border the sands. Below Meall Mor, low grass-covered cliffs flank the beach.

Water quality No sewage is discharged in the vicinity of this beach. The RPB does not monitor this beach.

Bathing safety Safe bathing.

Access From the A836 north of Tongue, banks of grass-covered dunes descend to the beach. There is no proper footpath but it is an easy walk down to the sand.

Parking There is limited car parking in a layby off the main road above the beach.

Toilets None.

Food None.

Seaside activities Swimming.

Wildlife and walks The 1000 feet (300m) high peaks of Cnoc an Fhreiceadan and Ben Tongue rise behind the beach. From the road a footpath inland skirts the sides of the hills, passing a tiny loch to reach Tongue and the shores of the Kyle.

16 Balnakiel Bay, Durness, Highland   OS Ref: NC3869

There are in fact three beaches at Durness, all worthy of note. All have clean white sands, are unspoilt and are quiet, even at the height of the summer. To the east of Faraid Head peninsula, below the steep limestone cliffs on which Durness stands, are the twin beaches of Sango Bay and Sangobeg. The best beach, however, is Balnakiel Bay, a long curve of white sand and dunes on the western side of the peninsula. There is easy access at the southern end of the beach close to the ruined Balnakiel Church. The extensive wind-sculptured dunes stretch north along the low rugged headland. The bare and treeless landscape is dominated by wild windswept moorland in sharp contrast to the coastline made up of warm red sandstone cliffs, folded and faulted limestone, collapsed caverns, geos, rocky shores and sandy bays.

Water quality One outfall discharges primary treated sewage from 200 people at low water mark. The RPB does not monitor this beach.

Bathing safety Safe bathing although in this part of the country some might find it rather cold.

Access A road off the A838 from Durness village leads to a car park behind the beach, and from here an easy path leads to the sand.

Parking Car park with 30 spaces.
Toilets Portaloo at car park.
Food Sango Sands Oasis Restaurant in Sango.
Seaside activities Swimming.
Wet weather alternatives ½ mile (800m) inland is a craft village in the building of a disused early warning station. The workshops are open to the public during the summer months.
Wildlife and walks There are walks on the cliffs surrounding the bay, and much evidence of 1000 years of human activity, including slight remains of an ancient fortress on the Faraid Headland. Steps lead down from Durness village to the beach at Sango Bay where the high arched entrance to the Smoo Cave can be found. The Allt (river) Smoo flows from the cave. The first of three chambers can be entered. The Highland Regional Ranger Service organises guided walks in the area, and further information can be obtained from the information centre in Durness. The remote north-western tip of Scotland, Cape Wrath, can be reached by a small ferry across the Kyle of Durness followed by a mini-bus service to the Cape. The bus takes you across the wild moorland to the Cape Wrath Lighthouse and there is fantastic cliff scenery along this most isolated stretch of coastline. The most spectacular cliffs are along the northern coast, where, in places, the sheer cliffs fall 800 feet (250m) to the waters below.

17 Sandwood Bay, Highland   OS Ref: NC2364

Sandwood Bay must be one of the most remote beaches in Britain, but equally one of the most magnificent. Lying on the west coast of Scotland between Kinlochbervie and Cape Wrath, a 4 mile (7km) walk from Blairmore brings you to this outstanding beach with its huge sand dunes and gently sloping pink sands, studded with rock outcrops. Towering sandstone cliffs extend away on either side of the bay, and to the west is a most impressive rock stack. For those who do not want to venture to such an isolated and exposed beach, there are a series of pocket-handkerchief-sized sandy beaches that surround Blairmore, the starting point for the walk to Sandwood.
Water quality No sewage is discharged in the vicinity of this beach. The RPB does not monitor this beach.
Bathing safety Very dangerous.
Access The B801 leads along Loch Inchard to Kinlochbervie, and beyond this a steep and twisting road continues to Sheigra. Sandwood can only be reached on foot, 4 miles (7km) along the track which turns off the road between Blairmore and Sheigra.
Parking Limited parking at Blairmore.
Toilets None.
Food None.
Wildlife and walks The walk to Sandwood crosses the peat moorland of Sutherland before making a steep descent to the bay. This area is both wild and beautiful, but anyone thinking of walking here should be fully aware of the dangers of this remote and difficult terrain. Only those completely prepared should undertake the trip.

18 Scourie, Highland   OS Ref: NC1544

Unlike most of the crofting villages along the west coast, Scourie has some facilities to cater for the visitor. It boasts two hotels, a shop, a post office and a camp site, thus enabling the tourist to stop a while and enjoy this most picturesque district. Scourie is set at the head of a 1 mile (1.6km) rocky inlet, on the banks of a small river draining from a loch a short distance inland. There is a lovely sheltered beach on the southern flank of the bay. The wide, gently sloping sands are backed by a narrow storm beach, where small boulders and pebbles edge the sand. The irregular hummocks of this grey-green rocky landscape come down to the water's edge in the outer bay. This exposed rocky coast is coloured by bands of lichens and encrusted with barnacles and seaweed below high water mark where there are many rockpools to explore. This is a deservedly popular spot.

Water quality Two outfalls, each serving 100-200 people, discharge primary treated sewage at low water mark. The RPB does not monitor this beach.

Bathing safety Safe bathing.

Access There are gently sloping grass slopes down to the sand.

Parking Parking space available adjacent to the beach.

Toilets In village.

Food Hotel and shop in village.

Seaside activities Swimming.

Wildlife and walks A stroll around the loch, village and its quayside can be a most pleasant way to spend an afternoon. Alternatively follow the path north of the bay to Tarbet. Handa Island, lying just across the Sound of Handa, is an RSPB reserve. The numerous ledges on its vertical cliffs provide nesting sites for thousands of seabirds including guillemots, kittiwakes and fulmars. The island can be visited by boat from Tarbet daily, except Sunday, from April to August.

19 Clashnessie Bay, Lochinver, Highland   OS Ref: NC0631

Steep rocky cliffs, wide bays dotted with tiny islands, clean clear waters, beautiful sunsets, seabirds and seals: the perfect ingredients to make a good beach. Clashnessie is an attractive and safe beach. The 660 yards (600m) of gently sloping pink sands are framed by red sandstone cliffs. There are superb views north towards Oldany Island and east along the rugged cliffs of the Stoer Peninsula.

Water quality No sewage is discharged in the vicinity of the beach. The RPB does not monitor this beach.

Bathing safety Safe bathing.

Access A side road from the B869 at Clashnessie leads down to the shore, and then there is a short walk down to the beach.

Parking Car park at beach with 10–15 spaces.

Toilets None.

Food None.

Seaside activities Swimming.

Wildlife and walks To the east there is a clifftop walk on to the Stoer Point with views of the fine cliff scenery including the Old Man of Stoer, an isolated sea stack rising 200 feet (60m) above the waves. Further along the coast stands the Stoer lighthouse. A good variety of birds can be seen on the beach and cliffs. There are also a number of walks on the wide flat moors inland.

20 Clachtoll, Lochinver, Highland   OS Ref: NC0427

This is one of a series of sandy coves along this stretch of coastline, north of Loch Inver, which is scenically stunning. Clachtoll is a small cove, 275 yards (250m) of beautiful white shell sand backed by machair banks and grey and red cliffs. The quiet beach is washed by clear waters and seals can often be seen close to the shore. There is a camp site situated behind the beach.

Water quality No sewage is discharged in the vicinity of this beach. The RPB does not monitor this beach.

Bathing safety Safe bathing within the bay.

Access There is car parking off the B869 which runs along this stretch of coast. It is a short walk across the dunes to the beach.

Parking Car park with 20 spaces.

Toilets Toilets and showers at beach car park.

Food Take-away meals and snacks at the camp site.

Seaside activities Swimming, windsurfing, diving, sailing, canoeing and fishing. Boats can be hired for fishing. Details are available from the local Ranger.

Wet weather alternatives Teas and games at Stoer village hall.

Wildlife and walks There is a diverse range of plant and animal life around the bay, and an interesting variety of birds and mammals, including seals and whales, can be seen. Many rare plants can also be found. There is a wealth of material available for those interested in conservation and the history of the area. Full details are available from the interpretative centre at the beach, and coastal walks can be arranged by the local Ranger.

21 Achmelvich, Lochinver, Highland   OS Ref: NC0625

This is a small sandy cove at the southern end of Achmelvich Bay which can be reached fairly easily. The white sands of the bay are backed by an area of machair grassland. This sand dune type vegetation is very fragile and easily eroded, so great care must be taken not to cause damage in this area. Steep, grey, rocky cliffs rise on either side of the sands, creating a marvellous setting for the bay. Dogs are permitted on the beach under strict control but they are not allowed on the surrounding land.

Water quality No sewage is discharged in the vicinity of this beach. The RPB does not monitor this beach.

Litter Litter on the beach is collected by local volunteers.

Bathing safety Safe bathing.

Access A side road off the B869 north of Lochinver leads to Achmelvich. The car park gives direct access to the turf sloping to the sand.

Parking Car park with 60 spaces.

Toilets Public toilets in car park.

Food None.

Seaside activities Swimming, surfing, windsurfing, diving, sailing and fishing.

Wildlife and walks There is a 1 mile (1.6km) nature trail along the coast to the small sandy bay of Alltan na Bradhan. The walk leads from the machair grassland over the sand hills and then passes through heath and bog vegetation. A leaflet describing the whole trail is available from the Countryside Ranger Centre at the rear of the car park at Achmelvich. This area also has interesting geology. There is a combination of red sandstone and grey Lewisian gneiss (pronounced 'nice') with igneous dyke intrusions – dark rock squeezed in bands up through the surrounding rock.

22 Achnahaird, Enard Bay, Highland   OS Ref: NC0214

Flat windswept moorland with outcrops of grey gneiss leads down to the shore of Enard Bay, a magnificent island-dotted prospect. On the western side of the Rubha Mor headland is the narrow inlet of Achnahaird Bay. The bay, in the southern corner of Enard Bay, stretches nearly a mile (1.6km) inland and low tide reveals an expanse of flat white sand. On the western side of the inlet there are extensive dunes which give way to salt marsh at the head of the bay. Irregularly layered sandstone cliffs flank the eastern side of the inlet and a stream meanders across the centre of the sands.

Water quality No sewage is discharged in the vicinity of this beach. The RPB does not monitor this beach.

Bathing safety Bathe with caution as there may be some currents that could cause problems for the swimmer.

Access A side road from Achnahaird village leads to parking behind the beach. There is access to the sands on a path down the rocks (can be difficult) or through the camp site behind the dunes. Visitor pressure is causing damage to the dunes.

Parking There is limited parking behind the dunes.

Toilets None.

Food None.

Seaside activities Swimming.

Wildlife and walks The shores of Enard Bay are part of the Inverpolly National Nature Reserve, a large area of moorland, including the huge bulk of Suilven. There is a visitors' centre at Knockan some way inland, where there is an interpretative centre, a nature trail and a geology trail. This helps to introduce the visitor to an area that abounds in wildlife including red deer and otters. 100 bird species and 300 types of plant have been recorded within the reserve. Achnahaird Bay combines a wide variety of vegetation types: dunes, salt marsh, rocky and sandy shore. The salt marsh attracts waders and wildfowl. The rocky shore is banded with lichen and there are rock pools among the barnacle-encrusted rocks.

23 Achiltibuie, Badentarbat Bay, Highland   OS Ref: NC0309

Smooth heather-clad slopes descend to the crofting village of Achiltibuie which straggles 3 miles (5km) along the shore of Badentarbat Bay. The beach, which curves round the bay, lacks the sand so common on the west coast but to compensate there is a marvellous view across to the Summer Isles. A patchwork of islands and rocky skerries lies just off shore and provides the most wonderful seascape. From the pier the shingle and cobble beach stretches south to the rocky headland of Rubha Dunan.

Water quality No sewage is discharged in the vicinity of this beach. The RPB does not monitor this beach.

Bathing safety Bathe with caution as there may be some currents that could cause problems for the swimmer.

Access The road through the village continues along the edge of the bay and the sand can be reached across the grass which slopes below the road.

Parking Cars park on the grass between the road and the beach.

Toilets None.

Food Shops in village.

Seaside activities Swimming and fishing.

Wildlife and walks The Summer Isles fall within the Ben More Coigach Nature Reserve (Scottish Wildlife Trust – Royal Society for Nature Conservation). 15,011 acres (6,075 hectares) include the peak which gives the reserve its name, and whose purple and red slopes dominate the views inland from Achiltibuie. There is good walking along the Coigach Peninsula west of the bay. The Summer Isles can be viewed at closer range by taking a boat trip from the pier at Achiltibuie.

24 Gruinard Bay, Laide, Highland   OS Ref: NG9092

There are several excellent beaches dotted around Gruinard Bay, all of which overlook the lovely Gruinard Island, centrepiece of the bay. The island was used for anthrax experiments during the last war and has been out of bounds ever since. It is now being cleaned up, so hopefully the warning signs that have prohibited landing for so long will soon disappear. The A832 skirts the southern and eastern shores of the bay, giving easy access to the three lovely cove beaches on the eastern shore. Their pink sands are set among sandstone rock outcrops. In contrast, the south-eastern shore at Little Gruinard has the bulging hummocks of Lewisian gneiss as a most attractive backdrop. Gruinard Hill provides the best views of the bay, the island, and of the Summer Isles on the horizon. Wooded slopes above the beach provide a sharp contrast to the grey rocky outcrops. At Laide, the road runs parallel with the beach behind the machair turf, which slopes to the sand of this 1 mile (1.6km) beach. This most picturesque of bays, like most of the west coast beaches, is relatively quiet and unspoilt. A holiday spent walking the coast or exploring the lochans that speckle the surrounding countryside is an ideal way to escape and relax. Facilities for the tourist are limited and there is restricted parking. In many parts of the bay parking along the back-shore causes severe erosional problems for the machair grass. It is important that the grass cover is maintained and parking should be limited accordingly.

Water quality No sewage is discharged in the vicinity of this beach. The RPB does not monitor this beach.

Bathing safety Safe bathing.

Access The A832 follows the shore round most of the bay.

Parking There are two car parks in the south-eastern corner of the bay near Little Gruinard and another at Laide.
Toilets In Laide.
Food Hotel and shop in Laide.
Seaside activities Swimming and fishing.
Wildlife and walks There are trips around the bay available during the summer months which allow the visitor to take a closer look at Gruinard Island and enjoy the spectacular panoramas across the bay towards the mountains inland.

25 Gairloch, Highland   OS Ref: NG7679

Set among the stunning mountains of Wester Ross, Gairloch, although it is no more than a sizeable fishing village, is one of the few 'holiday resorts' on the west coast. It overlooks a fine sandy beach which curves north from the rocky promontory at Charlestown, round Strath Bay at the head of the loch, extending west of Gairloch to Big Sand. The bay enjoys the mild climate resulting from the North Atlantic Drift, and gardens nearby are filled with plants more commonly found in more southern locations. The A832 follows the shore at the head of the beautiful Loch Gairloch, where there are rocky outcrops of gneiss. The outer section of the bay is of red sandstone with safe, sandy beaches at Sheildaig and Badachro on the southern shores, and Big Sand on the northern shore. There is a large caravan site behind the extensive beach which is sheltered by Longa Island.
Water quality Three outfalls discharge primary treated sewage into the River Sand. There are complaints of sewage contamination at Redpoint beach. The RPB does not monitor this beach.
Bathing safety Safe bathing.
Litter Marine-borne domestic litter is a problem.
Access The A832 runs parallel with the shore between Charlestown and Gairloch. There are paths to the beach although erosion of the paths is extensive.
Parking Parking at Big Sand, in Gairloch and off the A832 to the south.
Toilets In Gairloch.
Food In Gairloch.
Seaside activities Swimming, windsurfing, sailing and fishing.
Wet weather alternatives Gairloch Heritage Museum.
Wildlife and walks From Badachro there is a footpath which leads south-west inland. It passes a small loch and leads to the cliffs of Red Point, where there are superb views across the Minch to the Hebrides. For those less able, there is road access and a car park at Red Point. A further mile to the south, there is a beautiful and remote sandy beach backed by dunes. The path continues to the south-east along the shores of Loch Torridon to Diabaig. This walk follows a spectacular length of coast which can only be reached on foot.

26 Applecross, Highland   OS Ref: NG7144

The dramatic and tortuous 'Pass of the Cattle' climbs over 2,000 feet (620m) as it twists its way from the A896, at the head of Loch Kishorn, across the wild mountains and moorlands to Applecross. There is a wooded approach to the cluster of white cottages which make up this remote village, on the southern shore of a wide bay. The sweeping sandy beach lies below limestone cliffs from which there are superb views across the Inner Sound to Raasay and Scalpay, with the Cuillins of Skye on the distant horizon. Having crossed desolate moorland, negotiated precipitous roads and revelled in vast panoramic views, one could be at the edge of the world. This lovely beach with its magnificent setting provides an ideal spot to rest and unwind.

Water quality No sewage is discharged in the vicinity of this beach. The RPB does not monitor this beach.

Bathing safety Safe bathing.

Access The Pass from Loch Kishorn should not be attempted by the caravanner or the faint-hearted; the alternative route which approaches the village along the coast from Loch Torridon is an easier drive. The village stands on the shore with easy access to the sands.

Parking Limited at Applecross.

Toilets None.

Food Shop in village.

Seaside activities Swimming and fishing. Picnic site behind the beach.

Wildlife and walks There are good walks along this beautiful stretch of coast with eider duck, mergansers and other seabirds to be seen in the bays.

27 The Coral Beaches, Dunvegan, Skye   OS Ref: NG2354

A pleasant, easy, ½ mile (800m) walk across grassland takes you to two small beaches which are beautiful and totally unspoilt. Known locally as the Coral Beaches, they are in fact white sand made up of broken shells. Grass banks slope gently down to the sand. The bays, each about 220 yards (200m) in length, are separated by a low grassy promontory around which there are rocky outcrops. There are lovely views across Loch Dunvegan whose clean, clear waters wash the beach.

Water quality There is no sewage discharged in the vicinity of this beach. The RPB does not monitor this beach.

Bathing safety Safe bathing.

Access The road north from Dunvegan becomes a narrow lane beyond Claigan. From the lane ending there is a well-defined path across the grassland to the sand.

Parking Limited parking along the lane.

Toilets None.

Food None.

Seaside activities Swimming and snorkelling.

Wildlife and walks There is excellent walking to the Coral Beaches and along the beautiful peninsula beyond. Numerous seals can be seen in the waters of the loch. They are often visible close inshore, and a short boat trip from Dunvegan takes you to the rocky islands where they can be seen basking on the shore.

28 Morar, Highland   OS Ref: NM6793

This stretch of coastline between Mallaig and Arisaig has to be one of the most memorable in Scotland. When you try to imagine the silver sands of the west coast you probably create a picture closely resembling this stretch of shore. The green crofting land, dotted with white cottages, slopes down to the white sands of the bays. South of Mallaig, with its busy harbour that links to the Islands, is the wide, sheltered Morar Bay. ⅔ mile (1km) of white sands fringes the wide Y-shaped bay which is set below undulating hills. The bay was originally the mouth of a sea-loch similar to many others that penetrate this coastline until the long finger of Loch Morar was cut off from the sea by an uplift of the land and glacial deposits. A fast-flowing river drains the freshwater lake over a weir, which is all that remains of once impressive falls which were sacrificed to a hydro-electric power scheme. The river meanders across the southern edge of the bay to the narrow sea opening.

Water quality There have been reports that some sewage from Morar village and the other villages along this coast ends up on the sands. The RPB does not monitor this beach.

Bathing safety Bathing is only safe close inshore due to strong under-currents 110 yards (100m) from the shore.

Access The main road runs parallel with the beach and it is a short walk from the road across the turf banks that lead down to the sand. The railway runs alongside the road and some trains will stop at Morar station.

Parking Along the road above the beach. Car park at toilets.

Toilets Toilets (including disabled) now available.

Food None.

Seaside activities Swimming and sailing.

Wildlife and walks At the southern end of the bay a turning off the main coast road leads along the shore of Loch Morar. Beyond the tiny hamlet of Bracora the road gives way to a path which can be followed through some spectacular scenery to Tarbet on Loch Nevis. Walking the shoreline around Morar there are stunning views east to the Inner Hebrides.

29 Camusdarrach Beach, Glenancross, Highland   OS Ref: NM6592

This beach was made famous in Bill Forsyth's film 'Local Hero' (although the actual village scenes were shot over on the east coast). The mile (1.6km) of gleaming white sands backed by dunes and undulating grassland is popular, but remains beautiful and unspoilt. There is easy access to the beach, by paths from the road above the beach. A series of delightful secluded bays can be reached by walking over the hills edging the shore, forming rocky outcrops. The area is popular with tourists and in summer many caravans appear. The approach to the beach is vulnerable to erosion and visitors should use the paths to avoid damaging the dunes. Those staying at this beach until the late evening will enjoy seeing the most breathtaking sunsets, as the sun sinks behind the rugged mountains of Skye.

Water quality No outfall in the vicinity of this beach. The RPB does not monitor this beach.

Bathing safety Safe bathing but beware of some offshore currents.

Access Camusdarrach is situated just south of Morar Bay. The road runs parallel with the shore between Morar and Arisaig. There are paths giving access at various points across the low turf-banks that descend to the beach.

Parking Cars can park on the turf behind the beach.

Toilets None.

Food None.

Seaside activities Swimming and windsurfing. Golf course.

Wildlife and walks All along the western coast there is much of interest for the naturalist. Underwater there is a rich and varied marine life which can only be glimpsed from the shore. The bobbing heads of seals are common, the outline of the basking shark a rarer occurrence. On the rocks that edge these beautiful beaches cormorants, shags, gannets and terns may be seen.

30 Traigh, Arisaig, Highland   OS Ref: NM6492

This U-shaped beach, some 2 miles (3km) west of Arisaig village is sheltered by the small dunes and elevated land behind it. The main road follows its perimeter and it is easily accessible. Immediately across the road is a small 9 hole course which is maintained by local voluntary effort and therefore the greens may not be up to the standard of a professionally maintained course, but it provides good practice and fun. The area is popular with tourists. Sunsets over the Western Isles viewed from Arisaig are often superb.

Water quality No sewage is discharged in the vicinity of the beach. The RPB does not monitor this beach.

Bathing safety Bathing is safe within the bay.

Access The trunk road A830 follows the perimeter of the site.

Parking Limited parking in a layby and on adjoining land.

Toilets Male and female toilets behind the beach with facilities for the disabled.

Food None

Seaside activities Swimming and sailing

31 Sanna Bay, Sanna, Highland   OS Ref: NM4368

On the northern side of Ardnamurchan Point, the most westerly point of mainland Britain, are the lovely white sands of Sanna Bay. This is a beautiful and unspoilt beach backed by impressive marram-covered dunes and ringed by craggy hills. There are a series of island skerries off Sanna Point at the northern end of the bay, as well as rocky outcrops along the beach, dividing the bay into three sections. The sands are washed by clean, clear seas. The south side of the bay is covered by extensive rocks encrusted with barnacles and many types of seaweeds. To the south is a second sandy cove which is shadowed by cliffs and the nearby Ardnamurchan Lighthouse.

Water quality No sewage is discharged in the vicinity of the beach. The RPB does not monitor this beach.

Bathing safety Offshore currents necessitate bathing with caution.

Access The B8007 from Kilchoran leads to the southern end of the bay, Portuairk, and from here it is a short walk across the dunes to the beach.

Parking Limited parking behind the dunes.

Toilets None.

Food None.

Seaside activities Swimming, sailing and fishing.

Wildlife and walks There is a string of small sandy bays along the north coast of Ardnamurchan, only accessible on foot. These deserted beaches offer much to interest the naturalist. Ardnamurchan Point itself is notorious in sailing circles for its unpredictable weather so do not be surprised if you see boats motoring past as quickly as possible!

32 Calgary Bay, Mull   OS Ref: NM3652

Calgary Bay has been described as Mull's most beautiful bay. It might best be considered as a small sea-loch with a sandy beach at its head. The gently sloping white sands are backed by small dunes and flat machair grassland. Rocky shores extend at right angles from both sides of the beach. There are areas of both flat rock and boulders amongst which there are numerous rockpools rich in animal and plant life. Steep cliffs and grassy slopes rising behind the rocky shore enclose the bay. This lovely beach is understandably popular with visitors in the summer. Emigrants from this area may well have founded the Canadian city which bears the same name.

Water quality No sewage is discharged in the vicinity of this beach. The RPB does not monitor this beach.

Bathing safety Safe bathing.

Access The B8073 from Tobermory leads south to Calgary. The road skirts the grassland behind the beach and continues along the southern shore.

Parking There is a car park at the northern end of the beach and a small parking area at the southern end.

Toilets At the southern end of the beach, on the road behind the dunes.

Food None.

Seaside activities Swimming and fishing.

Wildlife and walks From the car park at the northern end of the beach a track leads to an old pier. This continues for a short distance as a footpath above the rocky shore where a series of lava dykes can be seen as grey bands where the molten lava has been pushed up between the surrounding rocks.

33 Erraid, Fionnphort, Mull   OS Ref: NM3120

Mull has 300 miles (500km) of breathtaking coastline including sheer cliffs, stacks and arches. There are also tiny bays nestling below the cliffs with a backdrop of brooding mountains. The Ross of Mull, a long, low peninsula to the south of the island, has some of the best coastal features. There are cliffs of basalt columns, the Carsaig Arches at Malcolm's Point, numerous caves and secluded sandy bays which can only be approached on foot. The extensive sands at the western tip of the Ross are much more accessible. A road from Fionnphort, point of departure for the ferries to Iona, proceeds south along the Sound of Iona to extensive sandy beaches sheltered by Erraid Island. Between the island and the mainland, the Sound of Erraid is a sandy beach at low tide backed by sand dunes and machair grassland. At either end of the Sound there are rocky outcrops, and a host of islets and skerries lie just offshore. The grassland behind the beach is used for camping and as a result the beach can be quite crowded in summer. Those wanting to get away from the busier beaches should seek out the bays along the southern coast. There is easy access to Ardchiavaig with limited parking.

Water quality No sewage is discharged in the vicinity of this beach. The RPB does not monitor this beach.

Bathing safety Bathing can be dangerous due to the skerries and currents.

Access A side road from the A849 at Fionnphort leads south to Fidden skirting the dunes south to Knockvolgan.

Parking Parking space is available behind the dunes.

Toilets None.

Food None.

Seaside activities Swimming.

Wildlife and walks The lovely island of Iona is well worth a visit; boat trips leave from Fionnphort. There are sites of great historical interest including the St Oran Chapel and the Iona Cathedral. Scenically also, the island has much to offer with its beautiful shoreline, clear blue seas, and white sands.

34 Machrihanish, Campbeltown, Strathclyde   OS Ref: NR6521

A ribbon of pale sand edges the undeveloped west coast of the Mull of Kintyre, from West Loch Tarbert to Machrihanish. All along this western shore there are sea views north to the mountains of Jura and the low lying Islay. Ireland, only 20 miles (32km) away, is clearly visible on a good day. 4 miles (6km) of sandy beach studded with rocky outcrops sweep north from the headland at Machrihanish. Pounding surf washes the gently sloping sands which are backed by mountainous dunes. There is a championship golf course at the southern end of the beach and an airfield on the grassland stretching inland. This delightful beach is popular in summer.

Water quality One outfall serving 200 people discharges untreated sewage at low water mark. The RPB does not monitor this beach.

Bathing safety Dangerous undertows just off shore can cause problems for bathers.

Access There is access from either end of the beach with a short walk to the sands. The B483 from Campbeltown leads to Machrihanish at the southern end of the beach. The A83 hugs the western shore from Tarbert to Machrihanish Bay where it swings inland crossing the Mull towards Campbeltown.

Parking There is off-the-road parking at Machrihanish and at Westport off the A83 at the north end of the beach.

Toilets None.
Food None.
Seaside activities Swimming, surfing and fishing.
Wildlife and walks The plain that spans the peninsula from Campbel-town on the east coast to Machrihanish is in contrast to the tree-clad slopes to the north and the windswept Mull to the south. The Mull coast has cliffs dotted with caves, and most of its length cannot be reached except on foot. It is well worth the effort. There are often seals, basking sharks or porpoises to be seen off shore.

35 Brodick Bay, Brodick, Isle of Arran   OS Ref: NS0237

Below the bare granite summit of the majestic Goat Fell, wooded slopes descend to the water's edge of Brodick Bay north shore. The busy pier on the rocky southern shore is the main landing point for the island. The rocky shore gives way to a 1 mile (1.6km) arc of sand and pebble beach extending around the head of the bay. The beach is bisected by a river which meanders across flat grassland behind the beach before crossing the sands. The beach has a most beautiful setting, overlooked by the impres-sive Brodick Castle. The bay enjoys a particularly mild climate which is reflected in the Castle Gardens where thriving semi-tropical plants can be found.
Water quality Two outfalls serving 700 people discharge untreated sewage, one below and one above low water mark. There have been reports of sewage solids and litter washing on to the beach. The RPB does not monitor this beach.
Bathing safety Safe bathing.
Access The car park at Brodick is adjacent to the beach. A few steps from the car park take you to the sands.
Parking Parking for 100 cars at Brodick and Claddach.
Toilets At Brodick and Brodick Country Park.
Food Several small cafés.
Seaside activities Swimming, windsurfing, canoeing and fishing. Canoes, rowing boats, windsurf boards and fishing tackle are all available for hire. Golf course.
Wet weather alternatives Brodick Castle, Heritage Museum and Transport Museum.
Wildlife and walks On the northern side of the bay is the Brodick Country Park. Its 173 acres (70 hectares) include the formal gardens and woodland of Brodick Castle which have a notable rhododendron collec-tion. There is a self-guided nature trail and access to a path climbing Goat Fell. There is a permanent Ranger Naturalist Service and a series of guided walks are organised during the summer months, which include a seashore life walk. A walled Victorian garden has been restored and there is an ice house, Bavarian summer house and a children's adventure play area.

36 Blackwaterfoot, Arran   OS Ref: NR8928

The northern half of Arran is scenically outstanding, with lush glens cutting deep into the massive granite mountains. This area has been classed as a

National Scenic Area. Beaches attractive to the tourist predominate around the south of the island and include Lamlash Bay, sheltered by Holy Island, Whiting Bay and Blackwaterfoot. The latter, on the western shore of the island, has 1 mile (1.6km) of sand and shingle with rocky outcrops containing rockpools that are worth exploring. Sand dunes and a links golf course stretch south round the bay.

Water quality No sewage is discharged in the vicinity of this beach. The RPB does not monitor this beach.

Bathing safety Safe bathing.

Access There is a short walk from car park to the beach.

Parking Car park next to golf club and Kinloch Hotel has 200 spaces.

Toilets At Blackwater harbour.

Food Kinloch Hotel.

Seaside activities Swimming.

Wet weather alternatives Kinloch Hotel has a swimming pool, squash court, sauna and solarium.

Wildlife and walks The lane past the golf course leads towards Drumadoon Head where there is a most impressive sill, produced when molten rock was forced upwards through other rocks. The path continues north along the line of a raised beach to the Kings Cave and can be followed along the wooded slopes to Tormore and Machrie Bay. There is much evidence of man's past activities in the area with standing stones, and hut circles on the hillside.

37 Troon, Ayrshire   OS Ref: NS3230

Troon is Old Welsh for nose, and describes the promontory which divides the town's shore into two distinct halves. A lighthouse stands at the end of the rocky promontory overlooking the traditional harbour and the modern marina which make this a popular spot with sailing enthusiasts. Gently sloping sands extend both north and south of the harbour. Victorian red sandstone houses and a low sea wall overlook the wide sweep of sands. Here the amusements of the holiday resort are to be found: the children's paddling pool, putting and a funfair. Troon is also a golfer's paradise, with five courses on the dunes north and south of the town. These include Royal Troon and three municipal courses.

Water quality South beach monitored by the River Purification Board and found to meet the EC Mandatory coliform standards for bathing water; ★★★ in this year's listed section. One outfall serving 6,300 people discharges raw sewage at low water mark on the north beach.

Bathing safety Safe bathing.

Access Direct from promenade.

Parking Two car parks with 230 spaces.

Toilets Two blocks on promenade.

Food Hotels and cafés close to beach.

Seaside activities Swimming, surfing, windsurfing, sailing and fishing. Windsurfing school and marina for sailing. Paddling pool and funfair.

Wildlife and walks From the South beach there are views across Ayr Bay to Lady Isle, a Scottish Wildlife Trust Nature Reserve, but access is by permit only. Fullerton estate on the edge of town has woods and parks.

Wales

Sand dunes of Anglesey, pounding surf on the Lleyn, miles of sand, cliffs and secluded coves of West Wales and the beautiful Gower – this is the coast of Wales. There are numerous lovely beaches which are comparable with the best anywhere in the country and they have the added advantage of not being too crowded. Unfortunately there are individual beaches throughout the region that have failed to meet the minimum EC standards for bathing water due to the discharge of sewage from their shores. Major schemes are planned, but two of the largest are not due for completion until 1997.

The north and south coasts suffer from the close proximity of large industrial centres. The large conurbations of South Wales – Swansea, Cardiff, Port Talbot and Newport – all contribute to the pollution of the south coast with discharges of domestic and industrial waste. The north coast is affected by pollution from Merseyside and the Wirral. Milford Haven has suffered from oil pollution problems from the terminals and refineries that line its shore. Further west, away from centres of population, some beaches remain clean and unspoilt; definitely worth exploring.

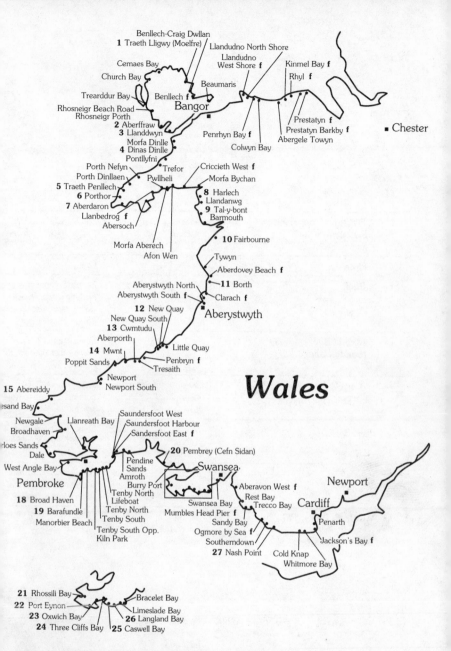

Benllech-Craig Dwllan
1 Traeth Lligwy (Moelfre)
Llandudno North Shore
Llandudno
West Shore **f**
Kinmel Bay **f**
Cemaes Bay
Rhyl **f**
Church Bay
Beaumaris
Trearddur Bay
Benllech **f**
Rhosneigr Beach Road
Bangor
Rhosneigr Porth
2 Aberffraw
Prestatyn
3 Llanddwyn
Prestatyn Barkby **f**
Morfa Dinlle
Penrhyn Bay **f**
Abergele Towyn
4 Dinas Dinlle
Colwyn Bay
Pontllyfni
Porth Nefyn
Trefor
Criccieth West **f**
Porth Dinllaen
Pwllheli
Morfa Bychan
5 Traeth Penllech
8 Harlech
6 Porthor
Llandanwg
7 Aberdaron
9 Tal-y-bont
Llanbedrog **f**
Barmouth
Abersoch

Morfa Aberech
10 Fairbourne
Afon Wen

Tywyn
Aberdovey Beach **f**
Aberystwyth North
11 Borth
Aberystwyth South **f**
Clarach **f**
12 New Quay
New Quay South
Aberystwyth
13 Cwmtudu
Aberporth
Little Quay
14 Mwnt
Penbryn **f**
Poppit Sands
Tresaith

Wales

Newport
Newport South
15 Abereiddy
esand Bay
Saundersfoot West
Newgale
Llanreath Bay
Saundersfoot Harbour
Broadhaven
Saundersfoot East **f**
rloes Sands
20 Pembrey (Cefn Sidan)
Dale
Pendine
West Angle Bay
Sands
Swansea
Amroth
Newport
Pembroke
Burry Port
Aberavon West **f**
18 Broad Haven
Tenby North
Rest Bay
Cardiff
Lifeboat
Trecco Bay
19 Barafundle
Tenby North
Swansea Bay
Manorbier Beach
Tenby South
Mumbles Head Pier **f**
Sandy Bay
Penarth
Tenby South Opp.
Ogmore by Sea **f**
Kiln Park
Southerndown
Jackson's Bay **f**
27 Nash Point
Cold Knap
Whitmore Bay

21 Rhossili Bay
Bracelet Bay
22 Port Eynon
Limeslade Bay
23 Oxwich Bay
26 Langland Bay
24 Three Cliffs Bay
25 Caswell Bay

■ Chester

f = failed to meet EC minimum coliform standards for bathing water in 1991.
Numbered beaches appear in the detailed section.

Coastal walk
Pembrokeshire Coast Path
Cardigan to Tenby 180 miles (290km) mostly in the
Pembrokeshire National Park.

Wales   *See page 19 for further details*

Beach No on Map	Rating. The more stars the better. f=failed	Resort	Pass/Fail track record	Sewage outlets	Population discharging from outlet	Type of treatment	Discharge point relative to low water mark, unless otherwise stated. Distance given in metres	Remarks
CLWYD								
	★★	Point of Ayr Lighthouse						
	f ★★ f ★★	**Prestatyn** Prestatyn: Barkby Beach	FPPPFF	1	16,246	Screens/ maceration	1000 below	Sandy. Safety patrols. Linked to Rhyl scheme.
	f ★★	Ffrith						Sandy.
	f ★ f ★★	**Rhyl** Rhyl (Splash Point)	FFFFFF	1	22,600	Maceration/ tidal tank	400 below	Sandy. Safety patrols. Bathing safe inshore except near river mouth £8 m LSO scheme.
	f ★★	**Kinmel Bay (Sandy Cove)**	FFFFFF					Sandy. Bathing safe except near river mouth Linked to Rhyl scheme.
	★★	Abergele (Towyn)	~~~~FP	1	4,237	Screens/ maceration/ tidal tank	100 above	Sand/shingle. Safe bathing. Linked to Rhyl scheme.
		Abergele (Pensam)		1	7,487	Screens/ maceration/ tidal tank	100 above	Sand at low tide. Safe bathing. Linked to Rhyl scheme.
	★★	Llandulas	~~~~PP	1	1,550	Screens/ maceration/ tidal tank	75 below	Sand/shingle. Storm overflow on beach. LSO improvement scheme.
	★★ f ★★ ★★	**Colwyn Bay** Colwyn Bay (end of Cayley Prom) Colwyn Bay (opposite Rhos Abbey Hotel)	PPPPPP	1	25,800	Screens/ maceration/ tidal tank	1000 below	Outfall extension planned.
GWYNEDD								
	f ★★	Penrhyn Bay	~~~~FF		3,500	Screens/ maceration/ tidal tank	100 above	Sand/shingle.
	f ★★ ★★	Llandudno (North Jetty) **Llandudno (North)**	PPPPFP					Sandy.

Rating. The more stars the better. **f**=failed	Resort	Pass/Fail track record	Sewage outlets	Population discharging from outlet	Type of treatment	Discharge point relative to low water mark, unless otherwise stated. Distance given in metres	Remarks
f ★ **f** ★★	**Llandudno (West Shore)**	FFFFFF	1	34,000	Screens/ maceration/ tidal tank	LWM	Sand/shingle. Bathing safe at high tide only. Some complaints due to unsatisfactory discharges in Conwy Estuary. Long sea outfall planned for 1993.
f ★	Deganwy (North)						
★★★ ★★	Dwygyfylchi (Conwy Bay)						
★★	Penmaenmawr (Conwy Bay)	~~~~FP	1 2	3,700 160	Maceration Raw	200 above 200 above	Sand/shingle Improvements planned.
★★★	Llanfairfechan						Safe bathing inshore only. Beware tidal currents.

NGLESEY

★★★ **f** ★★	Beaumaris: West of Pier Opposite swimming baths						Shingle/sand. Bathing safe on incoming tide, dangerous on the ebb.
★★★	Llanddona						
f ★★	Red Wharf Bay						Bathing safe except at ebb tide. Algal blooms reported. Sewage debris and litter left by users a problem.
f ★★ ★★	**Benllech** Craig Dwllan (Benllech)	PFPPFF	1	2,284	Raw	200 below	Sandy. Long sea outfall planned.
	Moelfre (Treath Lligwy)		1	894	Raw	100 below	Shingle. Safe bathing.
	Amlwch (Bull Bay)		1	4,200	Raw	50 below	Outfall ½ mile east of bay. Storm overflow below LWM. Water quality not monitored in 1991.
★★★	Cemaes Bay	~~~~FP	1	1,000	Maceration/ tidal tank	70 below	Sandy.
★★	Penrhos Beach (Centre)						
★★	Newry Beach, Holyhead		5	11,000	Raw	All above LWM	Docks area.

Beach No on Map	Rating. The more stars the better. f=failed	Resort	Pass/Fail track record	Sewage outlets	Population discharging from outlet	Type of treatment	Discharge point relative to low water mark, unless otherwise stated. Distance given in metres	Remarks
	★★★	**Trearddur Bay**	FFPPPP					Sand and rocks. Pollution incidents in 1991, including sewage solids and debris.
		Traeth Llydan (Broad Beach)						Dunes. Water quality not monitored.
	★★★ ★★	**Rhosneigr** Beach Road	~~~PPP	1	1,532	Raw	150 below	Outfall discharges from rocks. Many watersports.
2		Aberffraw Bay		1	534	Screens/ maceration	At HWM	Sandy.
3		Llanddwyn						Sandy.
	f ★★	St George's Pier, Menai Bridge						
	f ★★	Porth Dinorwic Sailing Club (Menai Straits)						
	★★	Plas Menai (Menai Straits)						
4	★★★	**Dinas Dinlle**	~~PPPP					Sandy.
	★★★	Pontllyfni						Sandy.
		Trefor		1	582	Secondary	At LWM	Sand/shingle. Water quality not monitored in 1991.
		Porth Nefyn		1	2,800	Maceration	At HWM	Sandy. Surfing.
	★★	Morfa Nefyn	~~~~PP	1	2,100	Maceration	At LWM	Sand/rocks.
	★★	Porth Dinllaen	~~~~FP					Sand/rocks.
		Rhos-y-Llan		1	420	Primary		Off rocks. Sandy. Water quality not monitored in 1991.
5		Traeth Penllech						Sand and rocks.
	★★	Porth Colman						Rockpools and safe bathing.
	★★	Porth Iago	~~~~PP					Sandy. Surfing.
6	★★★	Porthor	~~~~PP					Sandy.
7	★★★	Aberdaron	~~~~PP					Sandy. Surfing.

Beach No on Map	Rating. The more stars the better. f=failed	Resort	Pass/Fail track record	Sewage outlets	Population discharging from outlet	Type of treatment	Discharge point relative to low water mark, unless otherwise stated. Distance given in metres	Remarks
	★★★★	Porth Neigwl Beach						Surfing beach. Strong Atlantic rollers. Also called "Hell's Mouth"
	★★★★	Porth Ceriad Beach						
	★★	Machroes Beach, Abersoch						
	★★★ ★★★	**Abersoch**	PPFPPP	1	1,356	Secondary	100 below	Sandy.
	★★★	Afon Soch at Slipway						
	f ★★	Llanbedrog	~~~~FF	1	672	Maceration/ tidal tank	50 below	Sandy.
	★★★ ★★	**Pwllheli**	PPPPPP	1	4,107	Maceration/ tidal tank	At harbour mouth.	Sandy. LSO planned.
		Morfa Aberech						Sandy. Water quality not monitored in 1991.
		Afon Wen		1	46	Maceration/ tidal tank	At LWM	Sand/shingle. Water quality not monitored in 1991.
	★★ f ★★	**Criccieth** West Beach	PFPFFP	1	800	Tidal tank	50 below	Sand/shingle. New LSO proposed for 1994.
	★★★	**Black Rock Sands**						Windsurfing and surfing.
	★★★	Morfa Bychan	FFPPPP	1	800	Tidal tank	50 below	Sandy beach. Contaminated by local streams. Safe bathing except SE end.
8	★★	**Harlech**	PPPPPP	1	1,291	Primary	At LWM	Sandy beach. Bathing unsafe.
	★★★	**Llandanwg**	PPPPPP	1	258	Primary	At LWM	Sand/rock. Bathing safe at high tide. Visible sewage slicks.
9		Tal-y-Bont						Sand, dunes.
	★★★	Llanaber						Smuggling village.

Beach No on Map	Rating. The more stars the better. f=failed	Resort	Pass/Fail track record	Sewage outlets	Population discharging from outlet	Type of treatment	Discharge point relative to low water mark, unless otherwise stated. Distance given in metres	Remarks
	★★★ ★★★	**Barmouth**	PPPPPP	1	2,200	Screened	LSO	Sandy. Estuary unsafe for swimming.
10 ★★★		**Fairbourne**	PPPPPP	1	474	Primary/	400 below tidal tank	Sandy. Existing outfall to be replaced.
f ★★		Llwyngwril	~~~~~F	1	370	Raw	At LWM	Sand/shingle.
	★★	**Tywyn**	FPPPPP	1	2,811	Maceration/ tidal tank	Above LWM	Sandy. Surfing. Scheme under investigation, possibly including primary treatment.
	★★ f ★★ f ★★	**Aberdovey** Aberdovey Beach Aberdovey Beach East	~~~FFP	1	6,000	Primary/ tidal tank	At LWM	Bathing safe from beach north of village. Sewage outfall in estuary. To be combined with Tywyn scheme.
DYFED	★★★ ★★	Ynyslas (North) East Tywyni, Ynyslas						
11 ★★★		Borth	PPPPPP					Bathing dangerous near mouth of the estuary. Good elsewhere.
	f ★ f ★★	Clarach Bay: South of River North of River	~~~FFF					Bathing safe close inshore.
	★★ f ★★ ★★ f ★	**Aberystwyth North** Aberystwyth Harbour **Aberystwyth South (designated sampling point)** Aberystwyth South (non-designated sampling point)	PPPPPP FFPFFP	1	9,100	Screened		Bathing safe centre of prom and south of harbour in calm seas. New primary treatment works and outfall planned for 1994.
	★★★	Tanybwlch Beach, Aberystwyth						
	★★★	Morfa Bychan Beach (slipway)						

Beach No on Map	Rating. The more stars the better. **f**=failed	Resort	Pass/Fail track record	Sewage outlets	Population discharging from outlet	Type of treatment	Discharge point relative to low water mark, unless otherwise stated. Distance given in metres	Remarks
	★★★	Llanrhystud		1	500	Primary		Shingle. Sand at low tide.
	★★★	Llansantffraid		1	1,160	Primary	At LWM	Sand and shingle.
	★★★	Llanon Slipway						
	★★	Aberarth		1	470	Primary	At LWM	Shingle beach.
	f ★★ ★★ ★★★	Aberaeron: North of Outfall Fourth Groyne North Harbour South		1	5,000	Raw	At LWM	Sand and shingle. Under investigation.
	★★★	Little Quay Bay (Central Groyne)						Sand. Safe bathing.
12 ★★★ ★★★ ★★		New Quay: New Quay (North Beach) New Quay (South) **New Quay (Traeth Gwyn)**	PPPPPP	1	6,000	Maceration	1,300 below	Long sea outfall off Llanina Point.
13		Cwmtudu						Shingle and sand.
	f ★★	Llangranog	~~~~FF	1	400	Primary	75 below	Sand/shingle.
	f ★★	Penbryn						Sand.
	★★★	Tresaith	~~~~FP	1	180	Maceration	75 below	Sand and shingle. Safe bathing. Lifeguards.
	f ★★ **f** ★★	Aberporth Beach East Aberporth at Slip	~~~~FF	1	1,842	Maceration	75 below	Sandy. Bathing safe except when strong north winds blow.
14 ★★		Mwnt Beach						Sandy.
	f ★	Gwbert-on-Sea						
	★★★ ★★★	Poppit Sands				Secondary		Sand and shingle. Estuary polluted by outfalls at Cardigan. Bathing safe only at slack water.
	★★★ ★★★	Newport Newport Sands South	PPPPPP	1	1,400	Maceration	500 below LWM	Sand/shingle. Bathing safe in centre of beach except on ebb tide or when rough.

Beach No on Map	Rating. The more stars the better. f=failed	Resort	Pass/Fail track record	Sewage outlets	Population discharging from outlet	Type of treatment	Discharge point relative to low water mark, unless otherwise stated. Distance given in metres	Remarks
		Pwllgwaelod		1	880	Secondary	At LWM	Grey sand. Water quality not monitored in 1991.
		Fishguard		1	2,480	Screens/ maceration	At LWM	Water quality not monitored in 1991.
	★★★	Goodwick Harbour (South)		1	2,710	Raw	At LWM	Ferry terminal. Sewage reported in the water.
	★★★	Goodwick Sands	~~~~PP					
15 ★★★		Abereiddy Bay (at slipway)	~~~~PP					
16 ★★★		**Whitesand Bay**	PPPPPP					Surf bathing. Strong currents. Litter considerable.
	★★★	Caerfai Bay						Sandy beach under cliffs.
	★★★	**Newgale Beach**	FPPPPP					
	★★★	North						
	★★★	South						Shingle and sand. Surfing.
	★★	**Broadhaven**	FPPPPP	1	2,200	Secondary	At HWM	Sandy. Surfing.
	★★★	St Brides Haven						Safe bathing. Many rockpools.
		Musselwick Sands						Cliff-backed cove. Some monitoring in 1991. Nea Marloes.
17 ★★★		Marloes						Sand and rock.
	★★★	Dale	~~~~PP	1	600	Maceration/ tidal tank	Above LWM	Shingle and sand.
	★★★	Sandy Haven		1	1,360	Secondary	At LWM	Red sand.
	★★	Milford Beach						Near major refinery town
f ★★		Neyland Slip						Shingle bank and area for safe bathing.
		Angle Bay		1	500	Secondary	At LWM	Shingle and muddy sand. Water quality not monitored in 1991.
18 ★★★		Broad Haven (South Beach)						Sand, dunes.

Beach No on Map	Rating. The more stars the better. f=failed	Resort	Pass/Fail track record	Sewage outlets	Population discharging from outlet	Type of treatment	Discharge point relative to low water mark, unless otherwise stated. Distance given in metres	Remarks
19		Barafundle Bay						Sandy. Good bathing.
	★★★	Freshwater East	~~~~PP	1	600	Raw	At LWM	Sandy.
	★★★	Manorbier Beach Manorbier West	~~~~PP	1	520	Secondary	At LWM	Sand and shingle.
	★★★	Lydstep Beach						Privately owned beach. Lydstep Point owned by NT.
	★★★	**Tenby** **North**	PFPPPP	1	25,000	Screened/ maceration	2.7km below	Sandy. Highly effective beach management team on North Beach.
	★★★	North at Lifeboat Slipway						
	★★	**South**	FFPPPP					
	★★★	St Catherine's Island						
	★★★	Off Atlantic Hotel, Tenby						
	★★★	Kiln Park						
	★★	**Saundersfoot:** West		1	11,000	Primary	50 below	Sand and shingle. Sewage-related debris reported.
	f ★★	East						
	★★	**Beach**	PFPPPP					
	★★★	**Amroth**	FFPPPP					
	★★★	Amroth Beach East						
	★★★	Amroth Beach West						Sand and shingle.
	★★★	**Pendine** **Sands**	PPPPPP					
	★★★	West Beach						Sand and dunes. Part of beach often closed for MOD firing range.
20 ★★★		**Pembrey** **Sands**	PPPPPP	1	2,500	Secondary	Above HWM into channel towards Burry Port	Sand and dunes. Bathing safe except on spring high water.
	★★★	Burry Port Beach East		1	6,000	Primary	Below LWM	Industrial and muddy. Bathing unsafe.
	f ★	Llanelli Beach (fourth groyne)						
WEST GLAMORGAN								
	★★★	Broughton Bay						Sandy, bathing unsafe.

Beach No on Map	Rating. The more stars the better. f=failed	Resort	Pass/Fail track record	Sewage outlets	Population discharging from outlet	Type of treatment	Discharge point relative to low water mark, unless otherwise stated. Distance given in metres	Remarks
21 ★★★		**Rhossili Bay**	FPPPPP					Sandy. May be affected by animal faeces and algal blooms on rare occasions. Popular surfing beach.
		Fall Bay		1		Primary		South of the Worm's Head. Water quality not monitored in 1991.
		Ramsgrove		1	270	Primary	Below LWM	Sandy. Water quality not monitored in 1991.
22 ★★★		**Port Eynon Bay**	PPPPPP					Sand and dunes.
23 ★★★		**Oxwich Bay**	PPPPPP	1	500		Below LWM	Sand and dunes. (See Swansea Bay)
	★★★★	Crawley Woods, near Little Tor						
24		Three Cliffs Bay						Sandy.
		Southgate		1	500	Secondary	Below LWM	Rocky. Water quality not monitored in 1991.
	★★★	Brandy Cove		1	2,000	Secondary	Below LWM	Rocky.
25 ★★★		**Caswell Bay**	PFPPPP					Sandy. Surfing safe except on ebb tide. Very effective beach management with a high priority given to safety. (See Swansea Bay)
26		**Langland Bay:**						
	★★★	**West**	FPPFPP					
	★★★	East						Sandy. Popular surfing beach. (See Swansea Bay)
	★★★	**Limeslade Bay**	FFPFPP					Sandy. (See Swansea Bay)
	★★★	**Bracelet Bay**	PPPPPP					Sandy. (See Swansea Bay)
		Swansea Bay:		1	170,000	Screened/ tidal tank	Below LWM	Subject of many complaints. New projects totalling over £50 m for whole bay area but not due until 1997, covering Swansea, Bracelet, Limeslade, Langland, Caswell and Oxwich Bays.
	★★★	**The Mumbles**	FFFFFP					
	f ★★	Knap Rock						
	★★	Opposite Black Pill						
	f ★★	Mumbles Head Pier						

Beach No on Map	Rating. The more stars the better. f=failed	Resort	Pass/Fail track record	Sewage outlets	Population discharging from outlet	Type of treatment	Discharge point relative to low water mark, unless otherwise stated. Distance given in metres	Remarks
	★★	Jersey Marine, nr Swansea						
		Baglan (Neath)		1	60,000	Screened	3.1km below	Improvements planned as above. Water quality not monitored in 1991.
		Afan (Port Talbot)		1	60,000	Screened	2.4km below	Improvements planned as above. Water quality not monitored in 1991.
		Aberafan:						
	f ★★	West						
	★★★	**Aberafan at Slip**	FPPPFP					
	★★	East						
	★★★	Margam Sands (opposite steel works)						

MID GLAMORGAN

Beach No on Map	Rating	Resort	Pass/Fail track record	Sewage outlets	Population discharging from outlet	Type of treatment	Discharge point relative	Remarks
	★★★	**Rest Bay**	FPPPPP					Sand and rocks. STW in operation. Marine litter and heavy fuel oil pollution in 1991.
		Porthcawl						Sand and rocks. Sewage transfered to Penybont STW. Water quality not monitored in 1991.
	★★★	**Sandy Bay**	FFFPFP					Sand and rocks.
	★★★	**Trecco Bay**	FFPFPP					Sand and rocks.
	f ★★	Newton Bay (Newton Point)						
	f ★★	Ogmore by Sea	~~~FFF	1	140,000	Secondary/ other	Into River Ogmore approx 1.6km from sea	Sand and rocks. Lifeguards.
	★★★	**Southerndown**	FPFPPP					Sand and rocks. Strong currents off Trwyn y Witch headland. Lifeguards. Surfing except at high tide.
		Dunraven Bay						Glamorgan Heritage Coast project nearby. Polluted by oil in 1991. Water quality not monitored in 1991.

Beach No on Map	Rating. The more stars the better. **f**=failed	Resort	Pass/Fail track record	Sewage outlets	Population discharging from outlet	Type of treatment	Discharge point relative to low water mark, unless otherwise stated. Distance given in metres	Remarks
SOUTH GLAMORGAN								
27		Nash Point						Rocky. Bathing unsafe.
		Tresilian Bay		1	8,000	Maceration	At LWM	Rocky. Bathing unsafe. Water quality not monitored in 1991.
	f ★★	Llantwit Major Beach						
		Limpert Bay		1	4,500	Maceration	At LWM	Rocky. Overlooked by power station. Water quality not monitored in 1991.
	f ★★	Font-y-Gary Bay	~~~~PF	2	3,045 936	Raw Raw	At LWM At LWM	Rocky. Lifeguards. Sewage to be transfered to Barry West.
	★★	Watch House Bay, Barry						
	f ★★	Bendrick's Beach						
	★★★	Little Island Bay, Barry						
	★★★	**Cold Knap Beach**	FFFPFP	1	23,000	Screening	LSO. 1.5km below LWM	New scheme to transfer sewage to Barry West proposed for completion in 1997, with Whitmore and Jacksons Bay.
	★★★ ★★	Whitmore Bay: **Whitmore East Beach** Whitmore West Beach		2	21,000 23,000	Maceration Raw	At LWM At LWM	Sand, shingle and mud.
	f ★★	**Jacksons Bay**	FFFFFF					
	f ★★	St Mary's Well	~~~~FF					Shingle and rocks.
		Penarth		4				Shingle and rocks. Bathing dangerous. Water quality not monitored in 1991.

1 Traeth Lligwy, Moelfre, Anglesey   OS Ref: SH4987

A hard, flat, sandy beach ⅔ mile (1km) wide is revealed at low tide, ideal for sand castles and ball games. There are some areas of mud on the sand surface but signs indicate the areas to avoid. Gently sloping, grass-covered cliffs ring the bay to the south of the dunes that back the centre of the beach. A cliff path along the low rugged cliffs that rise to the north of the beach leads to the adjacent Dulas Bay. This more secluded bay has a fine sandy beach which can only be reached on foot.

Water quality One outfall serving 894 people discharges raw sewage 110 yards (100m) below low water mark at Moelfre south of the bay. The stream which crosses the beach may well be polluted; presence of solids and an unpleasant smell at times. The NRA does not monitor this beach.

Litter Beach is cleaned during the summer.

Bathing safety Safe bathing but beware of offshore winds.

Access Three lanes off the A5025, one at the Moelfre roundabout and two slightly further north, lead to the bay. The car park is adjacent to the sand.

Parking Two privately run car parks with 500 spaces, rough surfaced.

Toilets One block at car park.

Food Refreshment caravan and takeaway shop.

Seaside activities Swimming.

Wildlife and walks Cliff top paths can be followed in both directions from the beach. Walking south, the path over the headland provides excellent views of the rocky coastline. It leads to the picturesque little fishing village of Moelfre. Above the beach, in the rolling green field which slopes down to the shore, there are the remains of a 4th-century fortified village, Din Lligwy, and also a megalithic burial chamber.

2 Aberffraw, Anglesey   OS Ref: SH3568

A wide, flat, sandy beach is bounded landwards by a series of sand dune ridges, behind which flat grassland extends inland. This makes the dunes a prominent feature in a landscape that seems to be dominated by the sky. Aberffraw village is set back from the beach on the higher ground that rises to the west. The beach extends about ⅔ mile (1km) from low cliffs at the western end, below which the river flows.

Water quality One outfall serving 534 people discharges screened and macerated sewage at high water mark west of the beach. The NRA does not monitor this beach.

Litter The beach is cleaned during the summer.

Bathing safety Safe bathing, although the estuary area should be avoided on the ebb tide.

Access A lane off the A4080 just south of Aberffraw village leads to car parking behind the dunes. Easy walk through the dunes to beach.

Parking Parking for several hundred cars between ½ and 1 mile (0.75km-1.6km) from beach, on grassed common land. No parking on the beach.

Toilets In village and at Llys Llywelyn.

Food In village and at Llys Llywelyn.

Seaside activities Swimming.

Wildlife and walks The marram grass-covered dunes are well developed; depressions between the ridges (wet slacks) abound with wild flowers and low scrub, for example creeping willow. There is a 2 mile (3km) walk along the cliffs from Aberffraw leading to the church of Llangwfan. This area was the site of Llewelyn the Great, Prince of Gwynedd's Summer Palace although no trace remains.

3 Llanddwyn, Newborough, Anglesey   OS Ref: SH4163

From the rocky Llanddwyn Island a lovely sand beach curves 3 miles (5km) east to Abermenai point, the end of a sand spit at the mouth of the Menai Straits. The beach is backed by the extensive sand dunes of Newborough Warren. At the western end there is a conifer wood planted by the Forestry Commission. This remote, gently shelving beach is usually quiet and has superb views of Snowdonia and the Lleyn Peninsula.

Water quality No sewage is discharged in the vicinity of this beach. The NRA does not monitor this beach.

Bathing safety Safe bathing except at the eastern end; currents at the entrance to the Menai Straits can cause problems.

Access Road from Newborough village leads to a Forestry Commission car park within their plantation, and a path leads to the beach.

Parking Car park with space for several hundred cars in cleared forest areas behind beach.

Toilets At car park.

Food None.

Seaside activities Swimming and sailing.

Wildlife and walks There is a forest trail starting from the car park. The dunes of Newborough Warren behind the beach and Llanddwyn Island are both nature reserves; access to the dunes is restricted to prevent damage. Access to the island is by a causeway, and you get good views back along the beach and to the mountains in the distance. There is a ruined church and navigation beacon on the island. There are extensive cockle beds on the Straits side of Abermenai Point. Across the sand flats, a footpath leads through the Warren to Newborough Village.

4 Dinas Dinlle, Gwynedd   OS Ref: SH4456

Three miles (5km) of wide open beach stretches from Dinas Dinlle, a 100 foot (30m) hill which dominates the surrounding flat coastal plain, north to the mouth of the Menai Straits. The hill shadows the small village of the same name, with its string of bungalows, cafés and shops facing the beach. A moderately steep bank of large pebbles gives way to sand at low tide. The adjacent grassland, on which stands Caernarfon airport, is protected by a low sea-wall. Good surfing conditions frequently prevail.

Water quality No sewage discharged in the vicinity of this beach. Water monitored by the NRA and found to meet EC minimum coliform standards in 1991; ★★★ in this year's listing section.

Litter The beach is cleaned regularly throughout the summer.

Bathing safety Safe bathing except at the northern end.

Access Dinas Dinlle is signposted from the A499 south of Caernarfon. The road runs along adjacent to the beach, with easy level access.

Parking Parking along the whole length of the road, with about 1 mile (1.6km) of pebbled parking areas.

Toilets Blocks at either end of the beach and one at the centre.

Food Several shops and cafés at the southern end of the beach.

Seaside activities Swimming, surfing and fishing.

Wet weather alternatives Airport viewing pavilion and Caernarfon Airport Museum.

Wildlife and walks Good for a bracing winter walk.

5 Traeth Penllech, Llangwnnadl, Gwynedd   OS Ref: SH2034

A super beach; a wide sandy arc stretches over ⅔ mile (1km) below the rocky, grass-topped cliffs that fall steeply to the shore. A long strip of soft sand remains at high water and the wide flat sands studded with rocks towards the southern end are exposed at low tide. Traeth Penllech forms part of a larger indented bay on this northern coast of the Lleyn Peninsula. There are good views from the cliff top to the headlands in either direction. By following the clifftop path, small sand and shingle coves can be reached. The relentless waves that wash this coast make for excellent surfing conditions.

Water quality No sewage is discharged in the vicinity of this beach.

Bathing safety Safe bathing.

Access From the B4417 take the road through Penllech, turning left at the T-junction. There is parking off this road, above the beach. A steep path down a narrow valley leads to the shore ⅔ mile (1km) away.

Parking Summer parking on a private field off road north east of Pen-y-graig.

Toilets None.

Food None.

Seaside activities Swimming, surfing, windsurfing, diving and fishing.

Wildlife and walks The area is popular with divers because of its rich marine life; the rockpools give a hint of what can be seen below the waves. A path along the cliff top, above which choughs may be seen, leads to other delightful little sandy coves.

6 Porthor, Gwynedd   OS Ref: SH1630

This is the last and the most accessible in a series of long secluded bays along the north coast of the Lleyn Peninsula. This small cove is ringed by steep grass-covered cliffs, typical of this whole coastline. It is also called 'Whistling Sands' because the white sands seem to whistle or squeak as they are walked on. To really get away from it all try Porth Iago and Porth Colmon further north.

Water quality No sewage is discharged in the vicinity of this beach. Water monitored by NRA and found to meet the EC minimum coliform standards in 1991; ★★★ in this year's listing section.

Bathing safety Safe bathing.

Access From the B4413 south of Pen-y-groeslon lanes lead down to car park just before Carreg. Steep path down from cliff top.

Parking Car park on cliff top 220 yards (200m) from beach.

Toilets At car park.
Food Café on beach.
Seaside activities Swimming and fishing.
Wildlife and walks Low tide reveals rockpools at the western end.

7 Aberdaron, Gwynedd   OS Ref: SH1726

A sheltered bay except when a south or south-west wind blows and the waves come crashing in. The mile (1.6km) long sandy beach below the cluster of housing that makes up the fishing village of Aberdaron completely disappears at high tide. Take care not to get caught below the rocky cliffs that fringe the bay and extend south to the toe of the Lleyn.
Water quality Beach monitored by the NRA and found to meet the EC minimum coliform standards for bathing water in 1991; ★★★ in this year's listing section. No sewage is discharged in the vicinity of the beach.
Bathing safety Safe bathing.
Access Ramp to beach.
Parking and Toilets Adjacent to ramp.
Food Cafés and two pubs in village.
Seaside activities Swimming, windsurfing, diving, fishing and sailing.
Wildlife and walks Cliff top walks lead south to the 500 foot (150m) hill Mynydd Mawr that rises above the end of the Peninsula. There are spectacular views of the rocky coast and of Bardsey Island, 2 miles (3km) off shore. Westwards, the cliff paths lead to the cove of Porth Ysgo, not accessible by road. Boat trips to Bardsey Island leave from Aberdaron.

8 Harlech, Gwynedd   OS Ref: SH5831

From Harlech, with its castle perched on a rocky cliff 60 yards (55m) above the coastal plain, there are superb views over the dunes and golf links below and across Tremadoc Bay to the Lleyn Peninsula. 4 miles (6km) of soft sands, edged by a wide belt of dunes, extend from Harlech Point south to Llandanwg. There is masses of room on the extensive, flat, rather windswept sands. The fragile dunes have suffered from erosion and restoration work is being undertaken to help them recover; please assist this work by avoiding any further damage. There is access to the beach at Llandanwg, where board walks lead across the dunes to the beach. The church of old Llandanwg village can be seen half-buried in the sand dunes.
Water quality Harlech and Llandanwg are monitored by the NRA and were found to meet the EC minimum coliform standards for bathing water in 1991; ★★ in this year's listing section. One outfall at Harlech serving 1,291 people discharges primary treated sewage at low water mark. One outfall at Llandanwg serving 258 people discharges macerated and primary treated sewage at low water mark. A new sewage treatment works is planned for operation in 1995.
Litter Some marine debris is washed on to the shore.
Bathing safety The estuary and the area around Harlech Point is unsafe for bathing due to strong currents. Further south, the beach is safe for bathing. HM Coastguard search unit post at the car park. Emergency phone on path to beach and lifebuoys.

Access The beach is signposted from the A496 at Harlech. The road leads to car parking behind the dunes. A path leads through dunes.
Parking Car park with 300 spaces behind the dunes.
Toilets At the car park.
Food None.
Seaside activities Swimming, surfing, windsurfing, sailing, canoeing and fishing. St David's Golf Course.
Wet weather alternatives Harlech Castle, sports hall, indoor swimming pool, galleries and craft shop in Harlech.
Wildlife and walks The northern end of this beach and the shore of the estuary fall within the Morfa Harlech Nature Reserve; access is by permit only. The Snowdonia National Park Information Centre is in the town.

9 Tal-y-Bont, Gwynedd   OS Ref: SH5921

A first-class beach; miles and miles of golden sand backed by high dunes – 15 miles (24km) in all, unspoilt and set against the magnificent scenery of North Wales. The beach stretches from Shell Island Peninsula in the north, so called because of the variety of shells to be found there, towards Barmouth in the south. A road just north of Tal-y-bont leads to car parking behind the dunes. There are a lot of caravan parks along this section of coastline; at Tal-y-bont they remain hidden behind the dunes, but it does mean that the sands can be popular in summer. However, the wide flat sands revealed at low tide provide plenty of space.
Water quality No sewage is discharged in the vicinity of this beach. The NRA does not monitor this beach.
Litter Beach cleaned by the local authority.
Bathing safety Safe bathing. Emergency phone at the car park.
Access Beach signposted off the A496 north of Tal-y-bont, road leads to a car park behind the dunes. Good paths through the dunes lead to the beach.
Parking National Park car park behind the dunes has 120 spaces.
Toilets At the car park.
Food None, cafés in village.
Seaside activities Swimming, surfing, windsurfing, canoeing and fishing.
Wildlife and walks The dunes at the north end of the beach form the Morfa Dyffryn Nature Reserve; access is by permit only.

10 Fairbourne, Gwynedd   OS Ref: SH6116

Fairbourne has a magnificent setting at the mouth of the beautiful Mawddach estuary with the backdrop of the Welsh mountains. 2 miles (3km) of sandy beach stretch north from the small resort of Fairbourne to the mouth of the estuary. The promenade gives way to the dunes of Morfa Mawddach, a sand spit. A narrow gauge railway runs from Fairbourne along the beach to the point, where a ferry will take the visitor across the estuary to the old quay of Barmouth on the opposite shore. There are lots of shells to be found on this beach.
Water quality Beach monitored by the NRA and found to meet the EC

minimum coliform standards for bathing water in 1991; ★★★ in this year's listing section. One outfall discharges macerated and primary treated sewage through a tidal tank 440 yards (400m) below low water mark. A £1.7 million scheme will extend this outfall further out to sea.

Bathing safety Safe bathing except near the estuary mouth.

Access Beach signposted from the A493 through the town. Direct access from the promenade. Access for the disabled.

Parking Extensive car parking near the beach.

Toilets Near main access to beach.

Food Refreshment kiosks and cafés on the sea front. Restaurant at the point.

Seaside activities Swimming, windsurfing, sailing and fishing. Amusements. Narrow gauge railway. Windsurfing boards available for hire.

Wet weather alternatives Fairbourne railway and Butterfly Safari.

Wildlife and walks There is excellent walking country within easy reach of Fairbourne; footpaths lead along the estuary. The panorama walk above Barmouth provides superb views of mountains, river and sea.

11 Borth, Dyfed   OS Ref: SN6190

A former fishing village, Borth is a major centre for caravan and camping holidays. The sandy beach extends for some 2 miles (3km) north around the dunes of the National Nature Reserve at Ynyslas and to the Dyfi estuary. The Ceredigion Heritage Coast Path, southbound towards Aberystwyth, starts at Borth. Dogs restricted from May to September.

Water quality Beach monitored by the NRA and found to meet the EC minimum coliform standards for clean bathing water in 1991; ★★★ in this year's listing section. No sewage is discharged in the vicinity of the beach, but there is an outfall serving 6,000 people discharging primary treated sewage in the estuary.

Bathing safety Waters in the Dyfi estuary are dangerous, otherwise Borth and Ynyslas beaches are safe for responsible use.

Access Direct from the promenade in Borth or via footpaths through the dunes at Ynyslas.

Parking Parking for 200-300 at Borth and similar numbers at Ynyslas.

Toilets On the promenade (with facilities for the disabled).

Food Hotels, restaurants, cafés.

Seaside activities Swimming, surfing, windsurfing, sailing and sea angling. Golf course.

Wet weather alternatives Borth Livestock Centre, Tre'r Ddol Museum. A full list of all attractions and leisure facilities in the district is available from the Borth Tourist Information Centre.

Wildlife and walks Ceredigion Heritage Coast Path leads south through Clarach to Aberystwyth. Ynyslas Nature Reserve offers conducted tours and guided nature trails. Walks in the RSPB Reserve at Ynys Hir.

12 New Quay, Dyfed   OS Ref: SN3959

This traditional fishing town perched on the steep slopes above the harbour has three beaches. Treath-y-Dolau, to the south of the harbour, is backed by contorted shale cliffs. The harbour beach, bounded by the stone pier, and Traethgwyn stretching around the curve of New Quay Bay are both gently sloping sandy beaches. At low tide Llanina Point to the north can be rounded to reach Cei Bach beach, a quiet ½ mile (800m) of sandy beach, backed by a shingle ridge and shrub-covered slopes. Dogs restricted from May to September.

Water quality Beach monitored by the NRA and found to meet the EC minimum coliform standards for bathing water in 1991; ★★★ in this year's listing section. One outfall serving 6,000 people discharges macerated sewage from a tidal tank at low water mark off New Quay head.

Bathing safety Safe from all beaches.

Access Short walk down road which slopes down from town to the beach.

Parking Car parks in town.

Toilets Close to the beach.

Food Hotels, motels, and cafés.

Seaside activities Swimming, surfing, windsurfing, sailing and fishing. Boats and surf boards for hire.

Wet weather alternatives Bird hospital and lifeboat station. A guide to attractions and leisure facilities is available from Information Centre.

Wildlife and walks Ceredigion Heritage Coast Path provides walks with views of dramatic cliff scenery. Ceredigion District Council produces leaflets which describe each of the many beaches from Borth in the north to Gwbert-on-Sea in the south.

13 Cwmtudu, New Quay, Dyfed   OS Ref: SN3558

A small secluded cove among the rugged cliffs south-west of New Quay, Cwmtudu lies at the mouth of the wooded Afon Ffynnon Ddewi valley. A group of houses nestles in the valley. The shingle beach has a small amount of sand at low tide and is edged by cliffs with striking rock formations. Caves among the folds and faults were once used by smugglers. Dogs restricted from May to September.

Water quality No sewage is discharged in the vicinity of this beach. The NRA does not monitor this beach.

Bathing safety Safe.

Access The beach is signposted from the A487 south of New Quay, several miles' drive along lanes. A steep path leads down to the cove.

Parking Car park with 30 spaces.

Toilets None.

Food Café.

Seaside activities Swimming.

Wildlife and walks The Ceredigion Heritage Coast Path, 110 yards (100m) up the road from the beach, leads around the headland to the north and gives good views over the bay. Earth banks above the craggy inlet are the remains of an Iron Age fort. From here the path continues along the coast for 3 miles (4.8km) leading to New Quay Headland and Birds Rock.

14 Mwnt, Cardigan, Dyfed   OS Ref: SN1952

A natural suntrap and surrounded by National Trust land, this beautiful undeveloped sandy beach is quite easily accessible and can be very popular in summer. The 330 yards (300m) of gently sloping sands are fringed by folded and faulted shale and mudstone cliffs. The beach is shadowed by the imposing form of Foel-y-Mwnt, a conical hill on the headland. The tiny whitewashed church of The Holy Cross nestles in a hollow at its foot. The only other obvious sign of man is the remains of a limekiln adjacent to the path down to the beach; limestone was landed in the bay and fired ready for use by the local farmers. Dogs are banned from May to September.

Water quality No sewage is discharged in the vicinity of this beach. Water monitored by NRA and found to meet the EC minimum coliform standards for bathing water in 1991; ★★ in this year's listing section.

Bathing safety Safe bathing inshore; care is required as surface currents, due to waves breaking on the headland, deflect across the bay. Emergency phone on cliff path.

Access Mwnt is signposted from the B4548 north of Cardigan. Lanes lead to car park above the beach. Steps and a steep path down the cliff to the beach.

Parking National Trust car park with 250 spaces.

Toilets At the head of the steps to the beach (facilities for the disabled).

Food Refreshments available from Easter to October.

Seaside activities Swimming.

Wildlife and walks National Trust cliff top walks. A pack detailing walks in the Cardigan area is available from local tourist information centres. Foely-Mwnt hill on the headland provides good views of the bay south to Cardigan Island and the narrow rocky inlet to the north. On the cliff tops above the beach there is a small remnant dune system where marram grass covers the wind-blown sand. Dogs on leads are welcome on the footpaths.

15 Abereiddy Bay, Abereiddy, Preseli, Dyfed   OS Ref: SM8031

One of many small bays that have known a very different and more active past. The slate that gives the small beach its dark grey sand was quarried and the remains of the workings can still be seen at the northern end of the beach. A small harbour on the north side of the headland where the rock has been cut away forms a deep blue pool.

Water quality No sewage is discharged in the vicinity of this beach. Water monitored by the NRA and found to meet the EC minimum coliform standards for bathing water in 1991; ★★★ in this year's listing section.

Bathing safety Dangerous undercurrents and undertows off parts of the beach; life saving equipment and an emergency telephone are available. Power boat restriction of 8 knots in bathing area.

Access Lanes from the A487 north of St David's lead to Abereiddy.

Parking Large car park for 200 cars.

Toilets At rear of car park.

Food Ice-cream van and teas on beach.

Seaside activities Swimming, diving, canoeing, surfing and fishing.

Wildlife and walks The Pembrokeshire Coast Path leads in both directions along this most impressive and unspoilt stretch of rocky coastline, several stretches of which are owned by the National Trust.

16 Whitesand Bay, St David's, Preseli, Dyfed   OS Ref: SM7327

Gorgeous sunsets framed in the wide arc of Whitesand Bay, from the remote rocky headland of St David's to St John Point, are an added attraction of this lovely beach. There are splendid views away to Ramsey Island and the Bishops and Clerks; the South Bishop can be identified on the far horizon by its lighthouse. The wide white sands stretch for ⅔ mile (1km). Large pebbles are thrown to the top of the beach by the waves that frequently crash on to the sands, much to the delight of many surfers. Open fields slope down to the shore from the imposing craggy hill Carn Llidi, which provides good walking with excellent sea views. St David's Head is owned by the National Trust. There is a dog ban on the beach from May to September.

Water quality Beach monitored by the NRA and found to meet the EC minimum coliform standards for bathing water in 1991; ★★★ in this year's listing section. No sewage is discharged in the vicinity of this beach.

Litter Considerable quantities off the beach.

Bathing safety Dangerous and unpredictable currents off parts of the beach and at some states of the tide; warning signs indicate where to bathe. Flags indicate when it is safe to bathe. Lifeguards patrol the beach during the summer. Weever fish. Power boat restriction of 8 knots within bathing area.

Access Road off A487 north of St David's, signposted to Whitesand, leads directly to car park adjoining the sand.

Parking Car park behind beach, with approximately 400 spaces.

Toilets At car park.

Food Café/shop at car park.

Seaside activities Swimming, surfing, canoeing, diving, windsurfing and fishing.

Wildlife and walks The coast path north provides an interesting circular walk, taking in St David's Head with the remains of a fort and a burial chamber, and returning round Carn Llidi Hill. A guide describing the route is published by the Pembrokeshire Coast National Park and can be obtained at information offices locally. Ramsey Island lies just south of the bay, and boat trips from Whitesand (12-person inflatables, operating May-September) take you round the island to view the seabird breeding colonies.

17 Marloes Sands, Marloes, Preseli, Dyfed   OS Ref: SM7908

'Magnificent Marloes', a mile (1.6km) of wide flat golden sands, stretches from the imposing bulk of Gateholm Island in the north-west to Red Cliff and Hoopers Point to the south-east. Beds of rock laid flat on a sea bed long ago are tilted and seem to be pushing up through the sands. Their jagged outlines point skywards along the length of this glorious bay. The steep cliffs that bound the beach reflect these dipping strata; do not attempt to climb them as they are dangerous. The barnacle- and seaweed-covered rocky outcrops testify to the fact that the whole beach disappears at high water. There is only one access point to the beach where a tiny stream flows through a narrow valley, so take care not to get cut off at the extremities of the beach by the incoming tide.

Water quality No sewage is discharged in the vicinity of this beach. Water quality monitored by the NRA and found to meet the EC minimum coliform standards for bathing water; ★★★ in this year's listing section.

Bathing safety Beware of currents and rocks. Life-saving equipment is available. Take care as some areas of the beach are quickly cut off by the rising tide. The cliffs are dangerous; do not climb.

Access From Marloes village a lane, signposted Marloes Sands, takes you to the National Trust car park.

Parking National Trust car park with about 50 spaces.

Toilets None.

Food None.

Seaside activities Swimming and fishing.

Wildlife and walks The coast path that follows the cliff top round the bay provides excellent views of the sands. There is a 2 mile (3km) nature trail starting from the National Trust car park. Walkers using the trail are guided by a leaflet produced by the Dyfed Wildlife Trust (DWT). To the south-west, the coast path leads to West Dale Bay and a series of secluded sandy beaches around the Dale Peninsula that can only be reached on foot. To the north-east, the path heads to Albion Reach and Martin's Haven. A National Park guide, available from the DWT Information Centre, describes a walk around the headland. Boat trips run from Martin's Haven to Skomer Island, renowned for its seabirds, wild flowers and seal colonies, and a marine area now designated a Marine Nature Reserve.

18 Broad Haven South, Bosherston, Dyfed   OS Ref: SR9893

A classic golden beach with a clear stream meandering across a wide flat 'V' of golden sands, backed by dunes and with rocky cliffs rising at either side. A distinct rocky outcrop lies just off shore. This unspoilt beach is only accessible by foot across the dunes but still gets busy in summer. It is perfect for relaxation or for exploration. There are lily ponds in the nature reserve behind the dunes and surprises round every headland: tiny rocky inlets, deep crevices, stacks and blow holes, not to mention the wildlife.

Water quality No sewage is discharged in the vicinity of this beach. Water monitored by the NRA and found to meet the EC minimum coliform standards for bathing water in 1991; ★★★ in this year's listing section.

Litter Beach cleaned regularly by the National Trust.

Bathing safety Safe bathing. Life saving equipment available.

Access A lane from Bosherston leads to the National Trust car park; a path leads to the beach, and there is also a steep path to the beach from Bosherston a mile (1.6km) inland.

Parking National Trust car park on headland above beach, National Park car park in Bosherston.

Toilets At car park in summer.

Food None.

Seaside activities Swimming.

Wildlife and walks Separated from the beach by the dune ridge are the Bosherston Lily pools, three lakes created in the late 18th century by damming three narrow valleys behind the beach. Water lilies and freshwater wildlife abound. Paths and causeways form circular walks around the area, starting at the car park in Bosherston. South of the bay the coast path proceeds along the cliff top to the tiny rocky inlet where St Govan chapel stands at the foot of a long flight of steep steps down the cliffs. Further south there is a 130 foot (40m) deep cleft in the cliff known as the Huntsman's Leap: a local huntsman is supposed to have died of fright after realising what his horse had just leapt! The path continues along this most beautiful rocky coastline towards the Elegug Stacks, a series of impressive limestone stacks, about 3 miles (5km) away. A large arch carved by the waves from the limestone cliffs is known as 'The Green Bridge of Wales'.

19 Barafundle Bay, Stackpole, Dyfed   OS Ref: SR9995

The National Trust owns an 8 mile (13km) section of the coast around Stackpole, including the beautiful Barafundle Bay. The beach can only be reached by foot with a mile (1.6km) walk along the cliff top from Stackpole Quay. One of many tiny harbours that once proliferated in west Wales, the stone quay in this tiny inlet has been restored by the National Trust. From the clifftop path you get your first glimpse of the bay, an impressive view of soft golden sands backed by high dunes, with steep limestone cliffs rising on either side. The cliffs, with distinctive dark bands at their base due to the encrusting seaweeds, barnacles and lichens, extend to Stackpole Head which shelters the bay.

Water quality No sewage is discharged in the vicinity of this beach. The NRA does not monitor this beach.

Litter Clean; a small amount of litter is washed up. In summer the beach is cleaned daily by the National Trust.

Bathing safety Safe bathing. Life saving equipment at top of steps down cliff.

Access A lane east of Stackpole, signposted to Stackpole Quay and Barafundle, leads to the car park at Stackpole Quay. A 10-minute walk along the coast path, signposted from the car park, leads to the bay; follow the steps down the cliff to reach the sands.

Parking National Trust car park at Stackpole Quay with 230 spaces.

Toilets At car park.

Food None.

Seaside activities Swimming.

Wildlife and walks The coast path from Stackpole Quay crosses the beach and, climbing through the trees, the path tracks around Stackpole headland, passes Rame Blow Hole, and continues on to Broadhaven Bay. There are excellent views of the rocky coastline, and north-east the ranks of red sandstone headlands extend to the horizon. Walking south-east there are views down on to tiny sandy coves which cannot be reached because of the steep limestone cliffs that tower above.

20 Pembrey Sands, Llanelli, Dyfed   OS Ref: SN3802

A marvellous beach with 7 miles (11km) of sand edged by a belt of sand dunes, known locally as Cefn Sidan. The beach falls within the Pembrey Country Park which also covers the extensive grassland and forest behind the dunes. The middle of the beach near the visitors' centre can be very busy on a warm sunny afternoon, but the extremities remain relatively quiet although they are often used for marine sports. Land yachting by the local club is well worth watching. Whether you want to relax on the sand and enjoy the clear views to the Gower on the horizon, or be more active, the country park has lots of facilities, both natural and man-made, to keep the whole family happy. Dogs are not permitted in the central ¾ mile (1.2km) section of the beach although this may not always be observed by visitors.

Water quality Beach monitored by the NRA and found to meet the EC minimum coliform standards for bathing water in 1991; ★★★ in this year's listing section.

Litter Flotsam and jetsam are washed up on this beach. This may be on the increase, but it is cleaned regularly.

Bathing safety Safe bathing. Lifeguards patrol the beach near the main access point from June to September.

Access Country park signposted from the A484. Board walks from the car parks lead through the dunes to the beach.

Parking Several car parks behind dunes with about 1,000 spaces.

Toilets One toilet block with facilities for the disabled.

Food Permanent kiosk with outdoor seating provides snacks and drinks.

Seaside activities Swimming, windsurfing, sailing and fishing. Pitch and putt golf, miniature and narrow gauge railways, adventure play area and dry ski slope. Events are regularly staged on the beach, for example sand sculpture competitions and treasure hunts.

Wet weather alternatives Kidwelly Castle and Industrial Museum, Pembrey Motor Sports centre. The Country Park Information Centre presents displays and exhibitions about the beach and country park (open all year).

Wildlife and walks There are four self-guided nature trails around the country park: woodland walk, floral trail, the yellow post walk (which includes the beach, dunes, forest and grassland), and the leisure route, suitable for wheelchairs and pushchairs. There is a permanent orienteering course, a programme of guided walks by the Ranger service and a nature quiz for children. Full information is available from the visitors' centre.

21 Rhossili Bay, Rhossili, West Glamorgan   OS Ref: SS4287

A spectacular 3 mile (5km) sweep of golden sands edges Rhossili Bay, stretching from Worms Head north to Burry Holms. The sands are shadowed by Rhossili Down; its grass slopes rise 600 feet (200m) above the beach and are popular with hang gliders. The southern end of the beach is ringed by steep cliffs which fall away northwards, where the Down is replaced by sand dunes. Worms Head, contrary to its name, is in fact an island, only linked to the mainland at low tide. The remains of a wreck can sometimes be seen at low tide. This lovely beach and the adjacent Down are owned by the National Trust.

Water quality Beach monitored by the NRA and found to meet the EC minimum coliform standards for bathing water in 1991; ★★★ in this year's listing section. No sewage is discharged from this beach. Complaints of visible sewage have been received which may be linked to animal faeces washed from the north Gower marshes.

Litter Considerable quantities of marine litter, such as fishing gear in the strand line.

Bathing safety Safe bathing.

Access The B4247 leads to Rhossili village. There is a good path down the cliffs to the beach.

Parking Car park in village.

Toilets At the car park.

Food In the village.

Seaside activities Swimming, surfing (extremely popular) and fishing.

Wildlife and walks Worms Head island and the adjacent stretch of coast are a National Nature Reserve. The limestone cliffs are rich in flora, and nesting birds can be seen on the nature trail. The limestone rocky shore of the Gower is one of the best examples in Britain. There is a network of paths on the headland and the adjoining Down where superb views can be obtained.

22 Port Eynon, West Glamorgan   OS Ref: SS4685

The rocky headland, Port Eynon Point, to the south shelters this sandy cove. The road from the Post Office leads down to the shore where a short section of newly built promenade gives access to the beach. On either side, high dunes back the wide, flat sands. High cliffs rise on either side of the bay with rocky outcrops at their base. On the eastern side of the bay stand the newly excavated remains of a salt house and workings. The wide, gently sloping sands are safe for bathing, and an ideal spot for building sand castles or playing cricket. A dog restriction by-law is being considered.

Water quality Beach monitored by the NRA and found to meet the EC minimum coliform standards for bathing water in 1991; ★★★ in this year's listing section. One outfall serving 1,200 people discharges primary and secondary treated sewage at low water mark off Overton Mere, east of Port Eynon Point.

Litter The beach is cleaned daily in summer and twice weekly in winter.

Bathing safety Warning notices indicate where it is safe to bathe. The beach is patrolled by lifeguards from May until September.

Access From the village a road leads to main access point where there is direct level access to the sands. Board walks and marked paths through dunes.

Parking Car park behind dunes with 500 spaces.

Toilets At beach entry point.

Food Shop and café at beach entrance.

Seaside activities Swimming, surfing, windsurfing, diving, canoeing and fishing. A boat ramp leads from the car park to the tidal sand, providing easy access to the beach for boats.

Wildlife and walks The South Gower Coast Nature Reserve stretches from Port Eynon to Worms Head at Rhossili, comprising 6 miles (10km) of rocky shore with faulted and folded grey limestone cliffs. There is a most interesting limestone flora, and nesting birds can be seen on some ledges.

The limestone rocky shore of the Gower is one of the best examples in Britain. The footpath on to Port Eynon Point climbs the cliff from the eastern end of the beach. The path leads to the Culver Hole, a deep cleft in the cliff which has been sealed off with a wall. There is a nature trail starting from the Rhossili Bay car park at the opposite end of the Nature Reserve.

23 Oxwich Bay, Oxwich, West Glamorgan   OS Ref: SS4986

A superb beach; from the steep tree-clad slopes of Oxwich Point a sweep of very fine soft sand backed by high dunes curves 2 miles (3km) round the bay to Great Tor – a stretch of towering rocky limestone cliffs. At low tide wide, flat sands are revealed. There is only one indentation into the crescent of sand, where the dunes are interrupted by the river Nicholaston Pill which meanders through marshland before crossing the beach. The main access is from Oxwich village where there are full facilities. The North Devon Coast can be seen on the horizon and in the evening it appears as a string of lights. At low tide Oxwich Bay links with Three Cliffs Bay to the east, giving 3 miles (5km) of continuous south-facing sands.

Water quality Beach monitored by the NRA and found to meet the EC minimum coliform standards for bathing water in 1991; ★★★ in this year's listing section. No sewage is discharged in the immediate vicinity of this beach.

Bathing safety Safe bathing.

Access Narrow lanes lead to Oxwich village at the western end of the bay, and a car park next to the dunes faces directly on to the beach. There is a ramp for launching boats that could be used for easier access to the hard tidal sand. There is also access to the other end of the beach: a 15-minute walk from Penmaen along the footpath marked Tor Bay leads to a steep path down the cliff.

Parking Large car park at Oxwich village, plus limited parking at Penmaen. In summer, National Trust car park (a farmer's field) at Penmaen.

Toilets Two blocks at Oxwich car park.

Food The Oxwich Bay Hotel which stands at the eastern end of the beach provides meals and bar snacks. There is a kiosk for refreshments at the car park, and cafés and a shop within the village.

Seaside activities Swimming, windsurfing, sailing, diving, canoeing and fishing. A slipway across the sand enables boats to be launched and makes the bay popular with waterskiers. There is a windsurfing school on the beach.

Wildlife and walks The Oxwich National Nature Reserve covers most of the beach, backshore and the Oxwich Point headland. The reserve includes a wide variety of habitats: sandy beach, dunes, salt- and freshwater marshes, cliffs, woods and grassland. There are marked footpaths throughout the reserve, and board walks give access to the dunes. A path west of the hotel leads through the trees past St Illtyd's Church to steps which climb to the headland and along the coast to Horton. There is an interpretative centre at the car park at Oxwich. At the western end there are barnacle- and mussel-encrusted rocks below the cliffs, and low tide reveals pools full of life.

24 Three Cliffs, Parkmill, Glamorgan   OS Ref: SS5488

The ruins of the Pennard Castle stand above the river valley which opens out to the eastern corner of this lovely sandy bay, ringed by steep cliffs. A three-pointed outcrop of rock curving out from the cliffs on the eastern side gives the bay its name. Wind-blown sand has built a series of burrows at the back of the beach. At low tide the river Pennard Pill completes a wide oxbow meander behind the burrows and then flows across the beach. Beyond the three cliffs there are wide, flat sands at low tide that merge with the sands of Oxwich Bay to the east.

Water quality No sewage is discharged in the vicinity of this beach. The NRA does not monitor this beach.

Bathing safety It is dangerous to swim at middle tide near the three cliffs due to severe tidal conditions; notices at the entrance to the beach indicate where it is safe to bathe.

Access From Penmaen a lane leads to a steep path from the cliff top down to the beach. Another path leads from Parkmill. Also reached from Oxwich Bay.

Parking Car park at Penmaen, limited spaces at the post office, and a National Trust seasonal car park (a field) close by for summer use.

Toilets None.

Food None.

Seaside activities Swimming, diving, surfing, fishing, windsurfing and canoeing from the beach.

Wildlife and walks Footpaths criss-cross the bracken and heather-covered headlands offering good views of the bay and adjacent Oxwich Bay.

25 Caswell Bay, Mumbles, West Glamorgan   OS Ref: SS5987

Another of the lovely bays to be found on the Gower. High rocky cliffs shadow this ⅔ mile (1km) of golden sand. There are only 55 yards (50m) of soft sand remaining at high tide but low tide reveals wide flat sands with rocky wave-cut platforms bounding either side of the beach. Beyond the rocks there is the small Brandy Cove which can only be reached down a very steep cliff path or over the rocky shore. There is easy access to the main beach: the road runs adjacent to the beach and a few steps lead down to the sand from a neat paved area with shop and refreshment facilities. There is a dog ban from May to September.

Water quality Beach monitored by the NRA and found to meet the EC minimum coliform standards for bathing water in 1991; ★★★ in this year's listing section. One outfall serving 2,000 people discharges secondary treated sewage below low water mark in Brandy Cove. Both beaches will benefit from a proposed scheme for a long sea outfall in the vicinity. The beach is very effectively managed by the City of Swansea Council.

Bathing safety Bathing requires care due to severe tidal conditions; the beach is patrolled by lifeguards from May to September.

Access From the road there are steps down on to the sand.

Parking Car park on the landward side of the access road with 500 spaces.

Toilets In the car park. Facilities for the disabled.

Food Shop, and refreshments available at the beach entrance.

Seaside activities Swimming, surfing, windsurfing, diving, canoeing and fishing.

Wildlife and walks A network of paths cover the wooded headlands above the beach and follow the Bishopston Valley inland from Pwlldu Bay.

26 Langland Bay, West Glamorgan   OS Ref: SS6187

A lovely bay edged with rocky cliffs, with a golf course on the west side of the cliffs. There are rocky outcrops and reefs which restrict the amount of sand at high tide, but from mid-tide to low, golden sand abounds. The particular swell in the Bay makes this beach ideal for surfers. The bay's proximity to Mumbles and Swansea makes it extremely popular in fine weather.

Water quality Water quality is monitored by the NRA and found to meet the EC minimum coliform standards in 1991; ★★★ in this year's listing section.

Bathing safety Langland Bay is one of Gower's most popular surfing beaches due to its accessibility and quality of waves and consequently when a swell is running, bathing requires great care. The beach is patrolled by City Council lifeguards from May to September.

Access Steps down from the car park.

Parking Two large car parks adjacent to the beach area with spaces for a total of 247 cars.

Toilets Adjacent to the tennis courts on the east side of the Bay.

Food Cafés and a shop either end of the beach.

Seaside activities Swimming, surfing, canoeing and fishing. Five all-weather tennis courts situated immediately behind the beach area.

Wildlife and walks A coastal path runs around the Bay giving access to the Mumbles area to the east and Caswell and the rest of Gower to the west.

27 Nash Point, Marcross, South Glamorgan   OS Ref: SS9263

From the headland at Nash Point with its two lighthouses (one now disused) there are good views of the North Devon coast across the Bristol Channel and north-west to Swansea and the Gower. Paths lead down into a deep valley which opens out on to the beach. Impressive layered limestone cliffs, typical of this area of Heritage Coast, extend away in both directions. The sheer walls are very unstable so do not sit too close to them or attempt to climb on them. There is one small area of sand; otherwise the beach is composed of large flat rocks where the cliffs have been eroded. Although the main beach area has continuous access, the extremes of the beach can become tide traps as the beach becomes covered at high tide.

Water quality No sewage is discharged in the vicinity of this beach. The NRA does not monitor this beach.

Bathing safety Bathing is very dangerous because of submerged rocks and tidal races. Do not climb on the cliffs.

Access There are steep paths from the headland car park.

Parking Parking in private field on headland adjacent to lighthouse.

Toilets None.
Food Car park kiosk sells ice cream.
Seaside activities Fishing.
Wildlife and walks There is a nature trail through the wooded valley.

Northern Ireland

The coast of Northern Ireland remains largely undiscovered to those outside the province although its most famous feature, the Giant's Causeway, is one of the natural wonders of the world. It consists of huge basalt columns that disappear below the waves like a stairway to the depths. Rich in geology, the coastline is made up of a succession of bays and rugged headlands. There are the strands of County Londonderry with their popular holiday resorts, and the nine glens of County Antrim, each with a little beach nestling at its mouth. There are also the magnificent sea loughs of County Down: Belfast, Strangford and Carlingford, all rich in wildlife. Unfortunately, undiscovered does not necessarily mean unthreatened, and Strangford Lough in particular has been suffering from the effects of the scallop dredge in recent years. While this may not necessarily affect the quality of its beaches, the rape of such a beautiful and unique habitat should concern anyone who cares for our coasts and coastal life and an effective management plan is essential. The issues concerning Strangford Lough are being widely discussed and debated and progress is being made.

It is a shame that the beaches of Northern Ireland are not more widely appreciated in the UK. 1991 was a superb year for Northern Ireland's bathing waters – 100% compliance with the EC Bathing Waters Directive. Many congratulations !

Northern Ireland

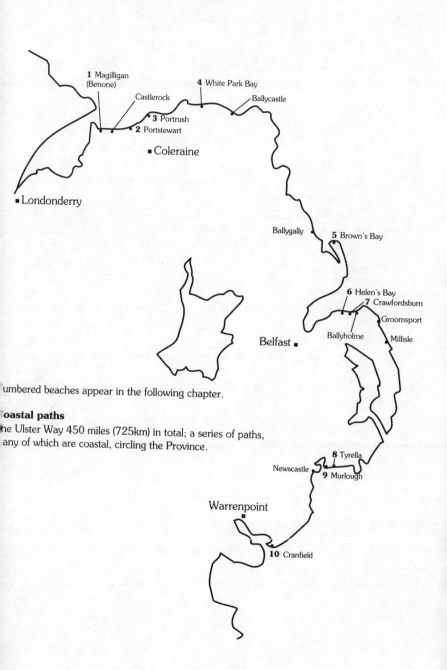

1 Magilligan (Benone)

Castlerock

3 Portrush

2 Portstewart

4 White Park Bay

Ballycastle

■ Coleraine

■ Londonderry

Ballygally

5 Brown's Bay

6 Helen's Bay

7 Crawfordsburn

Groomsport

Ballyholme

Millisle

Belfast ■

umbered beaches appear in the following chapter.

oastal paths

he Ulster Way 450 miles (725km) in total; a series of paths, any of which are coastal, circling the Province.

8 Tyrella

Newscastle

9 Murlough

Warrenpoint

10 Cranfield

Northern Ireland   *See page 19 for further details*

Beach No on Map	Rating. The more stars the better. f=failed	Resort	Pass/Fail track record	Sewage outlets	Population discharging from outlet	Type of treatment	Discharge point relative to low water mark, unless otherwise stated. Distance given in metres	Remarks
1	★★★★	**Benone (Magilligan)**	~PPPPP					Miles of sandy beach.
	★★	**Castlerock**	~FPPPP	1	1,060	Maceration	At LWM	Sandy.
2	★★★	**Portstewart**	PPPPP	1	6,040	Maceration	Above LWM	Miles of sandy beach.
3	★★★	**Portrush: Curran Strand**	PPPPP	1	5,560	Maceration	Above LWM	Sandy.
	★★★	**Mill Strand**	PPPPP					
	★★★	**Ballycastle**	~FFPPP	1	3,920	Maceration	At LWM	Sandy. Safe swimming
4		White Park Bay						Sandy, dunes.
5	★★★	**Brown's Bay**	~PPPPP					Sandy. Safe swimming
6	★★	**Helen's Bay**	~PPPPP	1	1,600	Tidal tank	At LWM	Sandy. Safe swimming
7	★★★	**Crawfords-burn**	~PPPPP	1	1,200	Secondary	Discharges to stream	Sandy.
	★★	**Ballyholme**	FFPPPP					Sandy.
	★★★	**Groomsport**	PFPPPP	1	40,000	Screened	At LWM	Sandy.
	★★	**Millisle**	~PPPPP	1	1,000	Primary	At LWM	Sandy.
8	★★★	**Tyrella**	~PPPPP					Sandy and very safe beach.
9		Murlough						Sandy.
	★★	**Newcastle**	FFFPFP	1	20,000	Secondary	285 below LWM	Sandy. New treatment works should ensure continued compliance future.
10	★★★★	**Cranfield: Nicholson's Strand**		1	2,200	Fine screens	410 below LWM	Long sandy south-facir beach.
	★★★	**Cranfield Bay**	~PPPPP					

1 Benone, Limavady, Co. Londonderry   OS Ref: C7037

Probably one of the best beaches in the United Kingdom. From Magilligan Point at the entrance to Lough Foyle, 7 miles (11km) of firm flat golden sand stretch east to the cliffs at Down Hill. Dunes fringe the wide curving beach, with sand hills covering the peninsula. The eastern end of the beach is backed by 750 foot (225m) cliffs, which are themselves shadowed by a heather-clad land plateau and the Binevenagh Mountains. The new leisure complex provides excellent facilities close to the beach. If you prefer to get away from the sandcastles and games, the miles of sand offer solitude with only the sea and sky for company. The 110 yards (100m) of sand virtually disappear at high tide, covered by waters which were only one of a handful to achieve a four-star Heinz Good Beach Guide grade. Dogs must be under supervision and on a lead.

Water quality Beach monitored by the DoE and found to meet the EC Guideline coliform standards for clean bathing water in 1991; ★★★★ in this year's listing section. No sewage is discharged in the vicinity of the beach.

Litter The beach is cleaned regularly.

Bathing safety Bathing from some areas of the beach is unsafe due to currents; notices indicate where not to bathe. The beach is patrolled by lifeguards from June to September.

Access It is a short walk from the car park on to the beach at Benone.

Parking There is a car park behind the dunes with 300 spaces. Car parking is also permitted behind the beach but should be avoided on any beach.

Toilets Public toilets at beach and also facilities at the leisure complex.

Food Refreshments are available at the leisure complex.

Seaside activities Swimming, surfing, windsurfing, sailing and fishing from the beach. Golf course, tennis and children's activity area are available at the leisure complex. A concrete ramp to the beach allows access to launch boats.

Wet weather alternatives Benone Tourist Complex.

Wildlife and walks It is claimed that up to 120 different species of shell have been found on Benone beach in one day, and an outdoor field studies recreation centre at Magilligan reflects the fact that the whole area is excellent for those interested in flora and fauna. 140 acres (56.6 hectares) of the sand dune system around the Martello Tower on Magilligan Point form a Nature Reserve and there is restricted access to protect this fragile environment. The coastline is the limit of the North Derry Area of Outstanding Natural Beauty. Inland, the Binevenagh mountains are good for hill walking and afford good views of the coast. An interpretative centre has been highly commended for its imaginative approach to the local marine environment.

2 The Strand, Portstewart, Co. Londonderry   OS Ref: C8338

This is a small, quiet resort compared to its near neighbour, Portrush. The town, set around its harbour, is located on a promontory. To the west are 2 miles (3km) of beautiful sandy beach, backed by 185 acres (75 hectares) of dunes owned by the National Trust. The flat sands are safe for swimming and good for fishing. There is good cliff scenery extending east towards Portrush, and the North Antrim Coast Path follows the cliff top.

Water quality Beach monitored by the DoE and found to meet the EC minimum coliform standards for bathing water in 1991 ; ★★★ in this year's listing section. One outfall serving over 6,000 people discharges untreated raw sewage at the low water mark.

Litter The beach is cleaned regularly.

Bathing safety Beware of currents that may affect bathing safety; the beach is patrolled by lifeguards during July and August.

Parking On the beach at low tide, but motorcycles are not permitted.

Toilets One for men and one for women.

Food One confectionery shop at the beach entrance.

Seaside activities Swimming, surfing, windsurfing, sailing, diving and fishing. Two golf courses. Boat trips from the harbour along the Causeway.

Wildlife and walks The dunes support a wide variety of fauna and flora, and offer attractive walks through the dunes from the beach to the estuarine shore of the river Bann. Bar Mouth, on the Castlerock shore at the mouth of the Bann, is a good birdwatching area noted for unusual passage migrants. The hide will accommodate wheelchair-users.

3 West Bay Strand, Portrush, Co. Antrim   OS Ref: C8740

Portrush is the largest seaside holiday centre in Northern Ireland. This Victorian and Edwardian resort is located on rocky Ramore Head and has all the facilities and amusements that might be expected of a traditional holiday town. From its elevated position there are excellent views along the coast to Donegal in the west and Rathlin Island in the east. A low sea wall bounds the soft sands of the west bay which curves gently south from the small harbour. The promenade which runs along the sea wall is on two levels separated by grassy banks. The larger East or Curran Strand is also backed by a sea wall but this gives way to dunes and a links golf course.

Water quality Beach monitored by the DoE and found to meet the EC minimum coliform standards for bathing water in 1991; ★★★ in this year's listing section. One outfall serving 5,000 people discharges macerated sewage at low water mark.

Bathing safety Beware of currents that may affect bathing safety. The beach is patrolled by lifeguards during July and August.

Access Steps and a ramp from the promenade.

Parking 150-200 spaces at West Strand, 250-300 at East Strand.

Toilets For men and women at each end of West Strand and on East Strand.

Food Promenade café.

Seaside activities Swimming, surfing, windsurfing, sailing, diving and fishing. Boat trips from the harbour.

Wet weather alternatives 'Water World' alongside the old harbour has a swimming pool complete with flumes and jacuzzis. Its facilities include an aquarium and light entertainments. Amusements.

Wildlife and walks A section of the rocky shore on the eastern side of Ramore Head between the Portandoo Harbour and Bath Road is a Nature Reserve noted for its fossil ammonites. Adjacent to the reserve is the Portrush Countryside Centre, an interpretative centre which can provide further information about the reserve and surrounding area. East of

Portrush there is superb cliff scenery, including towering limestone cliffs eroded by the waves to form arches and caves. The white cliffs are replaced by the brown basalt which forms the famous Giant's Causeway further east. The coastal path follows the clifftop to the picturesque ruin of Dunluce Castle which offers superb views along the coastline (the castle is closed on Sunday mornings and on Mondays during the winter).

4 White Park Bay, Portbradden, Co. Antrim   OS Ref: D0245

Stacks and rocky outcrops stud this magnificent bay owned and managed by the National Trust. The long curve of flat white sand is backed by dunes and circled by white chalk cliffs. On the western shore of the bay the whitewashed houses of Portbradden sit below the cliffs. The village's tiny church, St Gothan's, is the smallest in Ireland, a mere 11 feet by 6 feet (3.3m by 1.8m). Portbradden marks the junction between the chalk cliffs and the brown basalt of the Dunseverick and Causeway coast. The stretch of coast from Gid Point, the western boundary of White Park Bay, to Benbane Head is the Dunseverick Coast. The dipping rocks and basalt columns are less well-defined than those of the Giant's Causeway beyond Benbane Head. However, the series of rugged headlands and small indented bays, with the cliff top ruins of Dunseverick Castle and the numerous offshore stacks, make this section of quieter coastline extremely attractive. The bay is popular with naturalists, for nearly every type of maritime vegetation can be found along this section of coastline, including strand line, salt marsh, cliff grassland, maritime scrub and heath. There is a wide variety of bird and marine life to be seen.

Water quality No sewage is discharged in the vicinity of this beach. The DoE NI does not monitor this beach.

Litter The beach is cleaned regularly.

Bathing safety Strong currents make bathing dangerous.

Access There is car parking to the east of Templastragh on the A2 and on a minor road to Portbradden on the eastern shore of the bay. There is also a path from Ballintoy, 1½ miles (2.4km) east of the bay. During July and August an open-topped bus makes the journey between Coleraine and Bushmills with stops at Portstewart, Portrush, Portballintrae and the Causeway.

Parking Car park near the youth hostel east of Templastragh and on the cliff top near Dunseverick Harbour.

Toilets Near car park.

Food In village.

Seaside activities Swimming and fishing.

Wildlife and walks There is a 1 mile (1.6km) nature trail at White Park Bay, and a leaflet guide is available from the National Trust shop at the Giant's Causeway. The North Antrim Coast Path follows the cliffs west of the bay. It skirts Dunseverick harbour and castle and continues beyond Benbane Head to the Giant's Causeway. 40,000 basalt columns, formed by cooling lava, create the unique features of the Causeway. It has been estimated that somewhere in the region of 500,000 people view the Causeway each year. The main access point for those not wanting to walk the 5 miles (8km) to Benbane Head from White Park Bay is at Causeway

Head off the B146 north of Bushmills. There is parking and a National Trust Information Centre. The centre houses an exhibition of the history, geology, fauna and flora of the area. During the summer a bus will take visitors from the centre to the top of the Grand Causeway. To appreciate this magnificent scenery to the full, a walk to Benbane Head is recommended. There is a path along the base of the cliffs passing the Grand Causeway, and other features include the Organ, the Amphitheatre, the Wishing Well and Lovers' Leap. The return journey can be made along the cliff top. 2 miles (4km) along the coast path east of White Park Bay is the Carrick-a-rede rope bridge. The fragile swinging bridge spans a 60 foot (18m) wide by 80 foot (24m) deep ravine which separates Carrick-a-rede island from the mainland. The bridge is constructed each May by fishermen to provide access to their salmon fisheries. The walk across and back is not for the faint-hearted! A National Trust car park at Larrybane gives closer access.

5 Brown's Bay, Island Magee, Whitehead, Co. Antrim   OS Ref: D4303

Brown's Bay is at the northern end of Island Magee, a long peninsula which bounds Lough Larne. At the northern end of the peninsula two headlands, Barrs Point and Skernaghan Point, frame a deeply indented bay. A ⅔ mile (1km) crescent of sandy beach with rocky outcrops, containing numerous rockpools, is revealed by the falling tide. The beach is easily accessible and is a good amenity beach, suitable for a family day by the sea.

Water quality   Beach monitored by the DoE and found to meet the EC minimum coliform standards for bathing water in 1991; ★★★ in this year's listing section. No sewage is discharged in the vicinity of the beach.

Litter   The beach is cleaned regularly by the local council.

Bathing safety   Safe bathing.

Access   The B90 circles the northern half of Island Magee and runs parallel with the bay. A sea wall and promenade edge the sand.

Parking   Council car park with 124 spaces.

Toilets   Public toilets at car park.

Food   Nearby shop for confectionery and ice cream.

Seaside activities   Swimming, windsurfing, diving and fishing. Golf course.

Wildlife and walks   There are local walks on the headlands at either side of the bay.

6 Helen's Bay, Bangor, Co Down   OS Ref: J4683

This small sandy beach is sheltered by headlands at each end. From the Horse Rock below Grey Point the beach stretches to Quarry Point in the east and is backed by a stone promenade and a golf course on the grassland which slopes up from the promenade. Grey Point with its disused fort commands an excellent view of Belfast Lough and the Antrim coast. A wooded avenue leads from Grey Point 2½ miles (4km) inland. It was once a private carriageway built by the first Marquis of Dufferin and Ava, after whose mother, Helen Sheridan, the bay is named, and is now part of the Ulster Way.

Water quality Beach monitored by the DoE and found to meet the EC minimum coliform standard for bathing water in 1991 ; ★★ in this year's listing section. One outfall serving 1,600 people discharges sewage through a tidal tank at low water mark.

Litter The beach is cleaned regularly.

Bathing safety Safe bathing.

Access Helen's Bay Halt is ⅔ mile (1km) away and the car park is only 55 yards (50m) from the beach.

Parking There is a car park at the west end of the bay.

Toilets In the car park, including facilities for the disabled.

Food None.

Seaside activities Swimming and golf course.

Wildlife and walks The beach lies on the North Down Coastal Path. To the east is Crawfordsburn beach and country park. Seals and a variety of seabirds are just some of the wildlife of interest in this area.

7 Crawfordsburn, Bangor, Co Down.   OS Ref: J4783

Crawfordsburn and Helen's Bay are both within very easy reach of Belfast, by road along the A2 and also by train. As a result they can be very popular in summer. The 550 yard (500m) sandy beach at Crawfordsburn is divided in two by the stream that flows from the glen behind the sands. The beach and the glen fall within the Crawfordsburn Country Park. On the right bank of the stream stands the house of the Scottish family who settled here in the 17th century and gave the bay their name. For those wishing to escape from the busy part of the beach, Swineley Bay to the east is more secluded.

Water quality Beach monitored by the DoE and found to meet the EC minimum coliform standards for bathing water in 1991; ★★★ in this year's listing section. A sewage treatment works serves the Visitors' Centre and toilets, discharging fully treated effluent into a nearby watercourse which flows across the beach.

Bathing safety Safe bathing.

Access Crawfordsburn Halt is ¾ mile (1.2km) from the beach along the road through the country park. The country park car park is 440 yards (400m) from the beach.

Parking Large car park in country park.

Toilets In the car park (with facilities for the disabled).

Food Café.

Seaside activities Swimming, golf course. Orienteering courses held in the country park. Visitors' and interpretative centre.

Wildlife and walks The stream from Crawfordsburn village flows through a steep-sided valley, wooded with some exotic species. Below the village, it descends to a waterfall and flows under one of the railway viaduct's 80 foot (24m) high arches. Marked footpaths provide circular walks of varying lengths. Information about the park, including its walks and wildlife, is available from the interpretative centre. The beach is part of the North Down Coastal Path and also forms part of the Ulster Way. It follows the coast from Hollywood, passes through the glen to the Clandeboye Estate and on to Newtownards.

8 Tyrella Beach, Clough, Co Down   OS Ref: J4535

Situated in Dundrum Bay, Tyrella is a 3 mile (5km) stretch of unspoilt sandy beach facing south and backed by dunes. The clean, shallow water and safe bathing make this a very popular beach on sunny Sundays in the holiday season: at other times it is blissfully quiet. There are six golf courses within a 12 mile (20km) radius of the beach, including the excellent Royal County Down.

Water quality Beach monitored by the DoE and found to meet the EC minimum coliform standards for bathing water in 1991; ★★★ in this year's listing section. No sewage is discharged in the vicinity of the beach.

Bathing safety Safe bathing.

Access The A2 between Clough and Killough passes behind the beach.

Parking At present, some cars do park on the beach: this is a practice that the Marine Conservation Society strongly disapproves of. Alternative parking should be found.

Toilets On the beach.

Food Snack vans visit the site.

Seaside activities Swimming.

Wet weather alternatives Leisure centres at Newcastle and Downpatrick, each about 6½ miles (10km) away.

Wildlife and walks The Murlough Nature Reserve is close by – a dune system with plenty of wildlife and vegetation. There are signs of man's early habitation of the area: castles, dolmens (ancient cairns) and some of the earliest Christian remains (a result of St Patrick landing in the area). The Ulster Way goes past the beach.

9 Murlough, Dundrum Bay, Co Down   OS Ref: J4033

A long, broad, sandy bay lying at the foot of impressive 3,000 foot (1,000m) mountains, 'where the mountains of Mourne sweep down to the sea'. The beach and dunes extend over 4 miles (6km) northwards from the coastal resort of Newcastle to the Dundrum channel which connects Dundrum Inner Bay with the open sea. At the northernmost end some 2½ miles (4km) of beach and 700 acres (283 hectares) of sand dunes are owned and managed by the National Trust as a National Nature Reserve. The southern dunes are owned by the Royal County Down Golf Club. A narrow shingle beach lies between the wide sandy bay and the ⅔ mile (1km) wide sand dunes. The beach has long been popular with the holiday maker, walker and naturalist. The beach shelves gradually and is safe for swimming.

Water quality No sewage is discharged in the vicinity of this beach. The DoE NI does not monitor this beach.

Litter The beach is cleaned regularly.

Bathing safety Safe bathing.

Access Access from the main A24 Belfast to Newcastle road, 2 miles (3km) from Newcastle. Car parking available at Dundrum and Slidderyford Bridge, where there are two entrances. Access to the beach is on foot across the dunes by board walks. Tracks are suitable for wheelchair users.

Parking A small car park for eight cars at Dundrum. At Slidderyford there are some 600 car spaces on the road side, using the hard shoulder, or 350 spaces in a car park signposted Murlough Nature Reserve.

Toilets Toilets (with facilities for the disabled) at the car park, and at the Slidderyford entrance.

Food None.

Seaside activities Swimming, fishing, windsurfing. Other facilities at Newcastle, 2 miles (3km) away.

Wet weather alternatives Various facilities at Newcastle.

Wildlife and walks The beach lies on the Ulster Way, which continues through Newcastle and the Mournes to the south, and through Dundrum to the north. There are extensive paths through the nature reserve. Guided walks are organised by National Trust staff in the summer. The reserve is noted for its geographical development, its archaeological history and its rich variety of fauna and flora. The vegetation of the dunes includes strand line, dune grasslands, dune heath, scrub and woodland. Seals may be seen in summer months. Both Dundrum Inner and Outer bays are noted for their wintering sea duck, waterfowl and waders. A birdwatching hide is situated on the Inner Bay shore near Dundrum. There is a small interpretative centre situated in the car park. The imposing Norman castle at Dundrum gives magnificent views over the area.

10 Cranfield, Kilkeel, Co Down   OS Ref: J2611

An Area of Outstanding Natural Beauty and adjoining an area of Special Scientific Interest, Cranfield Bay is situated at the entrance to Carlingford Lough. The south-facing sand and shingle beach is backed by dunes and has the magnificent Mourne mountains as a backdrop. The beach stretches from the rocky outcrops at Greencastle Point to the boulders at Cranfield Point. There are good views across the Lough to Ballagan Point and away down the coast beyond Dundalk Bay. The water is some of the cleanest you will find in the UK – in 1991 it achieved ★★★★ status at one of the monitoring sites.

Water quality Beach monitored by the DoE and found to meet the EC minimum coliform standards for bathing water in 1991 in Cranfield Bay; ★★★ in the listing section. The water at Nicholson's Strand passed the Guideline standards; ★★★★ in this year's listing section. No sewage is discharged in the vicinity of the beach.

Bathing safety Safe bathing.

Access A road leads from Cranfield to the car park, from which there is a short walk across the grass to the beach.

Parking Car park with 150 spaces.

Toilets Public conveniences.

Food Hotel, two cafés and three shops.

Seaside activities Swimming, windsurfing, diving, waterskiing and fishing. Beach entertainment and band concerts. Golf course.

Wet weather alternatives Analong cornmill and marine park.

Wildlife and walks Mourne mountains are excellent for walking, with the Silent Valley Reserve just north of Kilkeel. A 3,000 million gallon (14,000 million litre) reservoir is set among the peaks and there is some fine parkland on the approaches to the dam.

What Can You Do To Help Clean Up The Beaches?

We compiled the 1992 Heinz Good Beach Guide using our own research, water quality data supplied by the National Rivers Authority and information given to us by the local authorities and other organisations concerned with the sea and the beach.

However, the most important source of information is YOU. We ask you to act as our ears and eyes around the beaches of the UK to help us know more about the problems around the coast. We cannot always act on individual cases, but we use your information in our national campaign to end sewage pollution of the seas around the UK. We can also supply you with the expert back-up knowledge of the issues to help you in your own campaign. Write to the Pollution Officer at the Marine Conservation Society for details.

If you have a complaint about a beach you visit, or think that we may have got something wrong in the 1992 Guide, or if you have found a beach to be clean or waters especially clear, then please write and tell us about it.

Please tell us all you can. The more we know, the more we can try to do about the problems around the UK coast. Send us slides and photographs of the worst and best beaches.

How To Make An Official Complaint And Report Pollution

If you go to a beach and find dirty water, badly littered beaches or dangerous items washed up, then register your complaint and report what you have found. If the authorities don't know about the problem, or think that people don't care, then nothing will ever improve. We cannot rely on government or industry to clean up the beaches and the water without prompting from us!

There are various local and national government bodies and water companies with whom to register your complaint or to whom you can report pollution (after you have told us about it!).

Here is a step-by-step guide of who to contact:

Local Authority Environmental Health Departments

Environmental Health Departments are responsible for keeping beaches clean of litter and safe from dangerous items washed up, such as chemical drums and canisters washed overboard or dumped at sea.

If you find items that you think may be dangerous call the Environmental Health Department straight away – do not touch whatever it is you find.

If the beach is badly littered with drink cans, plastic bottles, discarded fishing nets or whatever, register your complaint with the Environmental Health Department. The local authority has a legal duty under the Environmental Protection Act 1990 to keep beaches and other public places clean and free of litter. Tell them where the litter is and ask them to clear it up.

These departments are also responsible for displaying the results of bathing water monitoring at the beaches, in line with government policy. There should be posters giving the results in a clear, easy-to-understand form at the beaches themselves. If there are no posters, contact the Chief Environmental Health Officer to ask why. Ask them to put posters near the beach showing water quality monitoring results. The address and phone number of the local authority will be in the phone book.

Please send us copies of their letters.

Local tourism departments

Although these departments have no responsibility for pollution on the beach or out at sea, they have a lot to lose if a resort gets a bad name. When they receive complaints, they act quickly to get the other departments in the local authorities and the NRA (see below) to do something about the problem.

The National Rivers Authority, the River Purification Boards and DoE-NI

The National Rivers Authority (NRA) has responsibility for water quality and pollution incidents. The NRA also carries out the routine monitoring of bathing waters on which compliance with the EC Bathing Waters Directive is assessed. The River Purification Boards (RPB's) in Scotland and the Department of the Environment for Northern Ireland (DoE-NI) carry out broadly similar roles to those of the NRA in England.

If the waters appear to be badly polluted with sewage or there is any other pollution (such as oil) in the water, contact the local National Rivers Authority. They will be able to investigate the pollution. The NRA may even be able to track down and prosecute the polluter.

Also, if you suspect that the water may be affected by an algal bloom (heavy frothing of the water, excessive foam on the beach or possible red-brown discolouration of the water – 'red tides') then ask the NRA to investigate.

Here are the addresses and telephone numbers of the regions of the NRA, RPB's and DOE-NI:

THE NATIONAL RIVERS AUTHORITY

Head Office NRA Head Office
Rivers House, 30–34 Albert Embankment, LONDON SE1 7TL
Tel 071-820 0101

South West NRA – South West Region
Manley House, Kestrel Way, EXETER, Devon EX2 7LQ
Tel 0392-444000

Wessex Region NRA – Wessex Region
Rivers House, East Quay, BRIDGWATER, Somerset TA6 4YS
Tel 0278-457333

Southern Region NRA – Southern Region
Guildbourne House, Chatsworth Road, WORTHING, West Sussex
BN11 1LD *Tel* 0903-820692

Thames Region NRA – Thames Region
Kings Meadow House, Kings Meadow Road, READING, Berkshire
RG1 8DQ *Tel* 0734-535000

Anglian Region NRA – Anglian Region
Kingfisher House, Goldhay Way, Orton Goldhay, PETERBOR-
OUGH, Cambs PE2 0ZR *Tel* 0733-371811

Severn-Trent Region
Severn Estuary:
NRA – Lower Severn Region
Riversmeet House, Newton Industrial Estate, Northway Lane,
TEWKESBURY, Gloucestershire GL20 7JG *Tel* 0684-850951

Trent Estuary:
NRA – Lower Trent Region
Trentside Offices, Scarrington Road, West Bridgeford, NOTTING-
HAM NG2 5SA *Tel* 0602 -455722

NRA – Severn Trent Region
Sapphire East, 550 Streetbrook Road, SOLIHULL, West Midlands
B91 1QT *Tel* 021-711 2324

Yorkshire Region NRA – Yorkshire Region
Rivers House, 21 Park Square South, LEEDS LS1 2QG *Tel* 0532-440191

Northumbrian Region NRA – Northumbrian Region
Eldon House, Regent Centre, Gosforth, NEWCASTLE-UPON-TYNE NE3 3UD *Tel* 091-213 0266

North West Region NRA – North West Region
PO Box 12, Richard Fairclough House, Knutsford Road, WAR-RINGTON WA14 1HG *Tel* 0925-53999

Welsh Region NRA – Welsh Region
Rivers House, St Mellons Business Park, St Mellons, CARDIFF
CF3 0FT *Tel* 0222-770088

SCOTTISH RIVER PURFICATION BOARDS

Highland RPB,
Carr's Corner, Lockybridge, FORT WILLIAM, Inverness-shire
PH33 6TQ *Tel* 0397-704351

North East RPB
Greyhope House, Greyhope Road, Torry, ABERDEEN AB1 3RD
Tel 0224-248338

Forth RPB
Heriot Watt Research Park, Avenue North, Riccarton, EDIN-BURGH EH14 4AP *Tel* 031-449 7296 (out of hours Pollution
Callout 031-449 7292)

Clyde RPB
Rivers House, Murray Road, East Kilbride, GLASGOW G75 0LA
Tel 03552-38181

Tweed RPB
Burnbrae, Mossilee Road, GALASHIELS TDI 1NF *Tel* 0896-2425

Solway RPB
Rivers House, Irongray Road, DUMFRIES DG2 0JE *Tel* 0387-720502

Tay RPB
1 South Street, PERTH PH2 8NJ *Tel*: 0738-27989

DEPARTMENT OF THE ENVIRONMENT FOR NORTHERN IRELAND (DoE-NI)

DoE-NI Environmental Protection Division
Calvert House, 23 Castle Place, BELFAST BT1 1FY
Tel 0232-230560

The Water Service Companies

The Water Services Companies (WSC's), the newly privatised 'water plc's', are responsible for the operation of the coastal sewage works and outfall pipes around the coastline of the UK. They are currently investing large sums of money in a range of projects, but the pressure must be maintained to ensure the job is done properly.

If you see any outfall pipes discharging raw sewage near any beaches, write to the water company and ask them:

✳ whether they think it is still acceptable in 1992 to pump raw sewage into the sea and expect the public to swim in it?

✳ whether they are aware of the damage that sewage pollution causes to marine life?

To understand the problems around the coast, also ask them for the latest up-to-date information about your area, or the beaches you visit:

✳ how many outfall pipes there are in the area and how many people do they serve?

✳ what sort of treatment is given to the sewage before it is discharged to sea?

✳ are all these outfalls are clearly marked with signs giving details of such sewage is discharged and what sort of treatment it has received? If not, why not?

✳ are there are any 'improvement' schemes planned? What sort of treatment is considered to be adequate and why? When will the improvements be completed?

Here are the addresses of the ten water service companies of England and Wales:

South West Water Peninsula House, Rydon Lane, EXETER EX2 7HR *Tel* 0392-219666

Wessex Water Wessex House, Passage Street, BRISTOL BS2 0JQ *Tel* 0272-290611

Southern Water Southern House, Yeoman Road, WORTHING BN13 3NX
Tel 0903-64444

Thames Water Nugent House, Vastern Road, READING RG1 8DB
Tel 0734-591159

Anglian Water Ambury Road, HUNTINGDON PE18 6NZ
Tel 0480-433433

Yorkshire Water Broadacre House, Vicar Lane, BRADFORD BD1 5PZ
Tel 0274-206063

Northumbrian Water Abbey Road, Pity Me, DURHAM DH1 5FJ
Tel 091-384 4222

North West Water Dawson House, Great Sankey, WARRING-TON WA5 3LW
Tel 0925-234000

Severn-Trent Water 2297 Coventry Road, Sheldon, BIRMING-HAM B26 3PU
Tel 021-722 4000

Welsh Water Plas-y-Ffynnon, Cambrian Way, BRECON, Powys LD3 7HJP
Tel 0874-3181

Please send us copies of any replies you receive from the WSC's.

The Coastguard

The Coastguard is available to help anyone in danger at sea or on the beach. If you think that someone needs help at sea, *DON'T HESITATE* – dial 999 – *AND DON'T LEAVE IT TO SOMEONE ELSE!*

The Coastguard must also be told immediately of any dangerous items washed up on the beach, such as chemical drums and old wartime explosives. If you're in doubt, call anyway. Dial 999 and ask for the Coastguard. The call is always free.

Index

Aberaeron 163
Aberafan 167
Aberarth 163
Aberdaron 160, 172
Aberdeen 126
Aberdour Harbour 125
Aberdour Silversands 125
Aberdovey 162
Abereiddy Bay 164, 176
Aberffraw 160, 169–170
Abergele 158
Aberporth 163
Abersoch 161
Aberystwyth 162
Achiltibuie 128, 146–7
Achmelvich 128, 145–6
Achnahaird 128, 146
Afan 167
Afon Soch 161
Afon Wen 161
Ainsdale 120
Aldeburgh 82, 89–90
Aldingham 118
Allonby 116
Alnmouth 101, 109
Alum Chine 36
Amble 101
Amlwch 159
Amroth 165
Anderby Creek 96
Angle Bay 164
Annan Waterfoot 132
Anstey's Cove 33
Anstruther 125
Applecross 128, 148–9
Arbroath 126
Arbroath Victoria Park 126
Ardeer Beach 18
Ardwell Bay 131
Arisaig 151
Arnside 118
Askam-in-Furness 117
Ayr 130

Babbacombe 33
Badentarbat Bay 146–7
Baglan 167
Ballycastle 188
Ballyholme 188
Balmedie 126
Balnakeil Bay 128, 142
Bamburgh 17, 101
Bamburgh and Seahouses 111–12
Banff Links 127
Bantham 32
Barafundle Bay 165, 179
Bardsea 118
Barmouth 162
Barmston 96
Barricane Bay 24
Barrow-in-Furness 118
Barton-on-Sea 76
Beacon Cove 33
Beadfoot Beach 33
Beadnell Bay 17, 101, 111
Beaumaris 159
Bedruthan Steps 26, 44
Beer 34
Beesands 32

Belhaven Beach 124
Bembridge 37
Bendrick's Beach 168
Benllech 159
Benone 17, 188, 189
Berrow 23
Berwick-upon-Tweed 102
Bexhill 17, 78
Bexhill-on-Sea 87–8
Bigbury-on-Sea 32, 57
Biggar Bank 118
Birkdale 120
Birling Gap 78
Bispham 119
Black Rock Sands 161
Blackhall 99
Blackpool 119
Blackpool Sands (Devon) 32, 58
Blackwaterfoot 130, 153–4
Blue Anchor 23
Blundell Sands 120
Blyth 100
Bognor Regis 77
Borth 162, 174
Boscastle 25
Botany Bay 80
Bournemouth 17, 36, 71–2
Bovisand Bay 31
Bow 30, 53
Bowleaze 35
Boydston 130
Bracelet Bay 166
Bracklesham Bay 76
Brandy Cove 166
Branksome Chine 36
Branscombe 34, 62
Braystones 117
Brean 23
Bridlington 17, 96, 97, 103–4
Brighouse Bay 131
Brightlingsea 81
Brighton 18, 77
Brighton-le-Sand 120
Broad Haven 164, 178–9
Broad Sands Bay 124
Broadsands Beach 33
Broadstairs 80
Brodick Bay 130, 154
Broomhill Sands 79
Broughton Bay 165
Broughty Ferry 125
Brown's Bay 188, 192
Bude Crooklets 25
Bude Summerleaze 25
Budleigh Salterton 17, 34, 60–1
Bulverhythe 78
Burghead Bay 127, 139–40
Burnham-on-Sea 23
Burntisland 125
Burry Port 165
Burton Bradstock 34, 63
Butlins 130

Caister Point 82
Calgary Bay 129, 152
California 83
Calshot 76
Camber Sands 17, 79
Cambois 100
Camusdarrach Beach 128, 150–1
Canvey Island 81
Carbis Bay 27
Cardigan 176
Carnoustie 125
Carradale 129

Carrick Shore 131
Castle Cove 35
Castlerock 188
Caswell Bay 17, 166, 183–4
Cawsand Bay 31, 55–6
Cayton Bay 97, 105
Cemaes Bay 159
Challaborough 31
Chapel St Leonards 96
Charlestown 30
Charmouth 34
Chesil Beach 35
Christchurch 36
Church Beach 34
Church Cove 29
Church Ope Cove 35
Churston Cove 33
Clachtoll 128, 145
Clacton 17, 81
Clarach Bay 162
Clashnessie Bay 128, 144–5
Cleat's Shore 18
Cleethorpes 96
Clevedon 23
Cleveleys 119
Clovelly 25
Coatham Sands 98
Cobb Beach 34
Cocklawburn Beach 102, 113
Cold Knap Beach 168
Coldbackie 128, 142
Coldingham Bay 124
Collieston 126
Colwell Bay 36
Colwyn Bay 158
Combe Martin 24
Compton Bay 37
Constantine Bay 17, 26, 43
Cooden Beach 78
Coral Beaches 128, 149–50
Corton Sands 18
Coverack 29
Cowes 37
Crackington Haven 17, 25, 40
Craig Dwllan 159
Cramond 124
Cranfield 188, 195
Crantock 27, 44–5
Craster 101
Crawfordsburn 188, 193
Crawley Woods 166
Cresswell 101
Criccieth 161
Crimdon Park 98
Crinnis Beach 17, 30
Cromarty 127
Cromer 83
Crosby 120
Croyde Bay 24
Cruden Bay 126
Cruinard Bay 128
Cuckmere Haven 78, 85–6
Cullen Sands 127, 138–9
Cullercoats 17, 100
Curran Strand 188
Cwmtudu 163, 175

Dale 164
Dalgetty 124
Dalton Burn 99
Dartmouth Castle and Sugary Cove 32
Dawlish 34
Dawlish Warren 34
Daymer Bay 26
Deadman's Cove 27

Deal Castle 80
Deganwy 159
Denemouth 99
Dhoon 131
Dinas Dinlle 160, 170
Doniford 23
Doonfoot 130
Dornoch 128, 140
Dover Harbour 80
Dovercourt 82
Downderry 31
Drunmore 131
Druridge Bay 101, 107–8
Dunbar East 124
Duncansby Head 128, 141
Dunglass 124
Dunnet Bay 128
Dunoon 129
Dunraven Bay 167
Dunster 23
Dunvegan 149–50
Dunwich 82, 90
Duport 30
Durdle Door 35, 65–6
Dwygfylchi 159
Dymchurch 79
Dymchurch Redoubt 79

Earls Dyke 96
Easington 99
East Looe 31
East Quantoxhead 23
East Runton 83
East Wittering 76
Eastbourne 17, 78, 86–7
Eastney 76
Eaststoke 76
Elie Earlsferry 125
Embleton Bay 101, 109–10
Erraid 129, 152–3
Exmouth 34
Eyemouth 124
Eypemouth 34

Fairbourne 162, 173–4
Fairlie 129
Fairlight Cove 18
Fall Bay 166
Featherbed Rocks 99
Felixstowe 82
Felpham 77
Ffrith 158
Filey Sands 17, 97, 104–5
Findochty 127
Fisherrow 124
Fishguard 164
Fistral Bay 26
Flamborough 97
Fleetwood 119
Flimby 116
Folkestone 79
Font-y-Gary Bay 168
Formby 120
Fraisthorpe Sands 18, 96
Fraserburgh 126
Freshwater East 165
Friars Cliff 17
Frinton-on-Sea 82

Gailes 130
Gairloch 128, 148
Ganavan 129
Girvan 131
Glenancross 150–1
Goodrington Sands 33
Goodwick 164

Goring-by-Sea 77
Gorleston Beach 82
Gorran Haven 30
Gosford Sands 124
Gourock 129
Grange-Over-Sands and Kents Bank 118
Great Yarmouth 82
Greatstone Beach 79
Groomsport 188
Gruinard Bay 147–8
Gullane Bay 124, 133–4
Gunwalloe Cove 28
Gurnard Bay 37
Gwbert-on-Sea 163
Gyllyngvase 29

Hallsands 32
Happisburgh 83, 92–3
Harlech 161, 172–3
Harlyn Bay 17, 26, 42–3
Harrington 116
Hartland Quay 25
Hartlepool 98
Harwich 82
Hastings 79
Haverigg 117
Heacham 83
Helen's Bay 188, 192–3
Helensburgh 129
Hemmick Beach 30
Hemsby 83
Hendon South 99
Hengistbury 17, 36
Herne Bay 81
Hest Nank 118
Heysham 119
Highcliffe Castle 36, 72–3
Hightown 120
Hill Head 76
Holcombe 33
Holkham 18
Holland-on-Sea 81
Hollicombe 33
Holy Island 101
Holywell Bay 27, 45–6
Hope Cove 32
Hopeman 127
Horden 99
Hornsea 96, 103
Hove 77
Hoylake 121
Hunstanton 17, 83
Hythe 79

Ice House Burn 99
Ilfracombe 24
Ingoldmells 96
Instow 24
Inverboyndie 17, 127
Irvine 130

Jacksons Bay 168
Jacob's Ladder 17, 34
Jaywick 81
Jersey Marine 167
Joss Bay 80

Kames Bay 129
Kennack Sands 29, 51
Kessingland 17, 82
Kilchattan Bay 129
Kimmeridge Bay 35, 67
King Edward's Bay 100
Kinghorn 125
Kingsands Bay 31

Kinmel Bay 158
Kirkcaldy Linktown 125
Knott End-on-Sea 119
Kynance Cove 28, 50

Labrador Bay 17
Ladram Bay 34
Lamlash Bay 130
Lamorna Cove 28
Lancing 77
Langland Bay 166, 184
Lansallos Bay 31, 54
Lantic Bay 31, 53–4
Largs 129
Layde Bay 23
Leasowe Bay 121
Lee-on-the-Solent 76, 84
Leigh-on-Sea 81
Leonard's Cove 32
Lepe 76
Leven East 125
Leven West 125
Leysdown-on-Sea 81
Lido Peterhead 126
Lime Kiln 99
Limeslade Bay 166
Limpert Bay 168
Littlehampton 77
Little Island Bay 168
Little Perhaver 30
Little Quay Bay 163
Littlestone-on-Sea 79
Llanaber 161
Llanbedrog 161
Llandanwg 161
Llanddona 159
Llanddwyn 160, 170
Llandudno 158-0
Llandulas 158
Llanelli Beach 165
Llanfairfechan 159
Llangranog 163
Llangwnnadl 171
Llanon Slipway 163
Llanrhystud 163
Llansantffraid 163
Llantwit Major Beach 168
Llwyngwril 162
Lochinver 144–5
Lodmoor West 35
Loe Beach Feock 29
Longhoughton Steel 101
Longniddry 124
Long Rock Beach 18
Long Sands 100
Lossiemouth 127
Low Newton 101
Lower Largo 125
Lowestoft 17, 82, 91–2
Lulworth Cove 35, 66–7
Lunan Bay 126
Lunderston Bay 129
Lundin Links 125
Lydstep Beach 165
Lyme Regis 34
Lynmouth 24
Lytham St Anne's 120

Mablethorpe 96
Machrihanish 129,153–4
Machroes Beach 161
Maen Porth 29
Maidencombe 33
Maidens 131
Manorbier 165
Marazion and Mount's Bay 28

Margam Sands 167
Margate 80
Marine Lake 23
Marloes Sands 164, 177–8
Marsden Bay 100
Marske-by-the-Sea 98
Maryport 116
Mawgan Porth 26
Meadfoot 17
Meiklecross 129
Meols 121
Mevagissey 30
Middleton-on-Sea 77
Milford Beach 164
Milford-on-Sea 76
Mill Bay 32
Mill Strand 188
Millendreath 31
Millisle 188
Millom 117
Millport 129
Milsey Bay 124
Minehead 24
Minnis Bay 80
Minster Leas 81
Moelfre 159, 169
Moggs Eye 96
Monifieth 125
Monmouth Beach 34
Monreith 131
Montrose Links 126, 135
Morar 128, 150
Morecambe 119
Moreton 121
Morfa Aberech 161
Morfa Bychan Beach 161, 162
Morfa Nefyn 160
Mossyard 131
Mothecombe 31
Mother Ivey's Bay 26
Mousehole 28
Muchalls 126, 136-7
The Mumbles 166
Mundesley 83
Murkle Bay 128
Murlough 188, 194–5
Musselwick Sands 164
Mwnt 163,176

Nairn East/Central 127
Nash Point 168
Nash Point 184–5
Ness Cove 33
Nethertown 117
New Brighton 120
New Quay 163, 174–5
Newbiggin 101, 118
Newborough 170
Newcastle 188
Newgale Beach 164
Newhaven 78
Newport 163
Newquay Bay 26
Newry Beach 159
Newton Bay 167
Newton Haven 101, 110–11
Neyland Slip 164
Nicholson's Strand 188
Nigg Bay 127
Norman's Bay 78
North Berwick Bay 124
North Shields 100
Norton 36

Oddicombe 17, 33
Ogmore by Sea 167

Overstrand 83
Oxwich Bay 166, 182

Padstow 26
Pagham 76
Paignton Sands 17, 33
Palm Bay 80
Par Sands 30
Parton 116
Pathhead Sands 125
Pease Sands 124, 133
Peffersands 124
Pembrey Sands 17, 165,
    179–80
Penarth 168
Penbryn 163
Pendine Sands 165
Pendower Beach 29, 52–3
Penmaenmawr 159
Penrhos Beach 159
Penrhyn Bay 158
Pentewan 30
Penzance 28
Perran Sands 28
Perranporth 27
Pettycur 125
Pevensey Bay 78
Pilchard Cove 17
Pilling Sands 119
Pittenweem 125
Plas Menai 160
Plymouth Hoe 31
Poldhu Cove 28, 49–50
Polgaver Bay 17
Polkerris 30
Polpeor 28, 50–1
Polperro 31
Polridmouth Beach 30
Polstreath 30
Polurrian Cove 28
Polzeath 17, 25, 42
Pontllyfni 160
Poole 36
Poppit Sands 163
Porlock Bay 24
Port Eynon 166, 181–2
Port Isaac 25
Porth Beach 26
Porth Ceriad Beach 161
Porth Colman 160
Porth Dinllaen 160
Porth Dinorwic 160
Porth Iago 160
Porth Nefyn 160
Porth Neigwl Beach 161
Porthallow 29
Porthcawl 167
Porthcurnick Beach 29
Porthcurno 28
Porthgwarra 28
Porthgwidden 27
Porthleven West 28
Porthluney Cove 30
Porthmahomack 128
Porthmeor 17, 27, 46–7
Porthminster 17, 27
Portholland Beach 29
Porthor 160, 171–2
Porthoustock 29
Porthpean 30
Porthtowan 27
Portkil 129
Portland Harbour 35
Portloe 29
Portlogan Bay 131

Portmellon 30
Portobello 78, 124
Portpatrick 131
Portreath 27
Portrush 188
Portstewart 188
Portwrinkle 31
Powfoot 132
Praa Sands 28, 48–9
Prestatyn 158
Preston Sands 33
Prestwick 130
Priest's Cove 47–8
Pwllgwaelod 164
Pwllheli 161

Ramsgate 80
Ramsgrove 166
Ravenglass 117
Readymoney Cove 30
Red Wharf Bay 159
Redcar 98
Redgate 17, 33
Reighton Sands 97
Rest Bay 167
Rhos-y-Llan 160
Rhosneigr 160
Rhossili Bay 166, 180–1
Rhyl 158
Ringstead Bay 35, 64–5
River Aln Estuary 101
Roan Head 118
Robin Hood's Bay 97, 105–6
Rock 26
Rockcliffe 131
Rockham Bay 24
Rockley Sands 36
Roker 99
Roome Bay, Crail 125
Rosehearty 126
Rosemarkie 127
Rossall 119
Runswick Bay 97, 107
Ryde 37
Ryhope South 99

St Andrews 125
St Anne's North 120
St Anthony's Head 29
St Bees 117
St Brides Haven 164
St Combs 126
St Cyrus 126
St George's Pier 160
St Helens 37
St Ives 27
St Just Priest's Cove 27
St Leonards Beach 78
St Margaret's Bay 80
St Mary's Bay 33, 79
St Mary's Well 168
St Mawes 29
St Mildred's Bay 80
St Osyth 18
Salcombe 32
Saltburn-by-the-Sea 98
Saltcoats 130
Saltdean 77
Sandbanks 17, 36, 70–1
Sandend 17, 127, 137–8
Sandgate 79
Sandhaven 100
Sandhead 131
Sandown Bay 73
Sandown Esplanade 37
Sandsend 97

Sandsfoot 97
Sandside Bay 128. 141–5
Sandwich Bay 80
Sandwood Bay 128. 143
Sandy Bay 34. 167
Sandy Gap 118
Sandy Haven 164
Sandy Mouth 25. 39
Sandyhills 132
Sandymouth 17
Sango Bay 128
Sanna Bay 128. 151–2
Saundersfoot 165
Saunton Sands 24
Scarborough 97
Scourie 128. 144
Sea Palling 83. 92
Seaburn 100
Seacliff 124
Seaford 78
Seagrove Bay 37
Seaham Beach 99
Seaham Remand Home 99
Seahouses 101
Seamill 130
Seascale 117
Seaton 17. 31. 34. 124
Seaton Carew 98
Seaton Sluice 100
Seatown 34. 62–3
Seaview 37
Selsey Bill 76
Sennen Cove 17. 27
Shakespeare Cliff 80
Shaldon 33
Shanklin 37
Shanklin Chine 37
Sheerness 17. 81
Shell Bay 35. 125
Shellness 18
Sheringham 83
Shipload Bay 25. 38
Shoalstone Beach 33
Shoeburyness 81
Shoreham 77
Shoreham-by-Sea Beach 77
Siddick 95
Sidmouth 34. 61–2
Silecroft 117
Silloth 116
Silverknowes 124
Sinclair's Bay Wick 128
Skegness 96
Skelton Beck 98
Skinburness 116
Skinningrove 98
Skipsea Sands 96
Slapton Sands 32. 57–8
Snettisham Beach 83
Soar Mill Cove 32
Solent Breezes 76
South Shields 100
Southerndown 167
Southerness 132

Southgate 166
Southport 120
Southsea 76
Southwick 77
Southwold 17. 82. 91
Spittal 102
Spittal Quay 102
Stair Hole 35
Staithes 97
The Stell 98
Stevenston 130
Stokes Bay 76. 85
Stonehaven 126. 135–6
The Strand 189–90
Stranraer 131
Strathbeg Bay 126. 137
Strathlene. Buckie 127
Studland 17. 35. 69
Sunderland 99
Sutton-on-Sea 96
Swanage 17. 35. 68
Swanpool Beach 29
Swansea Bay 166

Tal-y-Bont 161. 173
Tanybwlch Beach 162
Tayport 125
Teignmouth 17. 35. 59–60
Tenby 17. 165
Tentsmuir Point 125. 134–5
Thornwick Bay 97
Thorpe Bay 81
Thortonloch 124. 133
Three Cliffs Bay 166. 183
Thurlestone 32
Thurso 128
Tintagel 25
Torbay 33. 59
Torcross 32
Torre Abbey Sands 33
Totland 36
Towan Beach (Newquay) 26
Towan Beach (Portscatho) 29.
  52
The Towans 27. 46
Traeth Lligwy 169
Traeth Llydan 160
Traeth Penllech 160. 171
Traigh 128. 151
Trearddur Bay 160
Trebarwith Strand 17. 25. 41
Trecco Bay 167
Trefor 160
Tresaith 163
Tresilian Bay 168
Trevaunance Cove 27
Trevone Bay 26
Treyarnon Bay 17. 43–4
Treyarnon Beach 26
Troon 130. 154
Tunstall 96
Turnberry 131
Tynemouth 100

Tyrella Beach 188. 194
Tywyn 162

Upper Largo 125

Vault Beach 30. 35
Ventnor 37

Wallasey 121
Walney Island 118
Walpole Bay 80
Walton-on-the-Naze 82
Warkworth 101. 108–9
The Warren 80
Watch House Bay. Barry 168
Watchet 23
Watcombe Beach 33
Watergate Bay 26
Waterloo 120
Welcombe Mouth 25
Wells-next-the-Sea 83. 93
Wembury 31. 56
Wemyss Bay 129
West Bay 34
West Bay Strand 190
West Hayling 76
West Mersea 81
West Runton 83
West Wittering 76
Westbrook Bay 80
Westcliff-on-Sea 81
Westgate Bay 80
Westhaven 126
Weston-Super-Mare 17. 23
Westward Ho! 25
Weymouth 17. 35. 63–4
Whitburn 100
Whitby 97. 106–7
White Park Bay 188. 191–2
Whitecliff Bay 37
Whitehaven 117
Whitesand Bay (St David's) 164.
  177
Whitesand Bay (Sennen Cove 48
Whitesands Bay 124
Whiting Bay 130
Whitley Bay 100
Whitmore Bay 168
Whitsand Bay 54–5
Whitstable 81. 88–9
Widemouth Sand 25. 39–40
Wide Pear Beach 17
Willsthorpe 96
Winchelsea 79
Withernsea 96
Woolacombe Sand 17. 24. 38
Worbarrow Bay 35
Workington 116
Worthing 77

Yarmouth 36
Yaverland 37
Yellowcraig 124
Ynyslas 162

Marine Conservation Society Membership Form

One of the best things you can do to help clean the beaches of the UK is to join the Marine Conservation Society. The Society relies on your support to protect the marine environment from pollution, not just for mankind but also for the thousands and thousands of different species that live in the seas around the UK and all over the world. Just because you can't always see them, doesn't mean they aren't as valuable as those land animals and plants that we all know.

MEMBERSHIP FORM

Yes, I want to join the Marine Conservation Society

Annual Member £12 ❑   Family Member £16 ❑
Life Member £200 ❑
Overseas members please add £4 a year postage
Institutions may join for £30.

Name _____

Address _____

_____

I enclose a cheque/postal order for:
Membership fee   £
Donation (if you wish) £
Total   £

❑ Tick this box if you would like to pay by Bankers Order or make your membership worth £3 more with a Deed of Covenant
❑ Tick this box if you would like a beach survey form to give us details of beaches you have visited in 1992

Send this form to:

The Marine Conservation Society
9 Gloucester Road
Ross-on-Wye
Herefordshire
HR9 5BU

HAVE A HAPPY HOLIDAY!